Sherman So
& J. Christopher Westland

Red Wired

China's Internet Revolution

First published in 2010 by Marshall Cavendish Business
An imprint of Marshall Cavendish International

PO Box 65829
London EC1P 1NY
United Kingdom

and

1 New Industrial Road
Singapore 536196
genrefsales@sg.marshallcavendish.com
www.marshallcavendish.com/genref

Marshall Cavendish is a trademark of Times Publishing Limited

Other Marshall Cavendish offices:
Marshall Cavendish International (Asia) Private Limited, 1 New Industrial Road, Singapore 536196 • Marshall Cavendish Corporation. 99 White Plains Road, Tarrytown NY 10591-9001, USA • Marshall Cavendish International (Thailand) Co Ltd. 253 Asoke, 12th Floor, Sukhumvit 21 Road, Klongtoey Nua, Wattana, Bangkok 10110, Thailand • Marshall Cavendish (Malaysia) Sdn Bhd, Times Subang, Lot 46, Subang Hi-Tech Industrial Park, Batu Tiga, 40000 Shah Alam, Selangor Darul Ehsan, Malaysia

A CIP record for this book is available from the British Library

ISBN 978-0-462-09967-5

Project managed by Cambridge Publishing Management Ltd

Printed and bound in Singapore by Times Printers Pte Ltd

Contents

Acknowledgments

No book is solely the product of its authors. First and foremost, our gratitude goes to James Allen; after spending long hours editing and reviewing, he is almost like the third author of the book.

We are indebted to Jacky Huang of IDC China, Dick Wei of J.P. Morgan, Richard Ji of Morgan Stanley, and Jason Brueschke of Citigroup for sharing their knowledge of the Chinese internet sector and their continual support for our research in the area.

We are also grateful to the following people who shared their first-hand experiences in the Chinese internet sector, either during our research for the book, or during co-author Sherman So's previous work at the *South China Morning Post:* Wang Zhidong, Lee Kaifu, John Liu, Jack Ma, Bo Shao, Joe Chen, Victor Koo, Gary Chen, Pang Shengdong, Merle Hinrichs, Foo Jixun, Jay Chang, Porter Erisman, Marc van der Chijs, T. R. Harrington, Fritz Demopoulos, Richard Robinson, Alvin Liu, Oliver He, Clement Song, Eric He, Bryan Yuan, Fan Min, Neil Shen, Justin Tang, Kevin Wang, Liu Dejian, Joe Wu, Chen Nian, Vincent Gao, JP Gan, Leong May Seey, and Lawrence Tse.

We want to especially thank Kou Xiaowei of the General Administration of Press and Publication for helping us to understand the Chinese government's role in the country's internet development.

We would also like to thank the many other people who contributed valuable information to the book, but all of whose names cannot be mentioned.

Thanks to Stuart Jackson, Mark Clifford, and David Savelson, who read and commented on all or part of the manuscript. Our thanks also go to some of the staff at the *South China Morning Post*—Edward Collis, Tim Leemaster, and Michael Logan, for their help in moving the project forward.

Finally we would like to thank our publisher, Marshall Cavendish, for publishing the book quickly at a time when the Chinese internet sector is still unfolding. We especially thank Martin Liu for his enthusiasm for the project, and Karen Beaulah and Jane Fieldsend for expertly handling our manuscript and dealing with the many last-minute changes.

Preface

The Chinese share an imprecation (the first of three)—*May you live in interesting times.*[1] The other two are considered even more forbidding—*May you come to the attention of those in authority*; and *May you find what you are looking for.* In contrast we, as authors, are blessed to live in interesting times; otherwise our search for discourse and rich veins of material might grow ever more taxing. And the internet's rise in China has made for very interesting times, to say the least. In the coming pages, intrepid reader, we will show how internet entrepreneurs have discovered and invented ways to thrive through clever adaptation to China's unique environment, and tell gripping tales of entrepreneurs who have gone from the brink of bankruptcy to huge riches.

Our interest in the Chinese internet grew out of a pivotal development. What was once an American Cold War invention has evolved into a major economic and social tool for America's erstwhile adversary, and now partner, on the world stage. By 2008, the number of internet users in China had outstripped America's at 298 million, and by 2009, China had 338 million internet users (more people than the entire population of America).

As a source of material, China *never* ceases to amaze and confound—its language, culture, business practices, and competitiveness all have taken their own paths, ones significantly different from those of their counterparts throughout the rest of the world. This makes it very challenging for foreign firms to craft strategies and business plans. What has worked in the West often does not work in China. The conundrums, idiosyncrasies, and constraints of the Chinese internet market both intrigued and motivated us to write this book. Our anticipated target audience for the book is executives and entrepreneurs in America, Britain, and other Western economies, who we think should be very intrigued and concerned by China's rise. The internet industry offers a superb opportunity to look closely at why those business models that seem to have worked so perfectly in their original countries may disappoint when exported to China. Every major company in the internet world—Google, Yahoo, eBay, Expedia, and so on—has entered China. Many have been great innovators on their home turf, only to find themselves outmaneuvered abroad.

1 An English paraphrase of the Chinese proverb, "It's better to be a dog in a peaceful time than be a man in a chaotic period."

Our book is divided into three parts—the first furnishing a brief history of the internet in China, the second dedicated to case studies and interviews with successful businesspeople, and the third summing up the lessons that aspiring businesses can use to craft their own success story. We hope, as readers, that you find our brief look into the Chinese internet market as rewarding as we found researching and writing it.

It was our goal as authors to lay out in broad strokes the factors, processes, and specific events that explain why particular internet business models did not work in their original forms when exported to China. We looked for the successful innovations that particular competitors crafted, and try to learn from the outcomes of their innovation. We also believed that the lessons learned while researching this book could apply to other industries in China, because internet industries are a reflection of the larger competitive world in which firms operate. Very often, something that works brilliantly in one culture can fail dismally in another—but not necessarily because the entire model was wrong, but merely because a few key aspects were lost in translation. We hope that our interviews and case studies will help aspiring business executives and entrepreneurs who want to take on the challenge of entering business in China to avoid some of the pitfalls into which their predecessors have fallen. May they live in interesting times.

Sherman So and Chris Westland
Hong Kong and Chicago,
October, 2009

The state of the revolution

In late 1957, at the height of the Cold War with China and Russia, America's President Eisenhower issued an aggressive military challenge to America's rivals that spawned the Advanced Research Projects Agency (ARPA). ARPA quickly moved to focus on computer science and information processing—in particular connecting mainframe computers at different universities around America, so that they would be able to communicate using a common language and a common protocol. ARPAnet morphed into the internet, which moved from military to commercial prominence in the 1990s. By 2008, in an ironic turnabout, China's population of internet users in this one time Cold War arena had surpassed America's at 298 million users, growing at 40 percent annually (according to China Internet Network Information Center, or CNNIC), and rapidly migrating off to nontraditional platforms such as telephones and personal digital assistants.

China is different—in language, culture, business practices, and competitiveness. And it is huge—the most populous country on Earth and, now, the biggest user of the internet. America's early dominance of the internet has not given it automatic license in China, and many early entrants to the Chinese internet business have found the challenges—along with the rewards—much greater than elsewhere in the world.

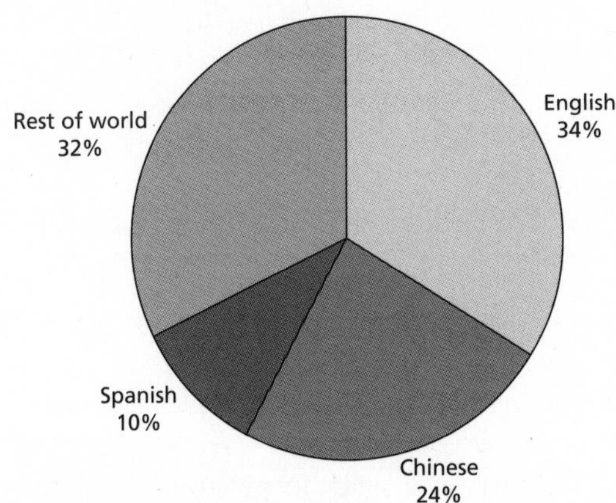

Figure 0.1: **Internet users by language (2006)**

Data source: *The Economist*

China's emergence from isolation to become one of the great cultural, economic, and of course internet, powerhouses in the world is remarkable, and in its own way, unique. China is not a monolith like America—the birthplace of the internet. It recognizes 55 ethnic groups and hundreds of dialects within 11 major language groups. Yet up to one fifth of China's population is learning English—British Prime Minister Gordon Brown estimated that the total English-speaking population in China will outnumber native speakers in the rest of the world within two decades.[2]

The internet, offering myriad resources in ubiquitous English, has become a Chinese passion; and the Chinese are returning the favor. Chinese is the second most widely used language on the internet.

We have been watching, with great interest, the transformation of China's internet for over a decade, and were curious about exactly what was taking place, and how it was happening.

Sector	Chinese companies	U.S. companies	Remarks
Search engine	Baidu: 62%	Google: 28% Yahoo: 4%	Market share measured by revenue of keyword ads
C2C	Taobao (owned by Alibaba): 86%	Eachnet (eBay): 7%	Measured by trading volume
Online chat	Tencent QQ: 77%	Microsoft Window Live Messenger: 4% Skype: 3% Yahoo Message: 0.4%	Measured by active users
Online portal	Sina: 27% Sohu: 19% Tencent: 13%	Yahoo: 3%[a]	Measured by revenue of display ads
Online travel	Ctrip: 51%	eLong (control by Expedia): 11%	Measured by revenue

***Table 0.1:* Market share of China's internet sectors (2008)**

Data source: Analysys International

Note: [a] including display ads in Yahoo China, Alibaba.com and Taobao.com

This book is our "report on a work in progress" which we hope you, the reader, will find as fascinating as we do. China never fails to

[2] Source: "The language business in China," *The Economist*, Apr 12, 2006.

impress because of its scale and influence. It is easy to get carried away and forget that the character of the Chinese internet, and the experience for China's internet users, is likely to remain substantially different from the experiences of those in the West.

The internet evolved in America first as an academic and military packet switching network then, after 1991, as a commercial tool that came of age with the introduction of the World Wide Web in 1993 for multimedia transfer. The technology that China embraced was already fully fledged, and the Chinese looked for ways to innovate on what was already a working technology platform. Consequently, all of the innovations we looked at in this book have been business and delivery innovations rather than being primarily technology innovations.

We also saw that most (but not all) Western firms trying to compete in China failed to understand fully the character of these innovations. As a result, they lagged behind their local rivals in market share by a huge margin (see Table 0.1). We were intrigued by how so many Western firms have gotten China's internet business so very wrong. We tried to assess what exactly it was that these expatriate firms must do if they are ever to succeed in China.

This perhaps would not matter, except that China now has the largest number of internet users in the world. We are of the opinion—and in good company worldwide—that the twenty-first century will be shaped by China's actions.

Scholarship, science, and other information-intensive activities have traditionally held sway in China's culture. It takes only a small leap of faith to assert that the internet will become central to China's growth and influence around the world, precisely because of its traditional strengths in information-intensive disciplines.

Our approach to this book, and to discovering in general what China's emerging internet industry is all about, has been to seek out successful internet firms and their management.

We wanted to build our conclusions on first-hand interviews and stories from the entrepreneurs and operations people themselves who have succeeded in China's internet markets. Many, if not most, of these individuals are self-made entrepreneurs—far removed from the academic types that have been instrumental in forging internet businesses in America and Europe. For this reason alone, their stories make for much more interesting reading than those of their Western counterparts.

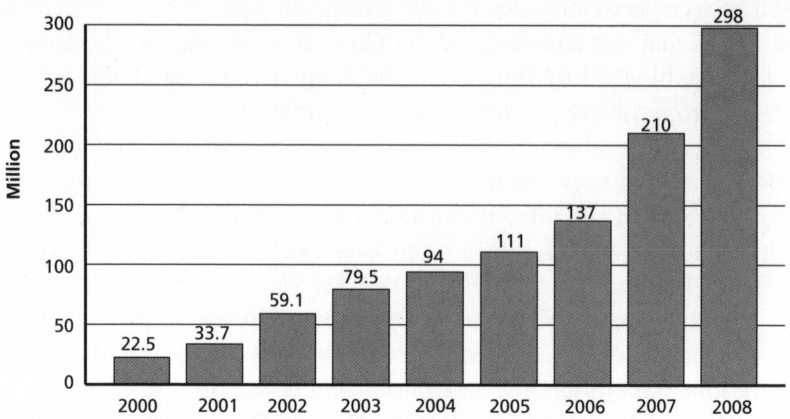

***Figure 0.2:* China's internet population (2000–08)**

Data source: CNNIC–China Internet Network Information Center

The trends are striking, the tales fascinating, and so, dear reader, without further ado, we invite you to press forward. We hope our book provides you with a captivating synopsis of what will surely be remembered as China's greatest cultural revolution—the explosion of China's twenty-first-century innovations on the internet.

1. News 24/7: Sina's story

While the internet was blossoming in America in the late 1990s, it was just getting started in China. Sina was among the earliest of China's internet startups, founded by Wang Zhidong, a computer engineer who had grown up in China, and backed by venture capitalists from Silicon Valley. Wang set his sights on the hottest startup in Silicon Valley at the time—Yahoo.

Wang soon discovered that the best way to attract viewers was with news—tons of it. News on an internet portal is like produce at a supermarket—it has to be fresh, and when it is, customers come back every day. Sina hired hundreds of editors to painstakingly gather stories from all the leading newspapers and magazines in China. News was not easy to come by in China then, and people were, and still are, hungry for it. Sina adopted a different layout and approach to that of Yahoo China, whose site was largely a replica of its American parent. News was just one part of the overall mix of content. Unfortunately, by using technology rather than people to gather and present news, Yahoo deprived itself of the sensational headlines that keep people coming back for more. Browsing on Sina was more informative, more exciting, and more sensational.

Build it and they will come

In the late 1990s, the so-called "web portal" was the definitive internet commodity. The portal concept was simple—build it and they will come. With the proliferation of web browsers in the middle of the decade, many companies tried to build or acquire portals, which were the starting point for around a third of searches on any browser. Like a shopping mall, the portal was supposed to attract traffic that then could then be directed to stores through paid advertising. It was a gateway that charged for its services.

Yahoo was one of the most successful portals. Founded in January 1994 by Jerry Yang and David Filo, both graduate students in electrical engineering at Stanford University, it began as a web directory, helping users to navigate the internet by organizing websites into categories and subcategories (this was accomplished through painstaking effort by a huge number of indexers on the Yahoo payroll). By the end of 1994, "Jerry's and David's Guide to the World Wide Web," as it was unpretentiously known, had received over 1 million hits.[3] Venture capitalists, following on the heels of Netscape's successful public stock offering, swooped in and took Yahoo public in 1996. The next phase of Yahoo's growth was a series of acquisitions that expanded its range of services—where it was once content to be the entry point to the net, it now aspired to be a one-stop shop, satisfying the user's every need. In March 1997, Yahoo acquired Four11. Its webmail service, Rocketmail, became Yahoo Mail. ClassicGames.com was acquired and transformed into Yahoo Games. In March 1998, it launched Yahoo Pager, an instant messaging service that was renamed Yahoo Messenger a year later. In January 1999, Yahoo acquired web hosting provider GeoCities. And eGroups became Yahoo Groups after its acquisition in June 2000.

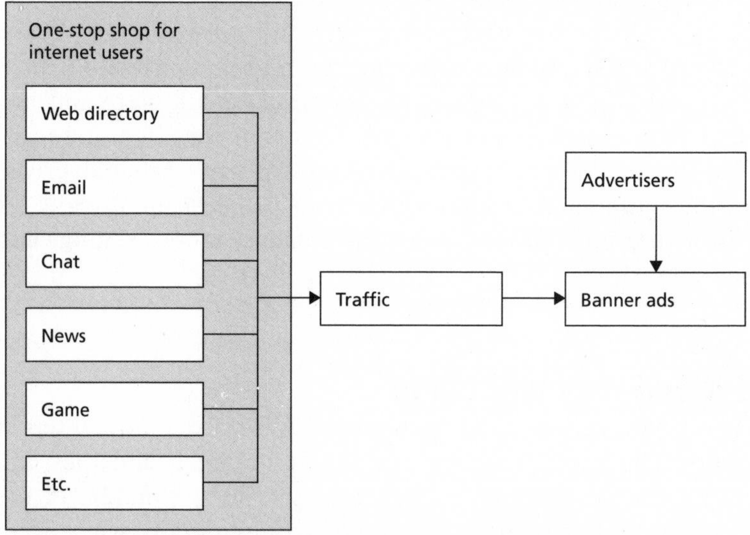

Figure 1.1: **Business model of web portals**

Portals get most of their revenue from advertising, selling banner ads on their pages. Banner ads are intended to attract traffic to the website of the advertiser. The advertisement is constructed from an image, perhaps employing animation, sound, or video to maximize presence,

[3] Source: *http://yahoo.client.shareholder.com/press/history.cfm*

and is either wide and short, or tall and narrow—hence the name "banner." The more visitors and the more pages they view, the more the portal can charge advertisers; most banner ads are sold on the basis of cost per thousand page impressions, similar to the formula employed by newspapers and magazines.

For portals, expanding services was a strategy to secure the user base and lengthen the user's time on site. Services that required registration, such as free email, customization features, and chat rooms, were added to encourage repeat usage. Games, news, and other services had the same effect. Everybody started to get in on the act. Portals such as MSN, Lycos, and Excite were also growing rapidly, following the formula pioneered by Yahoo.

America's experience was not lost on entrepreneur Wang Zhidong, who was determined to adapt Yahoo's model for China. In his eyes, one thing stood out—news. China's internet had a much greater appetite for news than for other services. Instead of imitating Yahoo's verbose, ill-organized and scattershot approach, why not focus on news alone?

Wang's insight paid off and Sina.com became not only the largest online portal in China, but also the dominant online media firm.

Zhongguancun

Wang Zhidong was born in 1967 in Guangdong, a province in southern China. He studied at Peking University, one of the country's elite schools, earning a bachelor's degree in electrical engineering. Wang stayed on afterward in the Haidian district of Beijing, close to Peking University, in an area called Zhongguancun, better known as China's Silicon Valley. Though a technology center from the 1950s, it became famous in the 1980s as the "electronics avenue," because of its connections to information technology and the preponderance of stores along a central, crowded street. After working for a year in Zhongguancun, Wang joined Founder Group, a technology company that had been spun off from Peking University. He worked at Founder from 1989 to 1991 before starting his own firm, Suntendy Electronic Information Technology and Research Company.[4]

The popularity of the personal computer in China dates from 1991, about the time that affordable PCs became available there. One of the

4 Source: Sina Annual Report 2000, Directors and Executive Officers of the Registrant.

major challenges facing their entry into the market was China's unique ideographic writing. For PCs to be widely used, they had to be able to easily process Chinese characters. Wang's answer to this problem, which ensured the success of his first company, was a piece of software known as Chinese Star, which helped users to input and print out Chinese documents.

Wang's success brought him influence and a modicum of fame among Beijing's technorati. Stone Group, one of the first successful privately owned technology companies in China, proposed a joint venture. Beijing Stone Rich Sight Information Technology Company (BSRS) was formed in 1993, using Stone's money and Wang's technology and research. The new company not only built on top of Chinese Star, it also developed a more powerful processing software, Richwin, which runs on top of English Windows and can support both the simplified Chinese characters used on the mainland and the traditional characters favored in Taiwan and Hong Kong.[5] Richwin benefited from the chaos in Microsoft's own move into China in the early 1990s, following the success of Windows 3.1. Microsoft had engaged a Taiwanese company to develop their Simplified Chinese language interface, but ran into trouble when rogue programmers began hiding anti-Communist slogans in the software in the hopes of extorting payments from Microsoft. Microsoft's Chinese interface was thwarted for several years, but came online after Shanghai firm Kingstar took over the effort. In the interregnum, Richwin profited. Before Microsoft launched a stable and functional Chinese Windows, almost every PC in Taiwan and Hong Kong was installed with a copy of Richwin.

By 1995, BSRS was doing very well, and a restless Wang started to think about new directions. In October 1995, he was invited to attend a conference hosted by computer giant IBM in Colorado. It was Wang's third trip to America. He had already visited the holiest shrines of the technological revolution—Microsoft, Apple, HP, Silicon Valley, and so on. And he knew from meetings with American investment bankers that venture capital could be beneficial to his firm's development.

Wang was bored with the daily routine in Colorado. "It was a one-week conference and there was nothing else to do besides skiing. But I did not know how to ski then, so I just read some of the magazines I had bought at the airport," said Wang.

[5] Simplified Chinese and traditional Chinese are two different forms of the written language.

Attached to those magazines were a few floppy disks. One of them invited users to connect to a telephone line before installation. "I did," said Wang, "and the next minute I was connected to the internet. My very first time." It was America Online's dial-up internet service. "Since I was on the net, I wondered what I should do next. Why not go to the IBM website?" There he was able to download a new driver to upgrade his IBM laptop. "I was amazed," said Wang, "Here I was in a hotel in Colorado and I could find all kinds of information, do different things and upgrade my laptop—all because of the internet. In theory, it could work in Beijing too, if only there was a network there."

Before returning home Wang made a second trip to California. "All my friends in Silicon Valley were talking about the net," said Wang. Netscape, maker of the first dominant web browser, had gone public on NASDAQ just a few months before. What was more significant was the wild success of Netscape's offering, despite the fact that the company had never made a penny of profit. Netscape offered a browser that had been "reverse engineered" from the founder Marc Andreessen's University of Illinois Mosaic browser, combined with a business model derived from founder Jim Clark's interactive television business. The public offering had been forced by Clark, because he needed the money to make a payment on his yacht. But it was wildly successful, and kicked off the phenomenon later called the dot.com boom. This success was not lost on Wang, who admitted, "The trip had a big impact on me." The first thing Wang needed to do after returning home was to find an internet service provider in Beijing. After an extensive search that lasted several months, he finally found a dial-up service offered by the information center of the Chinese Academy of Sciences.[6]

By December 1995, software giant Microsoft had done a volte-face, from a strategy that reflected Bill Gates' belief that the internet was just a "fad," to a conviction that the internet was the future. It put money and people in place to show that it was serious. "I thought that if Microsoft believed the future of software was the internet, China's future would be the internet. And BSRS's future would be the internet, too," said Wang.

[6] The Chinese Academy of Sciences (*http://english.cas.ac.cn*) is the national academy for the natural sciences of the People's Republic of China. It is an institution of the State Council of China, headquartered in Beijing with institutes all over China. It has also created hundreds of commercial enterprises, with computer maker Lenovo being one of the most famous.

But what was to be the business plan? What would be the model? And where would the revenue come from? For the moment, Wang had no answer to these questions. So he created a team of half a dozen people to explore different possibilities for BSRS. "There were seven to eight different directions," said Wang, "but there was one consensus—we needed a website." So SRSnet.com was launched in May 1996.

Wang went out to seek venture capital investment to fund the company's internet expansion plan. In September 1997, US$6.5 million was raised. However, the venture capitalists who joined the board of BSRS proved to be less enthusiastic about the internet than they had seemed at first. "They lied to me. They said they were interested in the internet. But that was just to keep me happy so I would let them invest [in BSRS]," said Wang. Later, the venture capitalists argued that as the internet division lacked any practical plans for making money, the company should maintain its focus on Richwin, its main revenue source.

"They would rather have used the money to acquire competitors of Richwin, such as America-based TwinBridge, or my old company, Chinese Star, than invest in the internet," said Wang. "But I believed the internet was the future of our firm. So I asked the board to give the internet team one last chance to prove themselves."

Goal!

In 1998, the internet division of BSRS received one more round of investment, with the warning that it might be the last. They tried many different initiatives, but one above all proved to be most important.

That year, the FIFA World Cup would be played in France. China's millions of soccer fans would be keen to follow the matches. So the internet team made SRSnet.com into a content site devoted to World Cup news. "It was a success. Traffic was up. The click-through rate was satisfactory and all the reviews from the industry were good. What's more, the site maintained its high traffic even after the World Cup," said Wang. "We were onto something."

Wang went back to his board. "Since the results of the website were quite good, I argued that they should not close the internet division just yet—'Keep it going and give me more time. Maybe I can find a way to sell it at a good price'."

In 1998, Wang went to America again. "I did a trip in May, seeking business partners," said Wang. He met with about ten companies. One of them was Sinanet, the largest Chinese-language website in North America. "I hoped they would be interested in our Chinese technology, or that they might want to be a distributor of Richwin in America," said Wang. But after Wang saw Sinanet in action he knew the direction that his own internet operation needed to take.

"Sinanet was a content site for Chinese news. It was very popular, but in terms of technology it was quite simple. Our website was not inferior to it—and this was the best Chinese site in North America," said Wang. He was so confident about SRSnet.com's prospects that he told the internet division to carry out several upgrades to the website.

In August 1998, the chairman of Sinanet, Daniel Chiang, a cheerful ex-basketball player who hailed from Taiwan, came to China to visit Wang. Before founding Sinanet, Chiang had been president of Trend Micro, a successful antivirus company that his wife, Eva Chen, had founded with Steve Chang in Los Angeles in 1988. Chiang had led Trend Micro to a successful Initial Public Offer (IPO) in Tokyo in 1988.[7] His connections in Silicon Valley and the capital markets would be beneficial if Wang wanted to take his firm public one day. The two executives hit it off immediately and quickly recognized that their companies complemented each other.

"After we met, I found that there was a lot that Daniel Chiang and Sinanet had that we needed. At the same time, we had something they lacked," said Wang. Sinanet had hired many ex-Yahoo people. At the time, Yahoo was the role model for many internet entrepreneurs. They could help Wang to figure out how to run an internet business. And as one of the top Chinese websites in Taiwan and North America, Sinanet would help Wang establish an international presence. On the other hand, if Chiang wanted to develop the mainland China market, potentially the largest in the world, he would need someone like Wang to help him. Moreover, Wang's BSRS had the strong technological development capability that Sinanet lacked.

It was corporate love at first sight for both parties. One month after their first meeting on August 26, 1998, Wang and Chiang decided to merge. The initial contract was signed on September 27. After board meetings at the two companies, the merger was formally announced on December 1.

[7] Source: Sina Annual Report 2000, Directors and Executive Officers of the Registrant.

"The public and the investment community were enthusiastic about the merger, because it was the first involving companies in Mainland China and Taiwan. As Sinanet was in fact America-based, it was also a merger between Chinese and American companies," said Wang.

The new company was named Sina Corporation. Its website, Sina.com, appeared on April 12, 1999 and almost immediately blew its competitors away. By May, all third-party measures indicated that Sina.com was the number one Chinese-language site in the world by traffic. It was voted number one by China's internet users in both the December 1999 and June 1999 semi-annual surveys conducted by CNNIC. As of February 2000, Sina.com was averaging 16.6 million daily page views and had 3.1 million registered users.

Competition

Despite a late start, Sina.com quickly surpassed its two main rivals. "China already had two major portal players, Sohu and Netease," said Wang. "Sohu's users were mostly white-collar workers, while Netease dominated the lower end, grass-roots internet market."

Sohu was founded in 1996 by Charles Zhang, who held a Bachelor of Science degree from Tshinghua University in Beijing, known as Asia's answer to the Massachusetts Institute of Technology and one of China's best schools, and a PhD in experimental physics from (the original) MIT.

Prior to founding Sohu, Zhang was MIT's liaison officer with China. In November 1996, two MIT professors, Nicolas Negroponte and Edward Roberts, gave Zhang his initial funding. By February 1998, he had built the first Chinese search engine, Sohu. Then the company received a second round of funding from venture capital investors including Intel, Dow Jones, and IDG. By March 1999, Sohu had developed into a comprehensive internet portal with various content channels.[8]

Sina's other rival, Netease, was founded in 1997 by William Ding, who had worked as an engineer for both China Telecom, the country's dominant fixed line phone company and internet services provider, and the Chinese offshoot of America-based database software company Sybase. In November 1997, he paved the way for Netease to become a major player by introducing China's first dual-language

[8] Source: *http://corp.sohu.com/companymilestones-en.shtml*

free email service. The email system was later licensed to other companies.[9]

Both Sohu and Netease were imitating Yahoo, though Sohu was putting the emphasis on its search engine function and Netease was focused on providing free email and free web hosting space. Wang was not impressed with either. "There was not much Chinese content on the web in those days. Therefore, in our opinion, there was not much a Chinese search engine could really do," he said of Sohu's business model.

As for free email and web hosting, Netease was hardly unique. Already plenty of other players worldwide, such as Hotmail and GeoCities, offered the same services. "There was no need for us to provide those [services] either," said Wang. Instead, Sina positioned itself as a "global Chinese website." But what did this mean, exactly?

"We figured out that many overseas Chinese were interested in news about their homeland. They were hungry for information about China," said Wang. "Besides, our past experience covering special topics, such as the soccer World Cup, had proved that news could work. We also gained quite a lot of popularity from organizing online Chinese forums." (Forums are discussion boards where users post their opinions about different topics.)

The Yahoo model—a diversified approach, with 10–20 different services—worked well in America in the early days. "But, Chinese internet users might not be ready for that yet," said Wang. "More importantly, our company could not afford to do that." Instead Wang chose to focus Sina's resources on a few services or channels.

The 3+2 strategy

Wang called it the "3+2" strategy. Sina has three websites: one for mainland China, one for Taiwan, and one for America. Three services or channels would be common to all three sites, while each site would have two extra services or channels unique to itself.

The three channels common to all Sina's websites are news, search, and "community," which comprises such things as forums, message boards, dating services, and clubs. "In hindsight, we were right on. The three main services are important even today. They are what people go online for," said Wang. (Today, search is the major internet application,

9 Source: *http://corp.163.com/eng/about/bod_wding.htm*

with Google dominating the space worldwide. Popular Web 2.0 applications, such as Facebook and MySpace, are extensions of simpler early community applications. And many people now read their news online.)

Sina outsourced its search function to others. "We had limited resources. Besides, we believed search was just a tool. We thought we just needed to partner with whoever was best in the market. Moreover, Yahoo was doing the same," said Wang. In 1999, Google was still very small, but AltaVista, Excite, and Openfind were all major search engines that were willing to partner with portals. Sina first partnered with AltaVista and Openfind but shifted to Baidu when the homegrown Chinese search engine came online.

The largest part of Sina's resources went into news. "Many overseas students in those days were interested in the news back home. The mainland students were interested in mainland Chinese news, the Taiwan students in Taiwan news," said Wang, "For world news they could turn to NBC, CNN, etc. But for Chinese news, we were the only source online."

Walking the line

Sina's editors painstakingly gathered news from all major newspapers and magazines in China. In the process they created a non-government national news channel the likes of which the country had never seen before. "It was the first comprehensive Chinese medium run by a nongovernmental organization," said Wang.

But Sina was walking a fine (and sometimes dangerous) line. Media is a tightly controlled business in China. All newspapers are state owned and all editors and reporters must adhere to strict guidelines on coverage. Reader interest takes a back seat to the government's official line. And when Sina was starting up, the restrictions were even tighter than they are now. Journalists who stepped out of line were routinely thrown in jail.

What's more, the media industry is very fragmented. There are no national newspapers apart from the central government's principal mouthpieces, *People's Daily* and *China Daily*, and they hold little appeal for the average reader. "Too dry and boring, unless you want to hear about government initiatives," said one Beijinger, summing up the majority view. There are few national magazines, either. Every city has its own three to five major newspapers and magazines. For example, the *South City Post* (南方都市报) is the most popular newspaper in Shenzhen, one of largest cities in South China, but finding a copy in Beijing or Shanghai is next to impossible.

In such conditions, creating a comprehensive national news channel focused on stories that people actually wanted to read was a tour de force. "We paid special attention to things like sport, entertainment, and technology. Those are the things people are interested in, and they are not politically sensitive," said Wang.

Sina also got some extra help from friends in the media. "There was a group of editors and reporters friendly to us those days. They gave us articles they could not use in their publications. Most of the time, it was not because the articles were bad, but because the publications had no space for them or the views clashed with those of the chief editors. We published the articles under the authors' names. They were happy about that as they gained recognition and their efforts were not wasted," said Wang.

Sina was also first to offer Chinese news updated in real time. "In the early days, websites were updated once every day, or every other day, or once a week, just like newspapers or magazines," said Wang. "We were the first to come up with an online publishing system where news is updated 24 hours a day. Staff are on shifts, so whenever news breaks we put it online. We also gave some columnists access to our online publishing system, so they can write and publish on our sites anytime." This was an early form of blogging, which has now become mainstream, but in 1999, and especially in China, it was quite a breakthrough.

On May 7, 1999, NATO bombed the Chinese embassy in Belgrade, Yugoslavia, killing three Chinese citizens and outraging the Chinese public. NATO later apologized for the bombing, saying that it occurred because of an outdated map provided by the CIA. Few Chinese accepted this explanation, believing the strike had been deliberate.

Sina's coverage of the bombing was fast and comprehensive and helped to make the portal a prime destination for news-starved users. "That's how Sina built up its reputation in news," said Wang.

Emulating *Reader's Digest*

As mentioned, news is a highly regulated business in China, and almost all media companies have to be state owned. So how did Sina escape the scrutiny of the Chinese government?

"In fact, building Sina's news operation was quite risky. We undertook two significant risks—one was political, the other commercial," said Wang. Without a license to operate a media firm, Sina could not hire reporters. But even if it had had such a license, the cost of hiring people to cover news, sport, finance, and entertainment would have been more than a startup could bear.

The experience of Jan Hung-Tse, founder of Taiwan's PC Home Publishing Group and book publisher Cite Publishing Ltd, shows how expensive it can be to get into the news business from scratch.[10] Jan founded Tomorrow's Paper (明日报), an online product, in 2000 to target the market in Taiwan, which imposes no tight restrictions on the media. After hiring up to 300 reporters, Jan needed the equivalent of US$642,000 a month to cover costs, but with internet advertising in its infancy, Tomorrow's Paper could manage no more than US$160,000 of revenue per month. Within three months it was in trouble and in February 2001 it folded.[11]

In those days, some websites in China routinely copied their content from others, but Sina, which wanted to go public one day, could not afford to get a reputation for copyright infringement. "So we took the Reader's Digest approach instead," said Wang.

US-based *Reader's Digest*, a popular monthly general-interest family magazine with a plethora of foreign editions, has thrived for decades by using mostly content from other publications. It is scrupulous about giving credit to authors and their publications, and paying all copyright fees.

Sina uses a similar approach, signing contracts with individual authors and media organizations in China, paying their copyright fees and crediting authors and publications by name. The beauty of the scheme was that it solved Sina's political and commercial problems in one. Since all articles originated with state-owned news organizations, the government had no reason to object to their content. And the costs were significantly less than if Sina had somehow tried to create its own news-gathering network.

Because the China media industry is so fragmented and most firms are small, Sina had plenty of bargaining power when it came to fee negotiations. Though some of the most prominent institutions, the Xinhua News Agency, for example, demanded high fees, others were happy to let Sina use their content for next to nothing. "Many of the

[10] Source: *http://www.publishing.com.hk/PubOrg/PubmanDetail.asp?ManID=20020907002*
[11] Source: *http://www.techvantage.com.tw/content/003/003098.asp*

small local newspapers loved for Sina to carry their articles, because Sina has a national audience and overseas readers. Their influence can be greatly amplified if Sina carries their articles," observed Wang.

	China	Taiwan	North America	Hong Kong
SinaNews	Xinhua News Agency China News Agency China Central TV HuaSheng News China Youth Daily Beijing Youth Daily Reuters AFP	Central News Agency China Times Interactive Formosa Television UDN News Power News	China Press Kwong Wah Ri Bao Singtao Daily Zhong Guo Daily Hwa Sheng Central News Agency	Metro Broadcast Corporation Limited Mingpao.com Limited Wisers Information Limited
SinaSports	Ballsweekly China Football News Sportsyouth	Min Sheng Bao	China Press	
SinaLiving	Life Week Neweekly AV World DaZhong Movie China Entertainment	Chinese Television System Crown Magazine Journalist Magazine	Hwa Sheng Togo Travel Crown Magazine	Easy Group Holdings Limited
SinaFinance	CITIC Securities Shanghai Securities News	Business Weekly Taiwan Economics News	CBS MarketWatch Dow Jones Reuters Stock 247	Core PaciNc-Yamaichi International (HK) Limited
SinaTechnology	ZDNet China Science & Technology Daily	OpenFind Search ZDNet	Isnet Zdnet OpenFind Search	PaceMaker Technologies

***Table 1.1:* Some of Sina's content partners in 2000**

Data source: Sina's Annual Report 2000

So Sina just hired editors and pocketed the change. They gathered news from other publications and put it online. While the traditional

Chinese media firms had to adopt the government's order of priorities, Sina was free to focus on what most people were really interested in, principally lifestyles, finance, entertainment, and sports. And to attract more eyeballs to the site, the editors did not hesitate to write sensational headlines that would have made tabloid newspapers proud.

China gate

As Sina's news focus gateway gained traction, generated revenues, and proved its detractors and competitors wrong, the other Chinese portals had to reassess their own models. Sina's gate was out-portaling the traditional portal concept of throwing up something for everyone.

Sina's success caused a crisis of confidence at Sohu, the original Chinese portal. It halted development of its search functions and followed Sina into news. Netease kept its email focus and became the largest free email provider in the country, though it also sharply increased its news content. At the end of 2002, these three portals controlled two thirds of the country's internet advertising market—Sina had 36 percent, Sohu 23 percent, and Netease 7 percent, according to iResearch, a China-based market research firm.

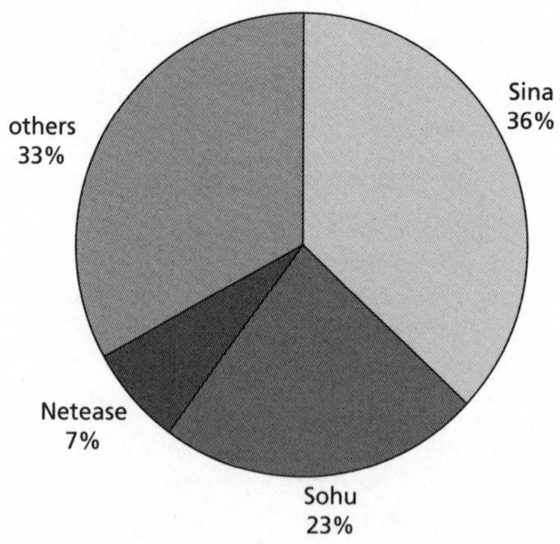

***Figure 1.2:* Online advertising market share in 2002**

Data source: iResearch

The format of Chinese online portals was now set. Instead of the diversified approach embodied by Yahoo, they would focus on news alone.

In 2003, the dominant Chinese instant messaging player, Tencent, wanted to branch out into the portal business. It followed the same path and built up its QQ.com site with news coverage.[12]

A typical Chinese portal, such as Sina.com.cn, is very different from Yahoo. Whereas Yahoo's introductory page is a tidy design featuring different services, Sina's is crammed with news headlines. Because of government regulations, "we dared not say we were a media company in those days," said Wang, "But in fact, Sina is the number one online media firm."

Today, Sina is tacitly recognized as one of the most powerful media companies in the land, with national coverage and a loyal user base consisting mainly of the better off. Its editorial staffers are no longer confined to their cubicles, but go out to interview people and cover news events, just like newspaper reporters. Sina's chief editor, Tong Chen, enjoys the same privileges as the chief editors of major publications.

Show me the money!

Although Sina had found a way to attract users, it did not become profitable until 2003. The reason was that online advertising was still in its infancy in China. iResearch estimated the country's total online advertising spending at only US$61 million in 2002.

Luckily, Sina was able to get listed on NASDAQ in 2000, just before the dot.com bubble burst. It raised US$68 million, which more than covered its US$24 million acquisition of a highly profitable independent mobile data service provider, MeMeStar, in January 2003.[13]

Mobile data services, which include SMS, ringtones, and WAP, quickly became an important revenue source and accounted for about two-thirds of Sina's revenue in 2003–04. Nevertheless, as China's internet population grew and advertisers increased their budgets for online media, Sina's online advertising revenue rose steadily. And by the end of 2006, it again accounted for the majority of the company's revenue—more proof that the original business model was the best.

[12] From Tencent's IPO prospectus: "Our QQ.com portal, relaunched in December 2003, is designed to provide users with information, community resources, and introductions to our growing number of value added services. The main portal channels currently include news, entertainment, sports, automobiles, games, jokes, fashion, and horoscopes."

[13] Source: Sina Annual Report 2004, Material acquisitions.

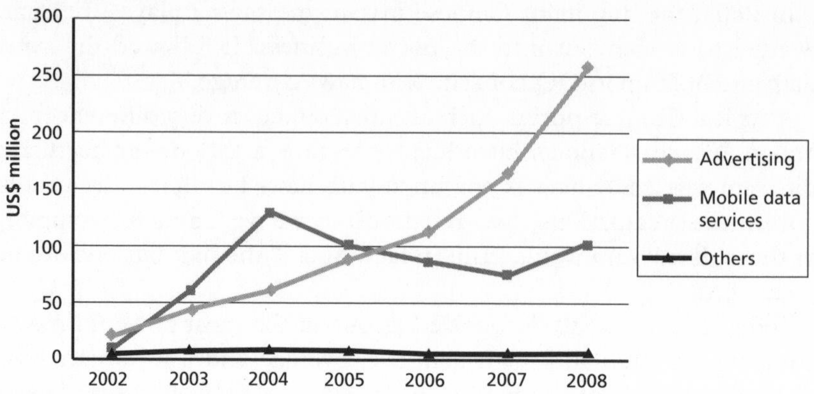

Figure 1.3: **Sina's revenue breakdown (2002–08)**

Data source: Sina

China's internet population grew over 33 times, from 8.9 million in 1999, when Sina.com was launched, to 298 million in 2008.[14] In the same period, online advertising spending soared over 350 times, from US$3.75 million to US$2.46 billion.[15]

Sina registered a profit of over US$88.8 million in 2008 on sales of US$369.6 million. From a team of six people whom the board directors once considered a waste of money, it has grown into an organization with over 2,000 staff.

Wang left Sina to start another venture, Dianji.com, in 2001, but his vision and model live on; Sina's foundation and its basic business model have not changed.

Sina is news.

"It's CCTV on the net," said an industry expert, referring to China Central Television, the nationwide TV network that is the country's most powerful media organization.

Yahoo vs Sina

There is one key difference to note when comparing Yahoo with Sina. Yahoo aspired to be the entry point—a portal or gateway—to the online world. It didn't so much matter where customers went from there. To the web directory developed by Jerry Yang, other services

14 Source: CNNIC.

15 Source: iResearch.

were added—email and news, for instance—designed to lengthen users' stay.

Sina, on the contrary, always wanted to be a "destination" site, one where people would stay. As a result it put great effort into content development. "When it's so difficult to get users to our site, why would we want to send them away," Wang reasoned.

"As Google's search engine replaces it as the preferred entry point to the web, and as more specialized sites steal traffic from its other services, Yahoo is doomed to fail," noted the prescient Foo Jixun, a venture capitalist and investor in the Chinese search engine Baidu, who was predicting Yahoo's troubles from around 2005. "Nowadays, if you want to read news, you go to the websites of the *Wall Street Journal*, the *New York Times*, etc. For community services, the new Web 2.0 players, such as Facebook, MySpace, and Flickr, provide much better services," said Foo.

"What was the value of Yahoo is being replaced and substituted by others," said Foo. "In 10 or 20 years, Yahoo will be gone." Sina should escape this fate, however, because its value is its content—it built itself into one of the most comprehensive news channels in China. And no search engine can replace this function. Despite the surging popularity of Baidu (and Google) in China, Sina has maintained its growth rate. Its imitators, Sohu, Tencent, and Netease, have managed to share in the limelight as they, too, have learned the trick of dumping news online. But Sina is still the leader in online display advertising.

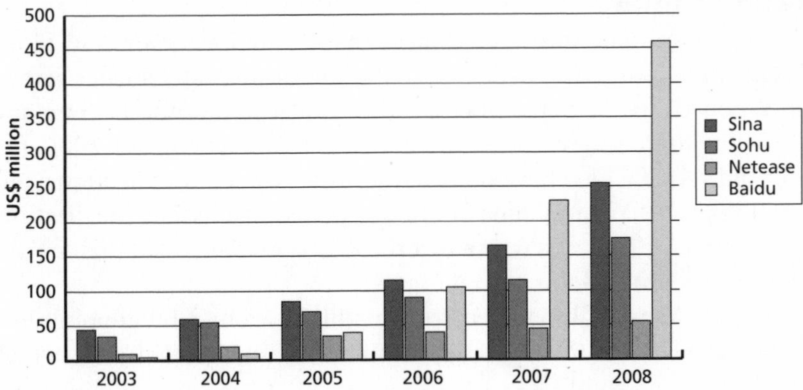

***Figure 1.4:* Online advertising revenue of the major Chinese players**

Data source: individual companies

Into the fray: Sohu and Netease

Sohu, which has always been the number two online portal in China, has largely followed Sina, building itself into an online media firm. It was the official internet sponsor of the Beijing Olympic Games in 2008, using more than 700 editorial staff to cover the events.

As Baidu's popularity grew, Sohu revived its search engine development program and launched a rival product, Sogou, in 2004. But it was too late; Sogou has never become mainstream. The company has had more success with Tian Long Ba Bu, an online game launched in 2007, which has more than doubled its revenue. Sohu's total revenues in 2008 reached US$429.1 million, 2.3 times that of the previous year, of which US$201.8 million was from games. It spun off its game division, Changyou.com, in a separated NASDAQ listing in 2009.

Netease has always been a distant third in the portal race, even though it discovered the magnetic attraction of online games before Sohu did. It started online game development in 2001, after Shanghai-based Shanda proved the business model could work. With hard work and some luck, Netease brought out the country's most popular online game, Fantasy Westward Journey, in December 2003. Most of its revenue now comes from online games, although it is also the country's largest free email provider.[16]

Yahoo China

Yahoo was tapping into the Chinese market via its Taiwan and Hong Kong operations, largely sticking to its American model, before setting up Yahoo China in September 1999.[17] But it lost traffic to Sina and Sohu due to inferior content. When the tech bubble burst in 2000, not only did Yahoo China have no revenue, but support from headquarters dried up, too. "Yahoo China could not match us in scale, localization, or investment. That was why it lost the China market," said Victor Koo, an ex-president of Sohu.

In 2003, Yahoo China tried to turn things around by appointing a local manager, Zhou Hongyi, who had been CEO of 3721.com, which

[16] From Netease financial release, Feb 25, 2009: "Total revenues for 2008 were US$436.2 million. Revenues from online games were US$366.2 million. Revenues from advertising services were US$59.5 million."

[17] Source: *http://cn.about.yahoo.com/company.html*

Yahoo purchased for US$120 million. Suddenly, Yahoo was more Sina than Sina, using sensational headlines and the sex appeal of young girls to drive traffic. It plunged into all kinds of businesses and partnerships, but it was already too late. Sina and Sohu had firmly established themselves as the prime online portals in China. (Zhou Hongyi's contract, being performance-based, would not pay out if he could not achieve certain revenue and profit targets. In the end, he left on bad terms, continuing to pursue his grievances through several lawsuits.)

Yahoo gave up. At the same time as it invested US$1 billion in the Chinese business-to-business site Alibaba in 2005, it gave its China subsidiary to Alibaba to run. But not even Jack Ma, a clever and persistent entrepreneur who had founded not only Alibaba.com but also the eBay slayer Taobao, could turn the situation around. Yahoo China's share of online advertising in China remained small.

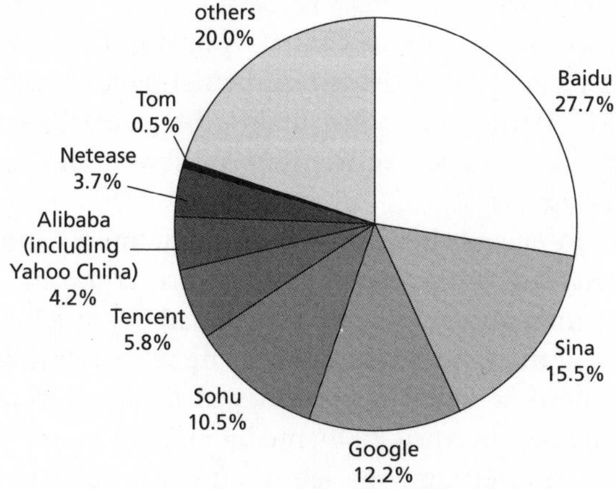

Figure 1.5: **China's online advertising market share**

Data source: Analysys International (2008, 3rd quarter)

Lessons learned

1 What works in your home country might not work in China. Where your options are constrained, you need to be innovative enough to spot the opportunities.

While trying to adapt Yahoo's model for China, the founder of Sina, Wang Zhidong, discovered an entirely different and more powerful formula—being an online aggregator of Chinese news. He changed the business model accordingly, and Sina became not only China's number one portal, but also its number one online media firm bar none.

Sina.com, which offers fast and comprehensive coverage of topics, aside from politics, that engage the wider public, stands out easily from traditional media companies that are either too small or too identified with the government to offer much competition. In fact, most have become Sina's partners, believing this can boost their reputation and influence.

Advertisers love Sina because of its national reach, a rather rare commodity in China. Apart from other online channels such as Sohu and Baidu, the national advertising alternatives are China Central Television (CCTV), whose high rates correspond to its virtual monopoly status, and the government newspapers *People's Daily* and *China Daily*, which are just too dull to achieve a mass readership.

Sina has found the sweet spot in China's media industry. Even if it were offline, Sina's status as a non-governmental national media firm would give it value. Being online just makes things easier—costs are lower, licenses are easier to get, restrictions are fewer, and scaling up and funding are easier.

In America, Yahoo lacked these advantages. The media industry in the West is concentrated in the hands of a few powerhouses. If Yahoo had wanted to use their content, it would have had to pay a high price.

Google has tried something similar with its news search function by aggregating many news sources on the web, which caused trouble with major media companies. In April 2009, media mogul Rupert Murdoch accused Google of committing copyright theft when borrowing material from news stories to assemble search rankings. Shortly after, the Associated Press, a 163-year-old cooperative owned by news organizations, weighed in with a similar charge (though it did not mention Google), announcing a content protection initiative and threatening legal and legislative action against news aggregators.[18] As the power of traditional media firms declines in the West though, they might find themselves more willing to cooperate with online portals. Recently, Yahoo has been successful in partnership with some smaller publications in the US, displaying their content on its site.[19]

[18] Source: Dirk Smillie, "AP's Curley Has Fightin' Words For Google," *Forbes.com*, April 30, 2009.

[19] Source: Evan Hessel, "Yahoo!'s Dangerous Newspaper Deal?" *Forbes.com*, June 22, 2009.

So, when adapting a business for China, it is important to remember to keep your eyes open. When in Rome, do as the Romans do. What is great in your home country may not be desirable in China. Conversely, what is not an option in your home country may be a great opportunity in China.

2 Take advantage of the internet's power as a marketing tool.

As the number of China's internet users rises—about 25 percent of the population is now online—advertising online is a viable alternative for a company looking to promote its goods or services.

For brand advertising, Sina and Sohu are effective in reaching the oldest, richest, and best-educated users. Tencent and Netease are good for younger and less affluent low-end users.

Baidu and Google China are the leading search engines. Generally, Google's users are big city folks who are older, richer, and better educated than Baidu's. However, Baidu's users are more numerous and can be found in all parts of the country.

2. Being there with Ctrip

With money raised from venture capitalists, Oracle consultant James Liang, investment banker Neil Shen, technical expert Qi Ji, and veteran travel agent Fan Min, set out to build a Chinese answer to Expedia, America's online travel leader—just as the internet bubble was bursting.

They set up a website, but real business did not come through until they bought a local travel agency, built a call center, and started dispatching promoters to places with high concentrations of travelers, such as airports and rail stations.

A new way to travel

By the time Ctrip was founded in 1999, millions of travelers had already discovered the World Wide Web. Travel had been revolutionized: people were booking their own hotel rooms, hunting for the cheapest airfares, and swapping travel tips with strangers around the globe via these new electronic means.

In the same year, software giant Microsoft spun off its highly successful subsidiary Expedia.com. Started just four years earlier as an internet experiment, the website, which allowed users to book airlines and hotels, was so popular that it was already a multi-billion dollar business.

The internet's broadly distributed and easily accessible environment is the ideal base for new travel marketplaces. People who had scarcely traveled before were presented with a vast array of choices at prices that seemed unimaginably cheap. They loved the freedom of being able to do their research and make their bookings whenever they liked. Forget 9 to 5, Monday to Friday—they could now book their dream holidays 24/7. And there was no need to go to the travel agent's office downtown. Booking a trip with a "human" travel agent was a thing of the past.

Expedia would soon be joined by other online travel agents. Travelocity.com was created in 1996 as a subsidiary of Sabre Holdings, itself a subsidiary of American Airlines. The airline began offering customers access to its electronic reservation system, SABRE, on the

CompuServe Information Service in the 1980s. This service was extended to America Online in the 1990s.

Orbitz was created as an airline industry response to the rise of online travel agencies. Continental Airlines, Delta Air Lines, Northwest Airlines, and United Airlines, later joined by American Airlines, invested a combined $145 million to start the project in November 1999.[20] It was code-named T2—for "Travelocity Terminator," according to some—but adopted the Orbitz identity when it commenced corporate operations in February 2000.

Priceline, the brainchild of venture capitalist Jesse Fink and digital entrepreneur Jay Walker, did something different with its "Name Your Own Price" system, where travelers essentially bid for airline tickets, hotel rooms, and car rentals.

Essentially, every online travel agency runs on the same model. The customer goes to a computer and finds a website like Expedia.com, which links him or her up with a database containing hundreds of airlines and tens of thousands of hotels.

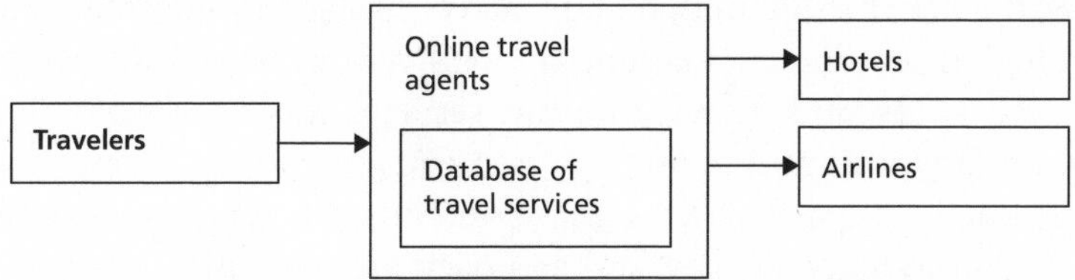

***Figure 2.1:* Business model of online travel agency**

However, for James Liang and his partners, there was just one problem: *Most people in China had yet to go online. How could they get them to visit Ctrip.com?*

Coming home

After years away, James was back in the city where he grew up, Shanghai—China's largest metropolis and its most vibrant business center. James was a computer whiz kid; he won a programming competition for teenagers at the age of 13. At just 15 he entered Shanghai's elite Fudan University, but rather than graduate there he took off for Georgia Tech in Atlanta, where he completed his master's degree when

[20] Since 2001, Orbitz has gone through a number of ownership changes and it is no longer owned solely by the airlines.

he was only 20. Oracle Corp, the world's third largest software company after Microsoft and IBM, hired him in 1991. Oracle specializes in enterprise software—particularly database management systems and enterprise resource planning (ERP) systems. By 1997, James had climbed the corporate ladder and become head of the ERP consulting division of Oracle China.[21]

The Chinese have a name for people like James—"Haigui," (海归) which means "someone who has returned from overseas," but which is pronounced just like the Mandarin words for "sea turtle." James's partner Neil Shen is another sea turtle. After Neil graduated with a Bachelor of Science degree from Shanghai Jiao Tong University, he, too, went to study abroad. He got an MBA from the School of Management at Yale University and started his career in investment banking. He worked for Chemical Bank, Lehman Brothers, and Citibank. Before founding his own company, Neil was a director and head of debt capital markets for China at Deutsche Bank, where he worked from 1996 to 1999.[22]

By 1998, the internet boom that had started in Silicon Valley reached China. Young entrepreneurs, teaming up with venture capitalists, were trying out all kinds of different internet services in China—portals, email, online shopping, and so on.

Qi Ji was one of them. The Shanghai Jiao Tong University graduate had spent a year in Silicon Valley, and had been amazed by its entrepreneurial culture and the internet. He returned home and founded his own company, Shanghai Sunflower High-Tech Group, in 1997, performing IT systems integration.[23]

Ji and Liang were old friends. They joined Shen to start up a venture in the middle of the Chinese internet frenzy. They decided to try an area that was not yet swamped with competitors—online travel. With a booming economy and a growing middle class, the travel industry in China was growing strongly, though the major players were all state-owned enterprises that were slow to seize the opportunities. The three major travel services in China at the millennium were China International Travel Service, China Travel Service, and China Youth Travel Service, all run by the government.

In the period from 1996 to 2006, overseas tourist spending in China grew from US$10.2 billion to US$33.9 billion, an annual growth rate

21 Source: Ctrip IPO prospectus, Management.

22 Source: Ctrip IPO prospectus, Management.

23 Source: Ctrip IPO prospectus, Management.

Item	1996	1997	1998	1999	2000
Total number of travel agencies	**4,252**	**4,986**	**6,222**	**7,326**	**8,993**
International travel agencies	977	991	1,312	1,256	1,268
Domestic travel agencies	3,275	3,995	4,910	6,070	7,725
Number of staff at travel agencies	**87,555**	**94,829**	**100,448**	**108,830**	**164,336**
International travel agencies	53,093	48,881	52,290	47,153	68,093
Domestic travel agencies	34,462	45,948	48,158	61,677	96,243
Total number of tourist hotels	**4,418**	**5,201**	**5,782**	**7,035**	**10,481**
Total number of international tourists arriving in China (10,000s)	**5,112.75**	**5,758.79**	**6,347.84**	**7,279.56**	**8,344.39**
Foreigners	674.43	742.8	710.77	843.23	1,016.04
Overseas Chinese	15.46	9.9	12.07	10.81	7.55
Compatriots from Hong Kong and Macao	4,249.47	4,794.33	5,407.54	6,167.06	7,009.94
Compatriots from Taiwan	173.39	211.76	217.46	258.46	310.86
Number of international tourists received by three major travel services (10,000s)	**171.46**	**189.68**	**167**	**205.11**	**223.3**
China International Travel Service	80.8	88.45	77.45	100.25	91.16
China Travel Service	59.25	66.94	53.79	65.1	88.32
China Youth Travel Service	31.41	34.29	35.76	39.76	43.82
Total number of domestic resident outbound (10,000)	**758.82**	**817.54**	**842.56**	**923.24**	**1,047.26**
For Private Purpose	241.39	243.96	319.02	426.61	563.09
Total number of domestic tourists (10,000s)	**6,3900**	**6,4400**	**6,9450**	**7,1900**	**7,4400**
Tourism receipts					
International tourism receipts (USD 100 million)	102	120.74	126.02	140.99	162.24
Domestic tourism receipts (100 million yuan)	1,638.38	2,112.7	2,391.18	2,831.92	3,175.54

Table 2.1: **Development of Chinese tourism (1996–2000)**

Data source: China Statistical Yearbook 2001, published by National Bureau of Statistic of China

Item	2001	2002	2003	2004	2005	2006
Total number of travel agencies	**10,532**	**11,552**	**13,361**	**14,927**	**16,245**	**18,475**
International travel agencies	1,310	1,349	1,364	1,460	1,556	1,688
Domestic travel agencies	9,222	10,203	11,997	13,467	14,689	16,787
Number of staff at travel agencies	**192,408**	**229,147**	**249,802**	**246,219**	**24,8919**	**29,3318**
International travel agencies	72,801	89,128	100,742	89,342	89,250	
Domestic travel agencies	119,607	140,019	149,060	156,877	159,669	
Number of star-rated Hotels	**7,358**	**8,880**	**9,751**	**10,888**	**11,828**	
Number of overseas visitor arrivals (10,000s)	**8,901.29**	**9,790.83**	**9,166.21**	**10,903.82**	**12,029.23**	**12,494.21**
Foreigners	1,122.64	1,343.95	1,140.29	1,693.25	2,025.51	2,221.03
Chinese Compatriots from Hong Kong and Macao	7,434.45	8,080.82	7,752.73	8,842.05	9,592.79	9,831.83
Chinese Compatriots from Taiwan Province	344.20	366.06	273.19	368.53	410.92	441.35
Overnight tourists	3,316.67	3,680.26	3,297.05	4,176.14	4,680.90	4,991.34
Number of Chinese outbound visitors (10,000s)	**1,213.44**	**1,660.23**	**2,022.19**	**2,885.00**	**3,102.63**	**3,452.36**
For private purposes	694.67	1,006.10	1,481.09	2,298.00	2,514.00	2,879.91
Number of domestic visitors (100 million person-times)	**7.84**	**8.78**	**8.70**	**11.02**	**12.12**	**13.94**
Tourism earnings						
Foreign exchange earnings from international tourism (100 million USD)	177.92	203.85	174.06	257.39	292.96	339.49
Earnings from domestic tourism (100 million yuan)	3,522.36	3,878.36	3,442.27	4,710.71	5,285.86	6,229.74

Table 2.2: **Development of Chinese tourism (2001–06)**

Data source: China Statistical Yearbook 2007, published by National Bureau of Statistic of China of 12.8 percent. Domestic travel was increasing as well, with total spending rising 14.3 percent per year from RMB 163.8 billion to RMB 623.0 billion during the same period.

Fan Min, a friend of Liang, Ji, and Shen, knew the travel industry inside out. Like Shen and Ji, he was a graduate of Shanghai Jiao Tong University, where he received his bachelor's and master's degrees. Fan worked at Shanghai New Asia Hotel Management Company, a leader in the field in China. From 1990 he served in a number of senior positions in the company, reaching deputy general manager level. He spent 1995 doing further study at the Lausanne Hotel Management School of Switzerland, and in 1997 Fan joined Shanghai Travel Service Company, a leading domestic travel agency, as chief executive officer.[24]

With Fan's knowledge of the travel industry and Ji's and Liang's technological skills, they had no trouble putting together a decent website. They named their company Ctrip (short for "China trip").

Selling a business plan to investors was not very difficult for Shen, who had mastered the art during years of investment banking. Given the chance, he could talk nonstop for 80 minutes, as a reporter who met him at the time recalls. Without any prompting, facts and figures would trip off his tongue—financial ratios, performance metrics, industry comparisons, the finances and strategy of competitors in and outside China.

They raised their initial investment capital in 1999 from a group of venture capital funds that included IDG, an early-stage fund run by IDC, a market research and analysis firm specializing in information technology, telecommunications, and consumer technology. The following year, heavyweight investors Softbank and Carlyle Group chipped in, too. In total Ctrip had almost US$17 million to build a Chinese answer to Expedia.

China's challenge

The internet arrived in China just a few years before Ctrip started. By 1999 there were about 2.1 million internet users in a country of 1.3 billion people, or roughly 1.6 persons per 1,000, according to a survey by government-backed researcher CNNIC. Most of them, 24 percent, were in the capital city Beijing, where many of the country's top universities are located. Over 90 percent used the internet to check

24 Source: Ctrip IPO prospectus, Management.

emails and instant messages. Only 15 percent had tried any form of e-commerce or online shopping. The odds of going online and booking a hotel in 1999 were close to zero!

Ctrip's website was ready by November 1999. The first version of Ctrip was more like a travel information site—a city guide. The main purpose was to attract eyeballs—to get people to visit the site. To help with this, writers were hired to produce travel-related articles for the site. But China was not ready for a web-centric operation like Expedia.com.

Liang and his partners could have waited until the online population in China was large enough to support a pure vanilla form of online travel like Expedia.com. But that might have taken another nine or ten years—by 2008, the country's internet penetration had reached about 22 percent,[25] still less than the level in America in 1999, which was roughly 30–40 percent.[26] And so, before their newly established start-up fell apart, they quickly had to find an alternative way to attract customers.

Metamorphosis

Ctrip was lucky enough to have raised sufficient cash before the internet bubble burst to buy up a traditional travel agency specializing in hotel bookings in China, Beijing Modern Express Corporate Travel Service. This meant that there were some customers and revenues in place. At the time of the acquisition, the agency had a monthly business volume of about 30,000 hotel nights. Ctrip went on to buy a few more travel agencies, which gave them the scale and the required licenses for their business. But the growth rate of a traditional travel agency was too slow, and the margin was too low. They needed triple-digit growth to satisfy their venture capital investors. There were clear yardsticks set for revenue and room booking growth in the second round of Ctrip's funding in November 2000, according to a venture capitalist who invested. If they did not meet those yardsticks, they would be punished—and that meant dilution of their ownership and a lower price for their shares.

Ctrip had another idea, though—why not send people out to office buildings to distribute pamphlets promoting its services? Many

25 Source: CNNIC.
26 Source: International Telecommunication Union.

companies promoted products and services this way in China—salespersons went door-to-door in downtown office buildings to solicit business. Unfortunately though, the result was unsatisfactory, recalled Fan years after. "How many people would be just about to take trips?" The concentration of travelers in a normal office was too low for the plan to succeed. Their formula had to change.

1 First, instead of office buildings, why not go to areas flooded with travelers—transportation hubs, such as airports and train and bus stations?
2 Second, instead of making people book through the website, why not give customers a number to call? People at airports and rail stations didn't have easy access to the internet, but many had their cellphones with them. By the end of 1999, there were 43.3 million cellphone users in China, the second largest contingent in the world. By August 2001, this number had jumped to 120.6 million, giving China the largest number of cellphones in the world (though that is still just one out of every ten Chinese, as services are inaccessible in large areas of rural China).[27]
3 Third, a call center would be needed to support the operation, not just a website. Most of the world's online travel agents give customers a number they can call—but that is usually just for exceptional situations. In Ctrip's case, the opposite is true. The website is the exception and the call center, which handles more than 70 percent of the reservations, is the rule.

By 2001, Ctrip had ceased to be a typical online travel agent. Most of its customers first encountered it not on the internet, but at the exits of rail stations and airports. Ctrip's promoters handed them a membership card, plus a booklet with hotel prices and a telephone number for reservations. The service is 24 hours a day, just like an online travel agent, but when they dial the reservations number, a real person picks up the phone.

When you think about it, after these transformations, Ctrip hardly even qualifies as an internet business. Only a small part of its traffic flows through the internet. It is actually quite labor intensive—over half of its employees are call center staff and "ground troops" at airports and rail stations.[28]

[27] Source: Ministry of Industry and Information Technology of China.
[28] According to Ctrip's IPO prospectus, as of October 31, 2003 it had 1,420 employees, including 554 in the customer service center, and over 300 on-site promoters.

Bricks (not clicks)

Ctrip bore only a faint resemblance to a proper internet travel site. The result, nevertheless, rocked. Ctrip broke even in March 2002, only two and half years after it started. Sales accelerated to over US$12.1 million in 2002 from a mere US$724,000 in 2000. It became one of the largest agents for hotel accommodation in China. By December 2004, it had registered over 1 million customers. It was booking 400,000 hotel nights and 180,000 air tickets every month.

Though it is not strictly an "internet business," it has enjoyed internet-like growth because it found a market that had previously not been well served—China's new business travelers. Ten to 15 years prior, there were very few small businessmen traveling around the country in search of clients, suppliers, and partners. Those who traveled a lot were government officials and managers of state-owned enterprises. They had the State to arrange their travel plans and they stayed in hotels set up by their own ministries or related organizations. The State Postal Bureau, for example, once owned hundreds of hotels around the country, all for the use of its own staff.

Today, managers of companies in China travel like their counterparts in America, and need fast and reliable services at competitive prices—and that's what Ctrip offers. Business travel accounts for 80 percent of Ctrip's business. Though there are still many traditional travel agencies in China, they tend to focus on package tours for leisure travelers. Guided tours are great for people who are unfamiliar with the destination and who want to travel cheaply. However, the schedules are too rigid for business travelers, who often have to fly at short notice.

The manager of an online game company used to travel out of his Shanghai office a few times per month. "I never book with a hotel. I just pick up a Ctrip booklet from the airport and call the number," said Joe Wu (in 2004). In early 2000, travelers could meet up to five Ctrip promoters during their trips from Beijing Rail Station, said an executive living in the capital city.

Today, in the major cities such as Beijing and Shanghai, Ctrip no longer needs to hand out as many booklets. But Fan said the practice still goes on, especially when Ctrip expands into new cities. Because of the low cost of labor in China, "on-site promoters" (Ctrip's official name for its ground troops) remain a cost-effective way for it to market its services. The average wage for call center staff was US$337 per month in October 2003. Each staffer takes on average 2,425 calls a month, so the average labor cost per call is US$0.14. Morgan Stanley estimated in September 2005 that labor costs consumed about 8 percent of Ctrip's commissions on air ticket bookings and 5 percent of its commissions on hotel reservations.

Of course, Ctrip also uses other marketing channels, such as online and offline advertising, strategic alliances with banks and airlines, telemarketing, and customer reward programs. But on-site promoters are still front and center when it comes to bringing in new customers.

With a brilliant financial record, the company went for an IPO on NASDAQ in December 2003. It was the first Chinese internet company to be listed on NASDAQ after the tech bubble burst. Online portals Sina, Sohu, and Netease were the lucky few that managed to get listed before the internet frenzy abated. Ctrip's share price shot up over three times its IPO level on the first day of trading.

The company continued its phenomenal growth in the next five years. In 2007, Ctrip booked 9.6 million hotel nights for its clients and sold 10.7 million air tickets.[29] Sales increased sevenfold to about US$164 million from 2003 to 2007. Its profit margin in 2007 was an exceptional 32.9 percent.

Apart from its Shanghai headquarters, Ctrip has branch offices in 11 other major cities in China. The company also maintains a network of sales offices in about 45 cities. It has over 7,100 employees, of which 3,000 work in its call center. It has become a well-known brand; many businesspeople and holidaymakers book their trips with it. Besides domestic destinations, they can book flights and hotels overseas, too.

	Ctrip	**Expedia**
Air tickets sold	10.7 million	45.1 million transactions
Hotel room nights booked	9.6 million	
Sales	US$176 million	US$2,665 million
*Annual growth rate (4 years)**	67.4%	3.3%
Profit	US$54.6 million	US$295.9 million
*Annual growth rate (4 years)**	70.2%	27.7%
Net profit margin	31%	11.1%
Number of staff	7,100	7,150

***Table 2.3:* Ctrip–Expedia comparison**

Data source: Annual reports from Ctrip and Expedia, 2007

* Result of 2003–07

[29] Source: Ctrip Annual Report 2007.

In hindsight, the bursting of the dot.com bubble in 2000–01 may have been a blessing in disguise for Ctrip, for three reasons.

First, it freed up management to try something new. Buying travel agencies, opening a call center, sending promoters to airports and rail stations—such unorthodox tactics were enough to drive plain vanilla internet zealots crazy. But after the bubble burst, ideology went out the window. What counted was what worked in real life, not what worked in theory.

A venture capitalist investor recalled why he invested in Ctrip. "Around June or July 2000, Ctrip changed its model. It said it was going to buy up traditional travel agents and focus on hotel bookings, with a call center operation," said the venture capitalist. "I liked the transformation. I thought that would work under the current business environment in China. So, we gave them the money, even though the internet bubble had crashed and we stopped investment in many other firms." This was the second round of Ctrip funding; it raised about US$12 million in November 2000. They had already used up the US$5 million raised in the first round. "Without that crucial investment, they would be gone," said the venture capitalist. The bold bet paid off handsomely. He sold his holding in Ctrip two years after the company listed on NASDAQ, making a 16-fold profit on his investment.

Second, the dot.com bust benefited Ctrip throught the impact on its competitors—they were wiped out when they were youngest and most vulnerable. Tom.com, a startup backed by a Hong Kong tycoon, Li Kashing, had been eyeing the online travel industry in China. It launched a China travel site in 1999, but the next year, when the bubble popped and easy money dried up, the operation folded.

"We were planning to set up a pure-bred online travel agency," said a former senior executive of Tom, who was in charge of its investment decisions, "but the market was not ready—not enough people online. And we could wait no longer—it took Ctrip about three years to break even, and it is a hybrid-model, 'clicks-and-mortar,' not a pure online operation. After the bubble burst, the Hutchison Group needed us to show profitability as soon as possible." The Hutchison Group is the flagship company Li used to control Tom. It operates many ports and telecommunication services around the world.

After Tom folded its online travel business, it went on acquiring a lot of traditional media companies, that, despite low margins, were cashflow positive. It eventually made a comeback by acquiring a successful mobile data service provider in China, which it built into the largest in the country. But that is for a later chapter.

Competition: Expedia enters China

Serious competition for Ctrip did not come until mid 2001. eLong, a travel information site set up in 1999 on the mainland, was pursuing the same opportunity with a business model similar to Ctrip's (on-site promoters plus call center). "In fact, eLong was the first travel site. But it was difficult to argue who imitated who, as Ctrip and eLong were pretty much doing the same thing at the same time," said J. P. Gan, a venture capitalist who invested in Ctrip when he worked for Carlyle. There were other players, too. But eLong was and is the largest.

eLong cofounder Justin Tang's background is similar to Neil Shen's and James Liang's. He too is a "sea turtle," someone born in China but who studied and worked abroad for some time before returning home. Tang studied first at Nanjing University then left for America. After receiving his Bachelor of Science degree from Concordia College, he worked for seven years in various investment and financial services companies, including Oscar Gruss & Son, Brookehill Equities Inc., and Merrill Lynch.[30]

eLong also sent promoters out to greet travelers at airports and other transportation hubs. It set up a call center. eLong has a website, too, though as in the case of Ctrip, 70 percent of its clients use the call center for their bookings. And like Ctrip, eLong enjoyed rapid growth. Its hotel booking volume increased from approximately 389,000 nights in 2001 to approximately 1,032,000 in 2003. eLong became the second largest online travel agency after Ctrip, with about half as much business volume.

When Expedia came looking for a foothold in China in 2004, its gaze fell upon eLong, although it was only marginally profitable. It acquired 52 percent of eLong in two rounds of investment, effectively making eLong its China branch. eLong, too, was listed on NASDAQ in October 2004. Insiders recalled that Expedia approached Ctrip first, but Ctrip refused to sell. The price was not right. "We talked. But Ctrip had always aimed for an independent listing—that would have given

30 Source: eLong IPO prospectus, Management.

the highest payback for investors like us. Large corporations, like Expedia, have many priorities other than maximizing minority shareholders' payback," said a Ctrip investor.

eLong, however, has never been as efficient as Ctrip. Analysts at Morgan Stanley compared their performance. They found that Ctrip produced 40 percent more sales with 30 percent lower costs per employee than eLong. "Ctrip practices Six Sigma in its operation and makes sure every step of its business process is running efficiently. Every operation detail is tracked and measured in Ctrip's system," said Gan. Six Sigma is a business management strategy, initially implemented by Motorola, that was originally developed to improve manufacturing processes and eliminate defects (defined as anything that could lead to customer dissatisfaction). It is widely used today in many sectors of industry.

For example, Ctrip was not the first to have promoters at train stations. Many small, local travel agents were doing the same in the late 1990s. "But Ctrip was the first one to offer a nationwide hotel booking service and professionally manage the process. The reference numbers on its membership cards were traced throughout Ctrip's system in an ongoing base. So, the company knows when and where a new member signs up, how many flights and hotel rooms he or she books over the years, and so on," said Gan.

In contrast, an industry insider has said that eLong's platform was never designed to support a large-scale operation—for example, if Ctrip receives 5,000 calls an hour from customers, only ten or 15 are likely to have problems. But if eLong receives 5,000 calls in an hour, 3,000 will have problems, said the industry insider.

David Savelson, an expatriate living in Hong Kong, once booked a five-star hotel in Guangzhou with eLong. "But when we showed up that evening, the hotel reception said they did not receive the reservation. Luckily, I printed out the confirmation page of eLong and the hotel staff trusted me and gave me the room," said Savelson.

Tang quit eLong one year after Expedia took over. Expedia appointed its own CEO, but even after several changes of management (or perhaps because of the changes of management), eLong still has not attained profitability. "And in retrospect, I thought Expedia's investment actually dragged down eLong's performance," one Ctrip investor observed. "Expedia did not invest a lot in eLong and it took away the incentives for the top executives to perform. The theoretical synergy between the two was never realized, either. There are not many overseas booking orders flowing from Expedia to eLong, and there are not many Chinese booking orders flowing from eLong to Expedia. I don't think the back-end platforms of the two are well integrated."

By 2008, eLong was no longer a serious threat to Ctrip. Ctrip continued its spectacular growth of 30–40 percent a year, compared with annual growth of 12–14 percent in the Chinese travel industry overall.

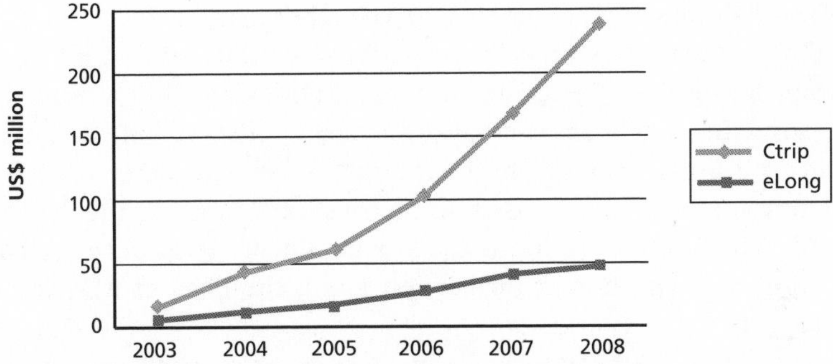

***Figure 2.2:* Revenue comparison between Ctrip and eLong**

Data source: Ctrip and eLong

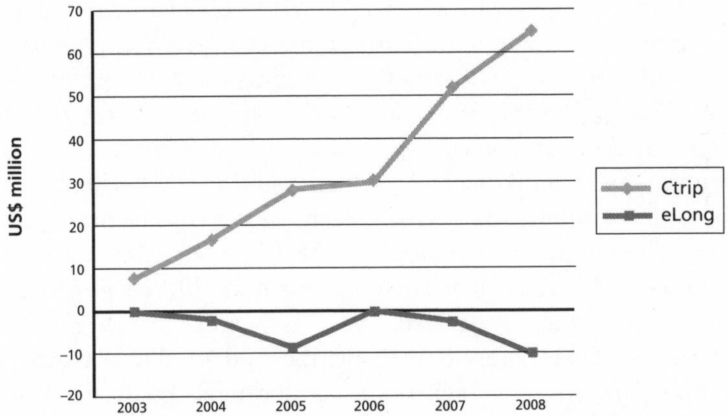

***Figure 2.3:* Profit comparison between Ctrip and eLong**

Data source: Ctrip and eLong

Other innovative ideas

Another important innovation at Ctrip was the way it managed its hotel inventory. In America, online travel agents do not have to deal with individual hotels or airlines if they don't want to. They can get flight information and room rates, determine room availability, and make reservations via Global Distribution Systems (GDS). For example, Expedia works with three of these GDSs—Sabre, Amadeus, and Worldspan. (Expedia has, however, started to link directly with hotels and airlines in an effort to achieve higher margins.)

In China, Ctrip uses TravelSky, a domestic GDS formed by all the domestic airlines, for flight information and bookings. But it must deal with individual hotels for reservations. Most hotels in China do not yet belong to a GDS because the membership fees are rather high. The hotel market, like many other industries in China, is highly fragmented. Most hotels are individually run. There are as yet no chains consisting of thousands of properties, along the lines of Marriott or Holiday Inn.

To build its hotel inventory, Ctrip must sign up hotels one by one. It has a team entirely dedicated to managing its relationship with hotels and maintaining the hotel room database. Luckily, hotels are in oversupply in China—many have occupancy rates below 70 percent. They are quite happy with the additional sales channel that they acquire when they sign up with Ctrip. Some even give Ctrip a guaranteed daily allotment of rooms without asking for any sort of down payment. This allows Ctrip to instantly confirm reservations. For hotels not on the guaranteed allotment list, Ctrip must check first to determine if a room is available, which could take anywhere from a few hours to a whole day. Ctrip reciprocates by recommending its guaranteed-allotment partners' hotels first. In 2005, although just 40 percent (or 1,300) of its hotel partners offered guaranteed-allotment rooms, they generated over 70 percent of Ctrip's hotel reservations, said Morgan Stanley. By the end of 2008, Ctrip had 7,700 hotel partners, of which 60 percent offered guaranteed hotel room allotments.

How to deal with payment was another difficult challenge facing Ctrip. In the West, payment is most often done by credit card. To book a hotel, you need to provide the online travel agent with your credit card number, to which it charges both the room rate and its commission.

In China, penetration of credit cards was practically zero when Ctrip started in 1999.[31] So Ctrip does not charge customers anything at all—after they have paid and checked out, Ctrip bills the hotel for its commissions, which are usually collected on a monthly basis.

Much depends on the hotels being honest. What if they were to lie about the number of nights a guest stayed, or simply say that the customer did not show up? Fan said Ctrip will randomly check with its clients to verify their stays. This is done by cellphone via SMS. In case of dishonesty, that particular hotel will be cut off. The whole process sounds rather complicated. True, but the profit is nice. Ctrip's commission rate on hotel booking reaches 10–15 percent. Its commission rate on air tickets is about 5 percent.

Weakness

Ctrip's weakness may be its strength. Its business model, so well adapted to the Chinese environment, may be difficult to export. For marketing and sales, it depends on a large team of low-wage workers—the call center staff, the on-site promoters, and so on. These are in abundant supply in China, but not everywhere else in the world.

A Ctrip executive talked about how hard it was to expand its business in Hong Kong.[32] In Hong Kong, sending promoters to the airport may not be such a good idea—salaries can be over five times higher than they are in the rest of the country. And the airport authority might not be keen to have salespeople accosting travelers as they leave the terminal. As for more traditional marketing channels, such as ads in the local papers—they did not work either. "The money for a full, front page ad in the city's dominant newspaper would be roughly my marketing budget for the whole year," said the executive.

Of course, at present, there is no pressing need for Ctrip to expand overseas, as the Chinese travel market is still growing fast and Ctrip's market share is still small. Morgan Stanley estimated that Ctrip accounted for only 1–2 percent of total travel industry revenues in China in 2008. The company did, however, revamp its English site in March 2008, just before the Beijing Olympics. Fan thought that since

[31] Credit card penetration is still rather low, but online payment by debit card has caught on and almost everybody now has one.

[32] Hong Kong, a city in the south of China, was a British colony until 1997. Its living standards are much higher than those in other Chinese cities. It is a busy financial center, on a par with New York and London.

the Chinese government had put so much money and effort into promoting China before the games, Ctrip might well benefit from an upsurge in foreign interest in the country—so why not upgrade its site?

As hotel chains and airlines organize their own web booking activities, online travel agents are bound to see their margins squeezed. International full-fare carriers, such as British Airways, typically sell 30 percent of their tickets directly, and budget airlines such as Ryanair sell more than half directly.

In America, Expedia has already started to suffer from such competition. Its revenue per air ticket decreased more than 10 percent a year in the 2005–07 period. In the long term, Ctrip will face the same threat. However, it will probably take longer for China's leading airlines, all of them run by the government, to adjust to selling more tickets themselves. In China, only 20 percent of air tickets are sold directly by carriers—80 percent are sold by travel agencies, and the large ones, such as Ctrip, have considerable clout with the airlines.

The agencies have even more bargaining power over hotels because China still lacks the big chains that can organize their own direct sales channels. Nevertheless, the rapid growth of budget hotel chains, such as Home Inns,[33] Hanting,[34] Jinjiang Inn, Motel 168, and so on, in China, is not to be underestimated.

In 2008, the financial crisis, which started from the subprime lending in America, caused a global economic slowdown that also affected China. Ctrip's profit grew just 23 percent to US$52.5 million in 2008, slowing down from the 74 percent growth rate it had had a year earlier. In 2008–09, it acquired 18.25% of Home Inns for US$92 million[35]; this was a budget hotel chain that it had once started and then spun off. While this could pave the way to future growth, most analysts believed Home Inns was competing in a tough environment.

While Liang's team could make Ctrip's operation stand out from the other online travel agents, they could not do the same with Home Inns. Although they pioneered the concept of budget hotel chains in China, Home Inns' competitors, or imitators, could come up with better services and lower prices.

33 Home Inns was started by Ctrip and spun off in 2004.
34 Hanting's founders included Qi Ji, a cofounder of Ctrip.
35 Source: Ctrip Annual Report 2008, p11.

Lessons learned

1 When adapting a business model to China, look at each part of your operation to identify what needs to be changed, what needs to be eliminated, and what needs to be added.

A detailed look at Ctrip's operation shows that in every area, from sales and marketing to payment and inventory management, it is different from Expedia, the American online travel agent it set out to copy.

Innovation is the act of introducing something new. And this is what Ctrip has done. It has introduced something new to almost every part of the formula, because Expedia's way did not work in China. The market was not ready. Credit cards were not available. There were no GDSs for hotels. There were not even enough people online. But unlike Tom.com, Ctrip's management was unwilling to see the company fail. They had no choice but to innovate.

	Expedia	Ctrip
Marketing	Online and offline ads	On-site promoters at airports, bus and train stations
Sales	Website	Call center
Payments (hotel)	By users via credit card	Users pay hotels directly—Ctrip settles its commission with hotels individually on a monthly basis.
Payment (air ticket)	By users via credit card	Initially, Ctrip partnered with small local travel agents, and sent people to collect cash payments from users and deliver air tickets to them. As airlines in China switched to electronic tickets, Ctrip allowed users to pay online with credit and debit cards.
Inventory (for hotel)	Through GDS	Through direct relationships with hotels

***Table 2.4:* Comparison between Expedia's and Ctrip's business models**

2 The "on-site promoters plus call center" formula.

One lesson to learn from the Ctrip story is that "on-site promoters plus call center" can be an effective sales and marketing channel in China, where labor is abundant and costs are low. In fact, in Ctrip's wake, other companies have begun to apply the same tactics successfully in their own businesses.

Founded in 2005 in Beijing, the United Automobile Association (UAA) wanted to be the country's answer to the American Automobile Association. At the core of its operation was a 400-person call center. It also dispatched promoters, not to airports or train stations, but to gas stations, to hand out leaflets and membership cards to passing car owners. "Ctrip on wheels" is how UAA describes itself on its website.

Still, your competitors can use the same tactics. Look at eLong—Expedia's Chinese branch. To maintain long-term competitiveness, your business must have other strengths—in Ctrip's case, their competitive strength is operational efficiency. Additionally, due to its larger scale and higher brand recognition, Ctrip enjoys a positive network effect—as more hotels pick it as their partner, more customers choose it as their preferred travel agent.

Ctrip's lead over eLong continues to widen. Its sales were 4.85 times eLong's in 2008, compared with 2.67 times in 2004. And while Ctrip's profitability reached about 30 percent, eLong was making losses.

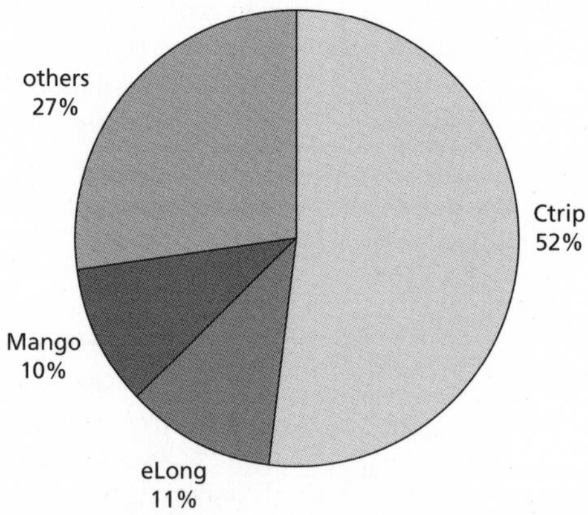

***Figure 2.4:* Market share of online travel (2008)**

Data source: Analysys International

Note: by revenue

3. Traffic alert: Baidu

The early history of Baidu, the largest Chinese search engine, is very similar to that of Google. It, too, started by licensing its services to other websites. But its founder Robin Li, a young computer engineer returned from America, decided to change the company's direction in 2001. He wanted to launch an independent search site, but to do so he had to address two problems:

1 *How to get advertisers*
2 *How to get traffic.*

The first problem he solved by recruiting sales agents. His solution to the second problem was much more risky. Though music downloads were still a gray area in China, Baidu's decision to offer its clients an MP3 search function brought down the wrath of the world's biggest recording companies on the young company's head. There was an advantage, however—American-based arch-rival Google dared not follow it onto such dangerous legal ground.

The 800-pound gorilla of search

As the World Wide Web increases in popularity and the amount of information on the web explodes, people need a quick way of finding the information they want. The first means to win acceptance was Yahoo—it offered web page directories maintained by indexers who ruled on the relevance of pages and entered them under categories and sub-categories. In many ways, this mimicked the traditional approaches taken in the news clipping and reference indexing service business that preceded the consolidation of information on the internet.

Machine-driven search engines, using computer algorithms and databases alone to return results, began to appear in 1993. The first was Wanlex (now defunct), followed the same year by Aliweb. The initial results of these systems were poor. Yahoo's human indexers were generally more successful at knowing what users wanted.

The breakthrough came in 1996 when two PhD students at Stanford University in California rediscovered a vintage search algorithm dating from the early 1950s. Eugene Garfield, the developer of this algorithm, was a structural linguist most famous for founding the Institute for Scientific Information (ISI), noted for its Science Citation Index (SCI) and other citation indexes of importance in academia. Garfield perceived science as a "web of knowledge" consisting of research papers (nodes) linked by their co-citation of other research papers (links). He devised "weights" called citation indices that tracked the propagation of scientific thinking. His work led to the discovery that in the natural sciences, a few journals like *Nature* and *Science* lay at the center of all research.

Four decades later, Larry Page and Sergey Brin adapted Garfield's 1950s work to the problem of web searches. Page and Brin looked at the internet as a "web of knowledge" consisting of web pages (nodes) linked by their hypertext citations of other web pages (links). PageRanks (a term the two used to describe relevance or importance of a web page) are the "weights" that are the web's counterparts to Garfield's citation indices; they track the propagation of web page usage and search. PageRank, eventually, became the core capability of a new search engine called Google.

For the initial users of Google it was love at first sight, and as their passion spread to others, it achieved the ultimate branding success—its name became a verb meaning "to search for information on the internet." Google went on to develop (or acquire) many beloved applications—Gmail, Google Maps and YouTube, for example—that have increased the site's "stickiness," or user loyalty.

How to profit from search traffic was Google's other major breakthrough. Although the idea was not original to Google, it perfected the concept of "cost-per-click" advertisements that appear alongside the search results, where the advertiser pays only when someone clicks on the ad. How much they pay is determined by a bidding process. Generally, the more an advertiser bids for a keyword, the higher up the list its ad will appear. Factors such as relevance and past performance also enter the equation—for instance, the more times an ad was clicked on when it appeared in the past, the higher its place in the list. Google calls this program for advertisers AdWords.

It has another program for website owners wishing to profit from their traffic—AdSense. For websites that join AdSense, the program automatically delivers text and image ads that are targeted to the sites and their contents. Whenever someone clicks on these ads, website owners share in the ad revenue with Google. Today Google derives about 70 percent of its revenues from its own website and 30 percent from the AdSense network. (For more about Google's Adwords and AdSense, please refer to this book's website: *www.redwiredrevolution.com.*)

Cost-per-click made Google rich. After introducing the charging formula in the first quarter of 2002, its revenue quadrupled within months, surging to US$348 million at the end of that year from a mere US$86 million in 2001.[36] Its profit shot up over 14 times to nearly US$100 million in 2002 from less than US$7 million the year before.

Search engines became the part of the internet business that everybody wanted a piece of. Yahoo, which had been happy to outsource its "insignificant" search functions to Google for almost four years until 2004, all at once became a competitor by acquiring and combining the search engines Overture, Inktomi, AltaVista, and AlltheWeb. Microsoft, the software giant which had missed the better part of the internet revolution, also launched its own search engine. Like Yahoo, Microsoft had used third-party search services at first. In 2004 it introduced a technology that made web search a more integrated part of its

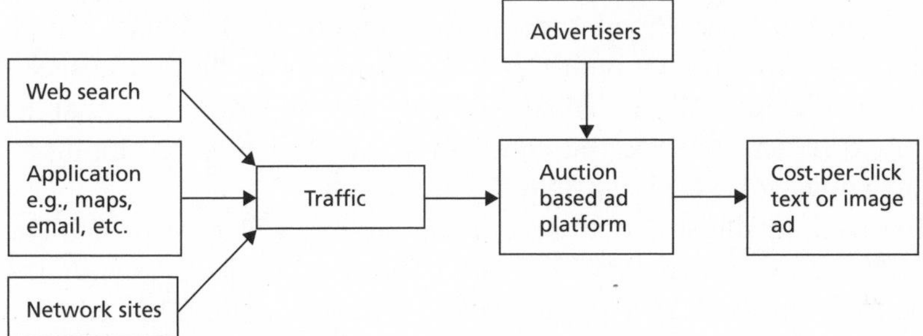

***Figure 3.1:* Search engine business model**

Note: How it works: search traffic is generated from users using web search functions and applications such as maps, email, etc. More traffic comes from users visiting network sites that have joined the search engine's partner program. Based on what users are searching for or reading about, the search engine's ad platform will show them relevant ads. The advertiser pays only when someone clicks on the ad. An auction process determines the ranking of ads.

36 From Google IPO prospectus: "In the fourth quarter of 2000, we launched Google AdWords, an online self-service program that enables advertisers to place targeted text-based ads on our websites. AdWords customers originally paid us based on the number of times their ads appeared on users' search results pages. In the first quarter of 2002, we began offering AdWords exclusively on a cost-per-click basis, so that an advertiser pays us only when a user clicks on one of its ads."

Windows operating system; this later became MSN Live search, which was relaunched as Bing in June 2009.

Search engine models, China style: Baidu

Born in 1968, Baidu founder Robin Li was the fourth of five children. He grew up during the uncertain times of China's Cultural Revolution. He was bright enough to get into the country's most prestigious school, Peking University, where he dabbled in computer science. Then he moved to America, enrolling at the State University of New York-Buffalo, where he completed his master's degree in 1994.

Around the same time as Larry Page and Sergey Brin were reading the indexing literature for search algorithms, Li, who had stayed on in America after college, was applying his skills to similar problems. He developed and patented a search mechanism that he called "link analysis," which ranked the popularity of websites according to the number of other sites that had linked to them.[37] However, his manager at Dow Jones & Company, where he helped develop software for the online edition of *The Wall Street Journal*, remained unimpressed.

Undaunted, Li attended a computer conference in Silicon Valley, where he set up his own booth to demonstrate his findings. Infoseek's chief technology officer William Chang was so impressed that he recruited him to oversee the company's search engine development. (Chang now works for Li as Baidu's chief scientist.)

However, pessimism about search engines was still widespread. The Walt Disney Company, which owned Infoseek, decided to shift the subsidiary's focus away from search and toward content. This led Li to form his own internet company with Eric Xu, who had a PhD in biochemistry and good contacts in Silicon Valley. During 1996–9, before founding Baidu, Xu worked for five different technology companies in Silicon Valley and found two different startups of his own. In 1998–9 he made the first Chinese TV documentary about entrepreneurs in Silicon Valley, for which he interviewed over 50 top venture capitalists, executives and entrepreneurs in the region.

A venture capital investor recalled meeting them in early 1999: "I remember Eric Xu coming to our office. He had studied biochemistry but he wanted to do internet business… It was something like selling

[37] Source: David Barboza, "The Rise of Baidu (That's Chinese for Google)," *New York Times*, Sept 17, 2006.

phone cards online. The model was not impressive and we ignored him. He later came back with Robin Li and said they wanted to set up a Chinese search engine. There were very few who had Robin's experience in search engines and, being Chinese, he figured to know the language well. We were impressed," said the venture capitalist, though his company, for reasons of its own, chose not to invest in Baidu.

By dint of sheer persistence, though, Li and Xu did manage to pry US$1.2 million out of several ex-Inktomi executives who had cashed out of that firm at the height of the internet boom in late 1999. The two went back to China, recruited a team of researchers from Peking University and started building their Chinese search engine. The first version took about a year to finish. They called it Baidu, a name that in Chinese means "hundreds of times," and refers to the persistent pursuit of the ideal of beauty.

Independence

Like Google, Baidu started out by licensing its search engine services to other websites. It partnered with the major Chinese portals Sina, Sohu, and Netease, and also tried to sell its search engine to companies and government agencies for use on their intranet sites. "We thought a search engine was just a tool. And if someone could provide that [to our users], we were glad to use their services," said Wang Zhidong, former CEO of Sina, China's top online portal. Before Sina used Baidu for searching, it had partnered with AltaVista and Openfind.

But by 2001, Li had come to the conclusion that there was no future in merely providing services to other sites. He was determined to launch an independent search website. And despite the misgivings of some of his board members, who were afraid of alienating Baidu's portal partners, he eventually got his way. Baidu.com was launched in September 2001 and is remarkably similar in design to Google.com. It, too, derives its revenue from auction-based cost-per-click or "pay-for-performance" ads. The Baidu Bid-for-Ranking service is its answer to Google's AdWords, while its Baidu Union, which allows website owners to share in the profits by showing Baidu's ads on their sites, corresponds to Google AdSense.

"Google's Adwords was inspired by Overtune. Baidu, at that time, also had its ideas from Overtune," said Foo Jixun, a venture capitalist whose former firm, Draper Fisher Jurvetson ePlanet, was an early believer in

Baidu. Together with other venture capitalists, it invested US$10 million in Baidu in September 2000.

As an independent website, two things needed to be addressed: 1) How to sell ads?; and 2) How to get traffic?

Tricks for selling keywords

Selling keywords is problematic in China. Like Google, Baidu uses its own sales force for dealing with major clients. But whereas in North America and Europe tens of thousands of small advertisers bid for keywords via Google's AdWords and pay by credit card, the vast bulk of potential Chinese users have yet to attain that level of sophistication.

"China is very different. There are hundreds of cities and advertisers who need to be educated," said Foo.

Online advertising is still relatively little used in China, especially by the small and medium-sized businesses that make up the majority of Baidu's customers. Many are not internet users, and most do not have credit cards for online transactions. China's internet penetration was about 2.5 percent at the end of 2001. And of the 33.7 million internet users, only 2.1 percent had used any form of online payment, according to CNNIC.

Online portals were selling their ads via third-party advertising agents. So Baidu began signing up agencies; these in turn would hire more agents, creating a sales force ready to "cold call" anyone who might listen and even go door-to-door if necessary. Agents taught potential customers the keyword bidding process step-by-step, and when that was too difficult they simply did the work for them. They also collected payment on Baidu's behalf.[38] Incredibly, it worked. Though some advertisers had bad experiences and quit, others liked the results and stayed, gradually increasing their online advertising budgets.

Pirate Bay

With advertisers in place, the last challenge for Baidu in turning profitable was getting traffic. Its portal partners Sina, Sohu, and Netease produced some traffic for Baidu; more came by word of mouth. But, it was not enough.

[38] Usually, clients will deposit their payments into the local agents' bank account. The agents take their commission, then transfer the rest to Baidu's account.

But there was one thing that people, especially teenagers, wanted from the internet—music, usually meaning pirated MP3 files. Despite all the potential legal ramifications, everyone in the Chinese internet business knew that whoever launched a complete MP3 search platform first could count on getting lots and lots of traffic. MP3 search was bound to be a "killer app"—the only question was: Who would be brave enough to go first?

The whole music industry was ready to come down hard on any Chinese search engine that attempted to do what the infamous Napster had done in America. Despite being wildly popular, the online music file sharing service had been shut down in 2001 by the legal might of the Recording Industry Association of America, which had no qualms about playing rough[39]—it even prosecuted students who were downloading music files in their dorms.

But this was China and the laws were different. "We debated about MP3. There were many gray areas," said Foo, a Baidu board member at the time. But the directors also knew that, risky as the move was, Google, their chief competitor, would not dare match it. Google at that time was the dominant search engine in China. "Baidu's popularity only began to surge in 2003–04. Before that, most people in China used Google, as there were few other choices of search engine," said Jacky Huang, China Internet Research Manager of IDC.

Baidu launched MP3 search[40] in 2002–03. Predictably, it was a magnet for young users. At the time of Baidu's IPO in 2005, the company said that MP3 search was generating as much as 22 percent of its traffic,[41] although some venture capitalists maintain the real figure was nearer 50 percent in the early days. In a 2004 survey, the China-based firm iResearch concluded that some 48 percent of the country's search engine users were downloading MP3 files. However,

[39] Source: Guy Douglas BA(Hons), LLB (Hons), PhD, "Copyright and Peer-To-Peer Music File Sharing: The Napster Case and the Argument Against Legislative Reform," *Murdoch University Electronic Journal of Law*, March 2004.

[40] Baidu's MP3 search was like an index service. It offered hyperlinks to the music files, which users could click on to download the files to their computers. Napster offered peer-to-peer software enabling users who installed it to freely share files on the internet—many of those pirated music files.

[41] From Baidu's IPO prospectus: "According to Alexa.com, 22 percent of our traffic went to mp3.baidu.com, our MP3 search platform, as of July 9, 2005. Should we face (as a result of the foregoing considerations or otherwise) a need or decision to substantially modify, limit, or terminate our MP3 search service, our business, financial condition, or results of operations could be materially and adversely affected."

venture capitalist Foo said MP3 search was just one of many applications Baidu developed to attract and retain users.[42]

"The problem with search engines is that user 'stickiness' is not high. If you cannot find the information you are looking for, you will immediately switch to another search engine," said Foo. "Just like Google has Google Maps, Gmail and many other applications, Baidu was making applications to attract users and increase user stickiness," he said. "MP3 search was just one of the applications."

With both traffic and sales problems solved, Baidu's numbers improved dramatically. At the end of 2004, total revenues were US$14.2 million, a tenfold increase from US$1.3 million in 2002. And what's more, Baidu had become profitable, earning US$1.5 million in 2004 after losing US$2.2 million in 2002.

	2002	2003	2004
Revenue	US$1.3 million	US$4.9 million	US$14.2 million
- online marketing services	38.9%	78.3%	91.0%
- enterprise search software	15.6%	6.9%	6.8%
- portal search services	45.5%	14.8%	2.2%
Net profit/(loss)	(US$2.2 million)	(US$1.1 million)	US$1.5 million

***Table 3.1:* Baidu's revenue, net profit, and revenue breakdown 2002–04**

Data source: Baidu IPO prospectus

By mid 2005, when just about everything related to China was attracting favorable reviews from foreign investors, Baidu was ready for an initial public offering of its stock. Its IPO on New York's NASDAQ market made headlines everywhere. The price of its shares shot up four times on the first day, as investors raced to grab a piece of the "Chinese Google."

R-E-S-P-E-C-T

Besides funds to grow with, the IPO gave Baidu a rather unexpected benefit: the high-profile news coverage made high-end internet users at home take it more seriously. "After the IPO, the white collar internet

[42] When interviewed by the author for a story in January 2008, Shen Haoyu, Baidu's vice president of business operations said, "After extensive research and user monitoring, Baidu determined that more than 50 percent of searches conducted were entertainment related. As a result, Baidu came up with the idea of providing a specialized search platform for entertainment needs, like our MP3 search."

users in China changed their minds about Baidu. It was a serious search engine, not just one for students and teenagers," said Jason Brueschke, head of Asia internet/media research of Citigroup.

Suddenly, it was cool even for older, richer, and better-educated internet users to use Baidu. It began to overtake Google in the choicest user group. CNNIC did three surveys on the country's search engine preferences in the 2005–07 period. The first, in August 2005, found 27.9 percent of high-end internet users preferred Baidu, compared with 58.7 percent for Google.

Two years later, the same researcher attributed 47.7 percent of high-end users to Baidu, versus 42.3 percent for Google. Such high ratings among the Chinese with the most purchasing power was great news for Baidu's advertisers.

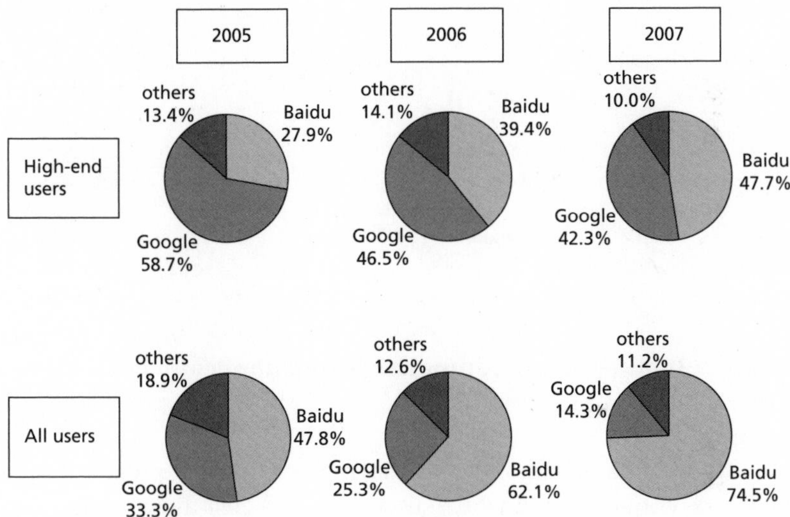

***Figure 3.2:* Change in users' search engine preferences: 2005–07**

Data source: CNNIC–China Internet Network Information Center

Note: The first row shows results for high-end users, i.e., those who are over 25 years old, with a bachelor's degree or higher and earning more than RMB3000 or US$375 per month. The second row shows results for all users.

Upping the ante

After raising about US$100 million with its IPO, Baidu quickly grew in terms of workforce and infrastructure. At the end of 2008, it had more than 6,300 staff in China, up from 750 before its stock market listing. The result was a faster pipeline for introducing new applications and better sales coverage.[43] At the end of 2008, Baidu.com contained 56 different applications. (Google listed 43 major applications in its annual report of 2008.[44])

Top 10 Baidu Applications			Top 10 Google Applications		
Apps	**Traffic contribution**	**Function**	**Apps**	**Traffic contribution**	**Function**
baidu.com	44.5%	Web search	google.com	55.2%	Web search
Tieba	14.5%	Virtual forum	Mail	24.7%	Email
Image	13.5%	Image search	Images	10.1%	Image search
Zhidao	8.4%	Community-driven knowledge base	AdWords	1.1%	Online auction base ad platform
Hi	3.5%	Instant message program	Translate	1.0%	Language translation
MP3	3.3%	MP3 search	picasaweb	1.0%	Photo album
Video	2.8%	Video search	Video	0.7%	Video search
Baike	1.6%	Encyclopedia	Groups	0.6%	Virtual forum
Zhangmen	1.6%	MP3 search	News	0.5%	News search
News	1.2%	News search	Docs	0.5%	Online word processor, spreadsheet, etc.

Table 3.2: **Baidu–Google comparison—top applications**

Data source: Alexa.com, end of 2008

Some of Baidu's applications have become extremely popular—Postbar (Tieba), a virtual forum where users choose their own topics, now accounts for 14 percent of the site's total traffic. Another service, Baidu Knows (Zhidao), a community-driven knowledge base where users answer each other's questions (just like Yahoo's Answers), has also been a hit. The applications attract more users and traffic to Baidu, which, in turn, generate more searches and clicks on advertisements.

"Many of Baidu's applications are gems for advertisers, for example, the Tieba. Imagine placing an ad for your skin care product beside a

[43] From Baidu's IPO prospectus: "We had 93, 143, and 328 employees as of December 31, 2002, 2003 and 2004, respectively. As of June 30, 2005, we had 750 employees, including 74 in management and administration, 234 in research and development and 321 in sales and marketing."

[44] Source: Google Annual Report 2008, Products and Services for our Users.

discussion about skin care in the virtual forum. It will be most effective," said T. R. Harrington, director of Darwin Marketing, a search engine marketing firm based in Shanghai.

Besides sales of keywords, Baidu also started to sell display advertising in some of its applications. "Recent research showed combining display advertisement with search engine marketing can be more effective than search engine alone," said Harrington, "Many of us do searches after reading or watching something interesting."

With more staff, Baidu has gathered more of its sales operations in-house. It decided its own sales force would handle the three largest cities in China—Beijing, Shanghai, and Guangzhou. Its call center now directly employs thousands of reps who cold-call anyone suspected of having an interest in buying keywords.[45]

Budding digerati

Baidu has also been smart to focus on first-time internet users. It has formed alliances with a number of directory websites, which are popular in the internet cafés where many Chinese teens get their first online experience. (The prices are low, only RMB2 per hour, or less than 30 American cents.) The café owners usually refer the novices to directory websites that show them how to find the sites that appeal to their particular interests.

By partnering with these directory sites, Baidu has built up a strong following among the newbies. Just before the IPO, Baidu purchased the most popular directory site Hao123.com, which, at 20 percent, was the largest traffic contributor among members of Baidu Union, the search engine's partner program.[46, 47] It also persuaded many internet café owners to make Baidu.com the default site on their web browsers.

Apart from these strategies, Baidu created a new method for inputting Chinese characters into the search box—the Pinyin input

[45] Of the 6,386 staff Baidu employed at the end of 2008, 3,855 worked in sales and marketing, according to Baidu's Annual Report 2008. Jacky Huang, China Internet Research Manager of IDC, believes two-thirds of them worked in call centers.

[46] From Baidu's 2005 annual report: "In August 2004, we acquired the domain name Hao123.com which was at the time the largest traffic contributor among our Baidu Union members. The traffic acquisition costs associated with click-throughs by users of the Hao123.com website during the period in 2004 prior to our acquisition accounted for approximately 20 percent of the total traffic acquisition costs in 2004, while the traffic acquisition costs associated with click-throughs by users of the Hao123.com website contributed approximately 18 percent to the total traffic acquisition costs in 2003."

method. Typing Chinese characters is not as simple as typing English words. There are different inputting methodologies, and the skill and effort required partly explain why, in the beginning, Chinese users were reluctant to use search.

Baidu's innovation was to create a system that recognizes Pinyin—the most commonly used romanization system for Standard Mandarin, which most kids in China master in primary school—and supplies the most likely corresponding Chinese characters. Most of the time, the system guesses accurately. This helps internet newbies to get used to Baidu search quickly.

Winning the allegiance of internet neophytes is good business for Baidu. Internet usership is growing fast. Of the 298 million Chinese online at the end of 2008, about 30 percent had come online within the previous 12 months, while 46 percent had less than 18 months of online experience.

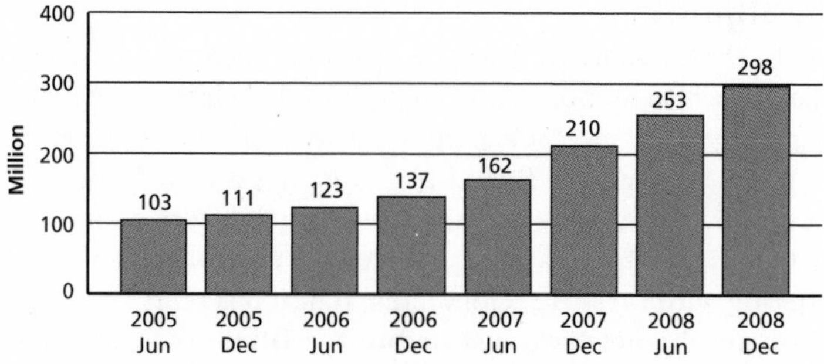

Figure 3.3: **Growth of China's internet population: Jun 2005–Dec 2008**

Data source: CNNIC–China Internet Network Information Center

With everything going well, Baidu's sales grew 33 times from 2004 (the year just before its IPO) to 2007, and profit shot up 106 times!!

47 From Baidu's IPO prospectus: "In August 2004, we acquired the domain name Hao123.com from its owner unrelated to us. At the time of the acquisition, Hao123.com was the largest traffic contributor to our Baidu.com website among our Baidu Union members. Pursuant to the asset purchase agreement, we paid the seller an aggregate purchase price consisting of RMB11.9 million (US$1.4 million) in cash and 40,000 ordinary shares of our company. In addition, we agreed to make a contingent payment of an additional RMB1.2 million (US$0.1 million) to the seller if certain traffic statistics of Hao123.com are achieved within 12 months of the acquisition."

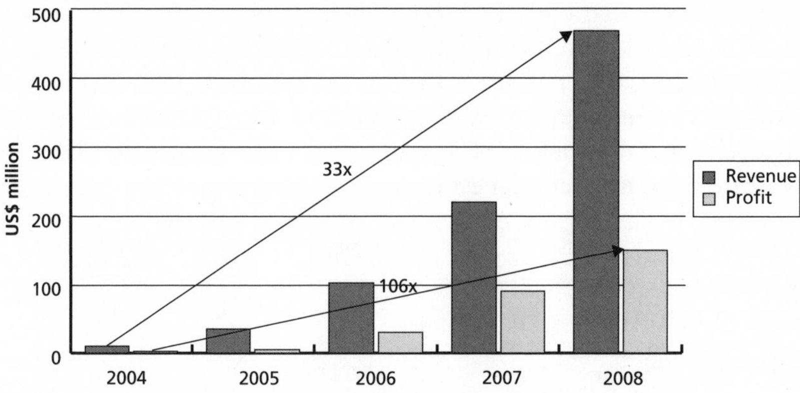

***Figure 3.4:* Baidu sales and profit (2004–08)**

Data source: Baidu

Baidu vs Google

Of all internet business models, the search engine may be the one that has changed least since migrating to China. Baidu's and Google's basic operations—how they get traffic and how they convert traffic into revenue—are almost identical, differing only in the details.

	Google	Baidu
Sales		
- the largest clients	Direct sales force	Direct sales force
- the majority of clients	Online (AdWords)	Call centers and sales agents
Generating traffic	From web search, applications, and network sites	From web search, applications, and network sites
Generate revenue	From auction-based ad platforms that charge advertisers on cost-per-click basis	From auction-based ad platforms that charge advertisers on cost-per-click basis Some banner ads

***Table 3.3:* Baidu–Google comparison—business models**

Therefore, much of the advantage enjoyed by Baidu over Google in China is due not to differences in the business model, but to differences in execution. "While Google China has done well, Baidu is much more resourceful and aggressive," said Jacky Huang, China Internet Research Manager of IDC.

While Google as a whole is much larger, its Chinese operation is much smaller than Baidu's. Baidu operates on a much larger scale than Google China, and has tried that much harder to win traffic and customers, sometimes crossing ethical and legal boundaries in the process. The table below is a summary of data gleaned from the companies and from analyst estimates.

	Baidu	Google China
Number of staff	6,387[a]	~800[c]
Number of applications	56[d]	29[d]
Number of third-party sales agents	~300[b,e]	25[c,e]
Size of direct sales force	2,900[a]	Nil[c]

Table 3.4: **Baidu–Google China comparison—scale of operation**

[a] From Baidu's annual report, 2008

[b] From analyst's estimate (Jacky Huang, China Internet Research Manager of IDC), end of 2008

[c] From Google, early 2009

[d] From Baidu's and Google's websites, end of 2008

[e] The difference in sales coverage may not be as large as this suggests, as Google's resellers are some of the largest in China, while Baidu's include agents both large and small

Baidu has **far more** people than Google China. It has developed **far more** applications to drive traffic. It has **much more** sales coverage, through both third-party agents and its own call centers. Google China uses only third-party agents. Baidu has also been careful to cater for the growing novice internet user population, which has been critical to its rapid growth (as discussed above).

State favoritism and Baidu's unfair advantages

But to be fair, not all of Baidu's early advantages over Google were deserved, and others will be hard to maintain.

1 In the early days, the Chinese government diverted traffic from Google to Baidu whenever there was politically sensitive news about China. [48]

2 Baidu initially used MP3 search—a service fraught with copyright infringement implications—to drive traffic, a move that Google, subject to stricter American laws, dared not imitate.

[48] Source: Clive Thompson, "Google's China Problem (and China's Google Problem)," *New York Times*, April 23, 2006.

3 Baidu mixes search results with advertisements (see below). This can lead to higher revenues as unwary users click on links that are, in fact, paid ads. Google, on the other hand, separates the two clearly, believing in the importance of objective search results: "The advertising is clearly marked and separated. This is similar to a newspaper, where the articles are independent of the advertising," its IPO prospectus stated.

State favoritism may also have worked in Baidu's favor. All governments have a strong incentive to help their local companies, and China's is no exception. The temptation to help Baidu may be particularly strong for the Communist Party, which sees the internet as a part of the media, and hence something to be controlled, just like the press, television, and radio. With search engines such an important gateway to the internet, the government may simply prefer to see the business dominated by a local player that it can control more easily than a foreign competitor. "Government relationships" and "insufficient localization" are Google China's biggest problems, according to a former Google China executive who has now left the company.

Mixing it up

As a user searches for a particular keyword, the search engine returns related websites from its database (natural search results) and its advertising serving platform returns relevant ads. While Google shows the two in separate areas that are clearly identified, Baidu allows ads to appear in areas that are supposed to be reserved for pure natural search results, with no indication that they are sponsored links.

One of the reasons that Baidu can get away with mixing natural search results and ads is that many Chinese internet users are so new to the game they don't know the difference. That, or they just don't mind very much. According to a survey carried out by CNNIC in August 2006, 66.8 percent of the respondents said they did not know about Baidu's practice of mixing ads with the natural search results, that is, allowing advertisers to bid for search ranking. Of those who were aware of it, 64.1 percent said they did not mind as long as they get highly relevant results.

However, Baidu's luck in this particular area may have run out following an embarrassing incident late in 2008. China Central Television (CCTV), the nation's dominant, state-run network, subjected the Baidu search engine to an investigation and broadcast the results. Its investigative reporters entered the keyword "癌症," cancer, in Baidu. Instead of the medical information about cancer that most users would probably expect, the results at the top of the list were ads for cancer treatments at various healthcare institutions.

The ads were not identified as "sponsored links," as they would be on Google. And they appeared on the left-hand side of the screen, where most users would expect to find unbiased results from the search engine, not paid advertisements. What's more, drug makers and hospitals need special licenses to advertise their products and services in China. But most of Baidu's medical products and services advertisers had no such licenses.

Since the report aired, Baidu has halted many of these ads and stated that in future it will only accept properly licensed clients.[49] And it has begun segregating natural search results from ads—"at least, in a small way," according to an investment bank analyst who tracks the company.

"Eventually, Baidu will have to clean up its act. This might lead to a short-term loss of revenue, but it will make the company much stronger and the industry much healthier in the long run," said Huang of IDC.

Traffic jam

Launching MP3 search was a fast and cheap way for Baidu to get traffic, but accusations of music piracy soon became a big headache.

In 2005, the four largest music companies in the world, Universal, EMI, Warner, and Sony BMG, and their local subsidiaries sued Baidu in a Beijing court for infringing the copyright of hundreds of songs.[50] After more than two years of legal proceedings, during

[49] From a Baidu press release, Nov 18, 2008: "Shortly after the CCTV program was broadcast, Baidu initiated dialogue with CCTV regarding this matter. At the same time, Baidu removed paid search listings of certain customers, particularly medical and pharmaceutical customers without licenses on file with Baidu. Baidu will allow these customers to resume access to Baidu's P4P paid search platform once their relevant licenses are provided to and reviewed by Baidu. These customers account for approximately 10–15 percent of Baidu's total revenues. Baidu believes this immediate measure is the most prudent way to protect the interests of Baidu's users. Currently, it is difficult to estimate how many removed customers will provide relevant licenses to Baidu and when they will do so. Baidu will work closely with customers to ensure those customers with proper licenses will be able to access Baidu's services again quickly."

[50] Lawsuits were filed by Gold Label on July 21, 2005, and EMI and Universal on July 28, just before Baidu's IPO. Warner Music filed its lawsuit on August 15, with Sony BMG going to court on September 8.

which Baidu argued that it was merely an electronic platform that automatically and indiscriminately identified music files on the internet, Baidu convinced the Beijing court that it was not guilty of copyright infringement.

But in 2006, the Chinese government changed its anti-piracy laws, which now say that it is illegal not only to be the source of pirated music files, but also to be a facilitator of piracy. The music companies were able to use the new laws to stop Yahoo China's competing MP3 search platform dead in its tracks. The music companies sued Yahoo China in January 2007; on December 20 the same year, a Beijing court found Yahoo China guilty.

During its own legal battles, Baidu approached the record companies about an out-of-court settlement, according to a person close to the music companies. EMI dropped its suit against Baidu, though the other complainants fought on.

By February 2008, the music companies were ready to take on Baidu in court again, this time under the new laws. The case is still unresolved. Many industry insiders expect Baidu to lose the second time. "Baidu will eventually stop its MP3 search. The only question is when," said an industry insider.

Lessons learned

In adapting the search engine business model to China, Baidu made two decisions that were genuinely smart at the time—enlisting agents to drive sales, and launching an MP3 search feature to drive traffic. Both measures were effective and cheap, but both have drawbacks that Baidu must deal with in the long term.

1 Beware of self-interested agents.

Using third-party sales agents is a very effective way to quickly build a nationwide distribution network in China. In many cases there is no other way to cover the entire country, which contains hundreds of cities, big and small. But controlling the quality of agents' services is crucial to a company's reputation and long-term success. In Baidu's case, quality control seems to have been insufficient.

For example, some of Baidu's agents have been guilty of telling website owners that their sites would be deleted from the search engine's index unless they agreed to join its advertising program, and that access to their sites would be denied even to users who specifically searched for it. Though Baidu publicly denied this bogus claim, its reputation did suffer damage.[51]

Another problem is that a sales agent's best interests and those of the company are not necessarily identical. Take for example "click fraud,"[52] a problem that all search engines face. Sometimes the perpetrators are the websites themselves that are showing the ads in question, profiting from inflated numbers. It could also be the advertiser's competitors, trying to drive up its costs. Or it could be sales agents trying to boost their commissions.

As Baidu has grown, it has concentrated more of its sales operations in-house. The potential benefits are twofold: it may increase its profit margin and it may eliminate many of the problems related to using external sales agents.

For companies building a distribution network in China, the wisest course may be to use sales agents at first, but gradually bring such activities under direct control. Many companies entering China have adopted such a strategy.

2 Weigh the merits of short-term vs long-term strategies and tactics.

Baidu's MP3 search story is not unique. Because China is an emerging market, there are many areas where laws are unclear and business practices unsound. Many companies in China take advantage of these "gray areas" to appear successful.

But to be successful in the long run, companies must gradually phase out the questionable parts of their business and concentrate on healthy activities that are sustainable. Baidu seems to be aware of the vulnerability of its MP3 search business to accusations of copyright violation. Subsequent applications, such as Postbar, its virtual forum, have managed to please users without containing such long-term negatives. It has also embraced serious marketing and promotion, by buying TV commercials, for instance, and outdoor display ads.

[51] From a Baidu press release, Nov 18, 2008: "Separately, Baidu would like to affirm that Baidu has never excluded websites of any customers because they did not pay for keywords, and Baidu does not tolerate such practices."

[52] Click fraud is a type of internet crime. It occurs in pay-per-click online advertising. A person, an automated script or a computer program imitates a normal user of a web browser clicking on an ad. The purpose is to generate a charge per click, but not actual interest in the ad. Click fraud is the subject of some controversy and increasing litigation.

The share of Baidu's traffic represented by MP3 search has gradually decreased, from as much as half at the start to less than 5 percent at the end of 2008, according to Alexa.com.

A lesson to learn: when assessing companies in China as potential partners, suppliers, or investment targets, be sure to *evaluate how much of their success is sustainable and how much rests on shaky ground.*

3 Never neglect internet neophytes.

In at least one area, though, Baidu was right from the very start. And that is its decision to engage closely with new internet users. This has meant not only partnering with directory sites and internet cafés, but also creating a new method for inputting Chinese characters into the search box—the Pinyin input method. The Chinese internet market is still in a high-growth phase, having achieved about 25 percent penetration in June 2009. Every year brings a flood of new users.

Be the first to reach the newbies and you can count on their loyalty over time.

4. Google's China odyssey

In the previous chapter we described how Baidu came to be the dominant search engine in China. In this chapter, we talk about its main competitor: Google.

Critics say that Google China adheres far too slavishly to its original American business model and ought to be doing much more advertising and promotion. Yet it is far too early to write off Google's chances in China. While Baidu has proved to be more resourceful and aggressive to date, the game is not over. Some of the most cosmopolitan and technologically sophisticated search engine users in the country are Google loyalists, and the US-based firm's advertising partnership program with other sites appears to be more successful than Baidu's. What's more, Google seems to be gearing up for the next big battle in the search engine war—mobile internet services via 3G technology, which is only now being introduced in China. Some experts believe that in the long run, Google China will be able to reduce its local competitor's big lead.

Competition

Apart from Google, Baidu has never had much competition. The profitability of search engines could not really be demonstrated until auction-based pay-per-click ads started to take off in 2002. Prior to that Baidu's only local rival was 3721.com, founded in 1998 by Zhou Hongyi, a computer engineering graduate from a university in Xian, a city in central China.

3721 was not really a search engine. Rather it was a name-matching service that linked Chinese company names with their web addresses. Users had to download 3721's program and install it on a Microsoft Internet Explorer browser. (The program ran on ActiveX, a proprietary Microsoft programming language.) When a company's Chinese name was typed into the web address field of the browser, 3721's server would do a match with its database and take the user to the company's website. The system could also match product names or English names.

Zhou promoted 3721 as a service that would spare Chinese users the need to input web addresses, with their unfamiliar English words and confusing letter codes. To be included in 3721's database, companies paid a fixed annual subscription fee.

The service was quite successful at first. At one point, 300,000 companies were registered and over 30 million users had installed the program. But it was ultimately no match for genuine search engines, which were far more powerful when it came to finding information.

The fatal blow for Zhou's company came in 2007, when Microsoft launched a new version of Internet Explorer and classified 3721's program as a virus that could no longer be installed on the browser. By this time, however, Yahoo had already bought 3721, paying US$120 million for it in November 2003. 3721 accounted for so much of Yahoo's market share in China that its failure doomed the American firm's efforts to penetrate the Chinese search market.

Zhou became president of Yahoo China and ran it until Alibaba's Jack Ma persuaded Yahoo to invest US$1 billion in his e-commerce empire and fold its China unit into Alibaba Group in 2005.

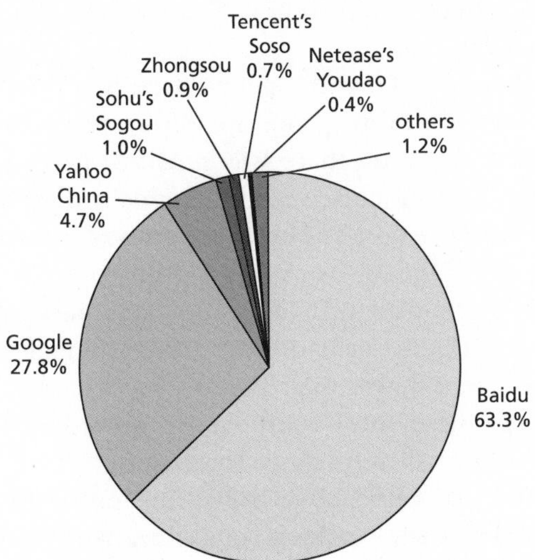

***Figure 4.1:* Search engine market shares in China, 2008 (3rd quarter)**

Data source: Analysys International

Several local companies sought to emulate Baidu's success by developing their own Chinese search engines. Instant messaging operator

Tencent and portals Sina, Sohu, and Netease all tried their hands, but they simply came to the game too late. Without any technological innovations to speak of, they never became mainstream.

Baidu's chief competitor has always been Google, the world's number one search engine. It opened a China office in 2005.

Google China

Even before it had an official presence in China, Google's services were being widely used there. "Baidu's popularity only began to surge in 2003–04. Before that, most people in China used Google, as there were few other choices of search engine," said Jacky Huang, China Internet Research Manager of IDC.

Some Chinese advertisers were already bidding for keywords on Google's American site. It was the search engine of choice for some of the country's most sophisticated internet users, those with the most income and education and with foreign experience or regular contact with foreigners. Such people have credit cards, and besides Google they also like Facebook and YouTube. The problem was that there were just not that many of them.

Another hindrance to Google's penetration was the behavior of the Chinese government. From 2002 to 2005, access to Google was routinely blocked any time there was sensitive news about China.[53] Local users would find themselves automatically diverted to Baidu or other Chinese search engines. The problem was most serious during 2003–04.

By mid 2005, partly due to Baidu's effort and partly due to government interference, the tables had been turned. Google's market share was about 23 percent, lower than Baidu's 37 percent, but still, it was well ahead of the other local competition, according to the Beijing-based market research firm Analysys International.

To reach more users and advertisers, and ensure a stable service in China, Google needed a local presence, with servers and staff inside the country. But it would have to tailor its services to Chinese laws. So it joined its local competitors in filtering out of search results all politically sensitive information—about the anti-communist

[53] Source: Clive Thompson, "Google's China Problem (and China's Google Problem)," *New York Times*, April 23, 2006.

Falun Gong religious sect, for example, or the June 4, 1989 Beijing massacre.[54]

Such compromises certainly clashed with Google's stated mission—"to organize the world's information and make it universally accessible and useful."[55] But the potential of the Chinese internet market, which was bound to become the largest in the world, was just too great for a company from Mountain View, California, to ignore. (China is not the only market where Google has modified its practices to suit local laws. In Germany, for example, access to neo-Nazi sites is banned.)

Despite a high profile in the media, Google China was on shaky ground in its early days. A year after setting up its office in China its market share had actually dropped, bottoming out at around 16 percent in mid 2006; Baidu, with its post-IPO momentum, had increased its share to 50 percent, according to Analysys International.

"The grassroots Chinese internet users had not heard of Google. The high-end users thought there was no hope for Google," said Lee Kaifu, president of Google China. Adding insult to injury, Baidu was even running a commercial on Chinese TV ridiculing the quality of Google's Chinese search. By the end of 2006, some of the local media were already anticipating the day when Google would exit China, just as eBay, another supposed American world beater, already had.

Teething troubles

There was a good reason for Google China's problems: It had few staff at the start, and soon found itself facing a host of unforeseeable obstacles.

"I was a general without an army," said Lee. The first employee he hired, a developer, did not start work until January 2006. In fact, a lawsuit brought by Microsoft, his former employer, had prevented Lee himself from taking up his duties before September 2005.

Born in Taiwan, Lee emigrated to America in 1973 while still in high school. He later earned a PhD in computer science from Carnegie Mellon University. While working as an assistant professor there, he

54 Because of its self-imposed censorship, whenever people search for interdicted Chinese keywords on a blocked list maintained by the PRC government, Google's China website, google.cn, will display the following at the bottom of the page (translated): "In accordance with local laws, regulations, and policies, part of the search result is not shown. Uncensored search results can be obtained from Google's main website, Google.com, but access to it is frequently blocked in China."

55 Source: Google's IPO prospectus.

developed the world's first speaker-independent, continuous speech-recognition system, which *BusinessWeek* honored as the "Most Important Innovation" of 1988. After leaving the university, Lee spent six years at Apple Computer, where he developed QuickTime, QuickDraw 3D, QuickTime VR, and PlainTalk speech technologies. In 1998 he joined Microsoft, where he was responsible for advanced natural language and user interface technologies and founded Microsoft Research Asia, now regarded as one of the best research centers in the world.

By 2005, he was ready to embark on a new journey with Google, but Microsoft was not ready to let go. It sued Lee over the one-year non-compete agreement that he had signed in 2000 on becoming Microsoft's corporate vice president of interactive services.

The lawsuit was barely out of the way when it became clear that while getting a license for Google's research and development center would be easy, the same could not be said of its website, Google.cn. "The government tightened the approval process for foreign companies to get ICP licenses," said Lee. An ICP, or internet content provider, license is a must for all websites in China. While obtaining an ICP license is a fairly easy matter for domestic players, Google did not get its own until mid 2007. So it had to use a license "borrowed" from a local player, Ganji.com, a classified advertising site that Google had once considered acquiring, said Lee.

As Lee recalls, much of 2005, the first year of Google China, was spent on preparation: getting licenses, signing deals with partners, recruitment, and market research. To better understand local requirements, Google interviewed the Chinese advertisers who were bidding for keywords via the AdWords service on its American site. But it understood that the majority of Chinese small businesses were not so tech savvy. Rather than rely completely on its online channel, Google followed Baidu's lead and used third-party sales agents to target small businesses.

Traveling executives from the American headquarters carried out most of Google China's work in 2005. They signed up 25 local agents to be Google's resellers in China.

Much of Lee's work in his early days was hiring staff. He trolled for young talent in China's top universities. Luckily, backing from headquarters was strong. "As long as I can find qualified talent, there is no limit on how many I can hire," said Lee in an interview in October

2006. By the end of 2006, Lee had recruited over 300 staff, and the hiring continued.

Growing up in China

Real work at Google China started in 2006. "The first thing we did was to improve Chinese search. And that occupied most of our time in 2006," said Lee. Google's search engine was designed to support multiple languages. At the time of its IPO in 2004, it supported at least 97 of them, including Chinese.[56]

The Chinese language presents its own peculiar difficulties, however. Chinese consist of phrases, equivalent to words in English, which are formed by multiple characters. A search engine must index and segment the Chinese text phrases before conducting keyword/phrase searches. Moreover, a Chinese language phrase generally has more synonyms and closely associated phrases than an English word. As a result, a Chinese language search engine must have a comprehensive database of these synonyms and phrases in order to function effectively. "For example, one of the top universities in China is Tsinghua University. It is commonly known as just Tsinghua (清华) in China. So if users search for the keyword university (大学), should pages that contain only Tsinghua be included in the search results?" said Lee.

Because Baidu was built to optimize Chinese search from the start, the developers bore all of these factors in mind when the system was built. Initially it was better at Chinese-language search than Google was. But by 2006–07, most analysts agreed that Google's Chinese search results were at least as good as Baidu's.

"In 2007, while we continued to improve our Chinese search, we started two major non-search development programs: mobile search and map," said Lee. Google China signed a deal with China Mobile, which serves more than 70 percent of the country's cellphone users, to be its mobile search provider in 2007. Developing mobile search features became a major task for Google China in the next few years. Its developments in map not only allowed users to find local businesses, view maps and get driving directions, it also resulted in some

56 From Google's IPO prospectus: "We make our services as widely available as we can by supporting over 97 languages and by providing most services for free."

applications with high social impact. For example, a real-time map could be viewed showing rail traffic around the Chinese New Year holidays, when people traditionally return to their families and train stations are packed.

In May 2008, an earthquake in Sichuan province killed close to 70,000 people. Google China launched a special real-time map that showed people who wanted to make donations or offer direct help what resources were needed in each of the affected districts. Such initiatives have helped Google to improve its relationship with the Chinese government, said Lee. "We now have regular meetings with the government to understand their policy about the internet," he added. (Improving the relationship with the Chinese government was important. A former Google staffer considered government relationships to be an obstacle that held back Google's development in China.)

After Google's CEO Eric Schmidt visited China in April 2007 to show his support for the China team, things started to improve. By mid 2007, Google's market share had rebounded to 22 percent, according to Analysys International. "Our efforts paid off. By 2008, our traffic in mobile search and map increased by four times," said Lee. Market share had reached 26 percent by the middle of the year. "Comparing the fourth quarter of 2008 to that of 2007, our sales in China increased 109 percent," he continued.

In 2009, Google China began a new project to develop its advertising products, AdSense and AdWords. In late 2009, it plans to start a music service that will resemble Baidu's controversial MP3 search feature, but run on legal music files.

"We have formed a joint venture with Top100 to offer ad-sponsored streaming music or music download services," said Lee. Top100.cn is a legitimate music site in China founded by NBA superstar Yao Ming, Gary Chen, and Erik Zhang in 2006. Google purchased a minority stake in 2007. The new service will offer free music; music companies, Google, and Top100 will share the revenue generated from selling ads on the site. Lee said the service may offer little profit in the near term, but in the long term it could change the way the music industry worldwide does business.

"The music industry is seeking new direction," said Lee. "China represents a good opportunity for testing. If our model works, it may become a global trend."

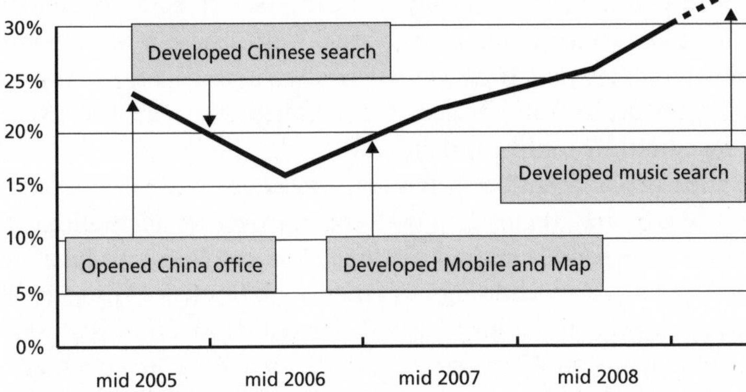

***Figure 4.2:* Google China's market share in search engines (mid 2005–end 2008)**

Data source: Analysys International

Transformation

In adapting its business to China, Google seems to be a faster learner than some of the American internet firms that entered China before it. "We are latecomers. But being a latecomer has its advantages," said Lee. "By the time we entered China, its importance had been proven. It was the largest internet market in the world. Our headquarters fully supports our operation and has delegated a lot of power to the local team."

Lack of local autonomy and lack of support from headquarters are factors that tripped up other American internet firms making forays into China. The importance and the complexity of the Chinese internet market were both underestimated. But Google seems to have learned from their mistakes. There is only one layer of management between Schmidt, the CEO, and Lee, the China head. And Lee said he meets Schmidt regularly, almost every month, to brief him on the situation in China.

How different from the experience of eBay. "When eBay China moved its computer platform from China to America in October 2004, traffic dropped by half on the very same day. But Meg Whitman, then CEO of eBay, didn't find out about it until a month later," said Bo Shao, founder of EachNet, which was sold to eBay in 2003 and became eBay China.

After the platform was moved to headquarters and consolidated, eBay China lost control over its website. "It took nine months to make any major changes and nine weeks to alter a word on screen," said Shao. "This is unthinkable for an internet business, which needs to be able to react rapidly to the market."

"Such things could not happen to us," said Lee.

Google China has relatively good control over its technology platform. The search service and ad platform (i.e., AdWords and AdSense) are core to Google's technology. As mentioned before, Google China started optimizing its Chinese search functions in 2006. In 2009, it started to develop its advertising product for China. It also seems to have studied Baidu's moves closely. And it is not ashamed to imitate the local market leader when it makes sense. "We are humble and we listen to what the local market wants," said Lee.

The first instance of this was Google China's decision to employ agents to sell keywords.[57] It also followed Baidu's lead in targeting the customers of internet cafés. After Baidu bought Hao123.com, the directory website most popular with internet café patrons, Google bought the second most popular, 265.com.

Taking another leaf out of Baidu's book, it lobbied with internet café owners to make its website (Google.cn) the default search engine on their computer browsers. Lee arranged for Google headquarters staff to visit internet cafés, so they would appreciate how important internet cafés were as the point of first contact with search engines for many young internet users in China.

In response to complaints that the "Google" name was too difficult for Chinese users to remember, it registered "guge.cn," which is the Pinyin of its Chinese name 谷歌, and a simpler version, "g.cn," at the risk of being accused of diluting its brand image.

Moreover, Google China has developed a lot of new applications for the local market. These include the Pinyin inputting method and Shenghuo, a website devoted to daily essentials, such as train timetables, apartment rentals, and job hunting. And there were many other small developments or adjustments that Google made as it acclimatized to the Chinese market.

By early 2009, Google had around 800 people in its China office. Most analysts believe its sales and profits have been growing at a

[57] Later Google set up a call center. However, it is just for customer support. Its own staff has never engaged in "cold-calling," as Baidu does—that was considered too much of a departure from its American model. The company was also afraid of being perceived as too aggressive.

healthy rate. Nevertheless, it still lagged behind Baidu by a wide margin. At of the end of 2008, the local rival controlled an estimated 60 percent of the search market, compared to 30 percent for Google, according to Analysys International.

Baidu was just more resourceful and aggressive. It operates on a much larger scale than Google in China, and has tried that much harder to win traffic and customers, sometimes crossing ethical and legal boundaries in the process. The Chinese government's interference also helped to divert traffic from Google to Baidu—a point we discussed in the last chapter. Moreover, a common criticism of Google China is that it is still not localized enough. "If more of its decisions were made locally, Google would be more successful in China," said T. R. Harrington, director of Darwin Marketing, a search engine marketing firm based in Shanghai. Darwin deals with both Baidu and Google on behalf of its clients.

Expatriate blues

Working for a multinational company, Google China's staff must always balance the headquarters agenda with their own. The expatriate Google China serves two masters, and its employees complain that they feel as if they are working for two bosses. What is a developer to do, for example, when headquarters is pushing for "cloud computing," while the local head is stressing Pinyin? Indeed, Google's move to cloud computing has become a topic of dissent at Google China.

Cloud computing is a style of computing in which scalable resources are provided as a service over the internet. The concept incorporates software as a service (SaaS), as well as Web 2.0 and other recent technology trends, which have the common theme of reliance on the internet for satisfying the computing needs of the users. However, its use in China is still limited.

As for Pinyin, an inputting method for Chinese characters, it is important to the Chinese market but not to the rest of the world. "I understand it would be very challenging for our staff," said Lee. "It's natural for them to want to be recognized by headquarters for their contribution." And there are limits to what Google China can do. "If a developer said he wanted to develop a completely new search engine, I could not possibly let him do so. That would be wasting our global research," explains Lee.

Baidu employees have no such worries. There is one boss and one agenda—to maximize sales and profit in China. Also, incentives for top management differ greatly. Baidu's CEO Robin Li founded the company and is its largest shareholder. He has everything to gain and lose from its success or failure.

Lee, on the other hand, is a salaried executive. He is undoubtedly well paid and enjoys a great bonus if Google China does well. But his gains will never be on the same scale as Robin Li's. Forbes ranked Li as the seventh richest person in China with personal wealth of US$1.7 billion in 2008. As a result, Google China seemed to adhere far too slavishly to its original American business model and lacked its local rivals' speed and flexibility in grabbing market share.

Darwin Marketing's Harrington thinks Google should have emulated Baidu, which has more sales agents plus its own in-house sales force targeting small business. "Baidu has 200–300 sales agents, while Google has only 25 in the whole country," said Harrington.

The difference in sales coverage may not be as large as the numbers suggest, though, as Google's resellers are some of the largest agents in China while Baidu's are a mix of large and small agents. Baidu more readily signs up new resellers, while Google has limited the size of its reseller network for reasons of quality control. But this strategy may hold back Google's sales growth.

Another problem is its hiring practices. "It used to take Google six to nine months to hire somebody, as the person has to meet the high standards Google sets in its headquarters," said Harrington. The reason for this was that, initially, the hiring of every senior executive at Google China had to be approved by Google founders Sergey Brin and Larry Page, according to a venture capitalist active in China. "There were tons of other matters the two have to worry about other than China. No wonder the hiring process took ages."

And Google did not hire the right people, either, said the venture capitalist. "Those who appealed to the Google founders were expatriate executives from top technology firms, such as Microsoft, HP, etc. But they were not the right persons for running [a] Chinese internet business. A friend of mine joined Google China. He was paid around US$285,000 a year, a huge sum according to the China standard. But after working hard for a year, he lost all his initiatives. He hung around the company for another year doing essentially nothing. Then he left. He is now thinking of starting his own business."

In fact, apart from Lee Kaifu, all of the senior executives that Google China first hired have left (by October 2009, Lee had also left Google China). "This might be good for them. The newly hired are more local and understand China better," said the venture capitalist.

Nor has Google promoted its brand in China as aggressively as Baidu has—a decision Harrington considers critical to Google's lack of recognition in China. "When Google started in America in 1996, it beat AltaVista, the dominant search engine then, by viral marketing alone. So it believed having a great product alone was enough to win market share. But the situation in China was different," said Harrington.

Internet penetration in China was too low for word-of-mouth marketing to be highly effective. Penetration was only about 22 percent in 2008, a far cry from the 50 percent already achieved in America by 2001,[58] when Google started to be popular and most people were already using search engines. Besides, the differences between Baidu and Google were not large enough to motivate people to switch immediately, according to Harrington. "Advertising is needed to educate people about the use of search engines and build brand recognition in China," he said.

In contrast, Baidu spent a lot on all kinds of advertising—TV, billboards, print, online—after raising money in its IPO "especially in the second and third tier cities and around the universities," said Harrington. "Eighty to 90 percent of internet users in the second and third tier cities use Baidu."

Google's edge

Nevertheless, Google has competitive advantages of its own, because of its technology and global presence. Three in particular stand out: 1) Google's advertising platform; 2) the size of its partner network; and 3) its global reach.

1 Google's advertising platform

Because of its more advanced technology, Google can match ads with keywords better than Baidu, giving it a higher traffic-to-sales ratio. Advertisers can also target their ads more precisely on Google, leading to a better response from users. "Third-party research has shown that

[58] Internet penetration in America was 50 percent in 2001, according to International Telecommunication Union (ITU).

while we have around 24 percent of total search engine traffic we have around 30 percent of total revenue," said Lee.

Of course, advertisers in China may not yet be technologically savvy enough to appreciate these differences. The average spending of Baidu's clients was only US$674 per quarter in late 2008. But as they gain in sophistication, the advantages of using Google's ad platform may become more apparent.

2 Its larger network of partner sites

"The virtuous cycle kicked in quickly for our partner program. As our technology is better, which results in a higher click-through rate of ads on our partner sites and more revenue for them, more websites became our partners," said Lee. Moreover, it gives its partners a bigger share of ad revenue: 60–70 percent, compared to Baidu's 30–40 percent, according to one industry insider.

"Google AdSense quickly became China's number one alliance program," said Lee. Over 200,000 sites have become Google partners, including some of the biggest names, such as Sina, the leading portal. The partner sites help Google to build its brand in China, as well as increase its traffic and revenues.

3 Global reach

Another advantage Google China has is its global reach. Many small businesses in China are using it to market their products and services overseas. Baidu cannot help them because it lacks an audience outside of China. (Baidu has launched a Japanese search site that has not proven very successful so far.) With time, some experts say, Google can become a more serious threat to Baidu.

"Among all the internet businesses, search engines are among the few that require core technology. That gives Google an edge. I believe it can narrow its gap with Baidu in the longer run," said Joe Chen, CEO of Oak Pacific.

Bo Shao, founder of EachNet, which was sold to eBay to become eBay China, said: "I believe search is still in its infancy, so if Google manages to come up with a technology breakthrough that dramatically improves its user experience, and if Baidu fails to catch up quickly, Google might have a chance in China. Barring that, I believe Baidu will remain the search leader in China."

Future tech

As computers and broadband services get cheaper, more people in China are going online. The internet is reaching beyond the big cities into remote areas. Users are no longer just university graduates, but also kids, teenagers, factory workers, and the elderly.

"Given that new internet users in China are currently concentrated in second- or third-tier cities and among low-end users, Baidu will continue to lead over the next five years," said a hedge fund manager who invested in Baidu.

Google, on the other hand, appeals to high-end and more experienced users. As the country's internet population matures, more users will prefer Google to Baidu. However, this could take a long time, as Chinese internet penetration was only at 25 percent in June 2009.

Around 2007–08, satisfied with its Chinese search engine performance, Baidu began casting about for new opportunities. It launched a Japanese search engine, and developed an online chat platform, Baidu "Hi," to challenge the dominant QQ, which belongs to local player Tencent. It also developed an online auction market, Baidu Youa, challenging e-commerce king Alibaba's Taobao. These initiatives could become profitable business lines, but they could cause Baidu to lose its focus, giving Google a chance to catch up in search. Or, to Baidu's peril, they could alienate Alibaba and Tencent, two of the strongest internet companies in China.

The next battlefield for Baidu and Google will almost certainly be mobile internet services.

Mobile dreamin'

China is already the world's largest market for cellphones, with over 640 million in service at the end of 2008.[59] And at the beginning of 2009, China started to roll out third-generation (3G) telecom technology, promising more and faster mobile internet services.

"As 3G starts in China, mobile internet will be an explosive opportunity," said Lee. He envisions a day when more people will be using cellphones than computers to go online in China. "Right now, the internet traffic from cellphones is about one twentieth of that from computers

[59] As of the end of 2008, there were 641.23 million cellphone subscribers in China, according to China's Ministry of Industry and Information Technology.

in China. But mobile internet traffic can catch up quickly once the infrastructure is ready," said Lee. In Japan, for instance, the amount of internet traffic generated by cellphones is almost the same as that generated by PCs.

Three factors are driving mobile internet business:

1 Internet-ready cellphones, such as Apple's iPhone, are popular, and Google is pushing its Android platform to make internet-ready cellphones less proprietary and easier to manufacture.
2 Mobile internet rates are declining. China Mobile cut GPRS fees[60] by as much as two-thirds in most cities in January 2009. Thanks to the government-mandated restructuring of the telecoms sector in 2008, China now has three cellphone operators instead of two, a situation that is likely to increase price competition.
3 Many internet applications become more enticing over the phone. Where location matters—in maps, directory search, locating friends, and so forth—a mobile application can be useful. Social networking applications such as Facebook will be even more attractive to customers who can use them anytime, anywhere.

An increasing number of competitors is preparing for the coming generation of mobile applications. In 2008, Google China hired as its head of sales John Liu, who comes from a telecoms background. He served for six years as CEO of SK Telecom China, a unit of the largest cellphone operator in South Korea. Before that he held senior executive positions at Singapore Telecom. During his tenure, SK Telecom bought a 6.6 percent stake in cellphone operator China Unicom, becoming its second largest shareholder. SK Telecom also became one of the first foreign firms to participate in the development of TD-SCDMA, China's very own 3G technology.

Baidu hired a new Chief Technology Officer and a new Chief Operating Officer in 2008, both with strong telecoms credentials. The technology chief is Li Yinan, a 16-year veteran of the industry who previously was the chief telecom scientist at Huawei Technologies, the largest telecom solutions provider in China, where he oversaw the

60 GPRS or General Packet Radio Service is a mobile data service available to the users of 2G and 3G cellphones. GPRS data transfer is typically charged per megabyte transferred, while data communication via traditional circuit switching is billed per minute of connection time, independent of whether the user actually is using the capacity or the phone is idle.

development of 3G cellphone chipsets. Operations chief Ye Peng was previously general manager of Apple China. Before that, he was managing director of SatCom AG and a vice president of Motorola Mobile Business North Asia.

Google has been the mobile internet search partner of China Mobile, the country's dominant cellphone operator, since 2007. In May 2009, Baidu became the internet search partner for a new mobile operator, China Telecom. As well as the search function, popular Baidu applications such as Baidu Knows, Baidu Post-bar, image search, news search, MP3 search, and so on, will be available on China Telecom's 3G platform.[61]

The country's second largest mobile player, China Unicom, has yet to pick an internet search partner. But Baidu also has an agreement with China Netcom, the country's second largest fixed line operator and internet services provider, to provide an internet search page for its users.

Under the telecoms restructuring plan implemented by the government in 2008, China Unicom merged with China Netcom. If Baidu can expand its contract with China Netcom to include mobile search, it will have the country's second largest cellphone operator on its side, too. And following industry restructuring, cellphone services market shares look likely to fluctuate more than they ever have.

The dominant fixed line operator, China Telecom, acquired the CDMA (Code Division Multiple Access) cellphone network of China Unicom and is developing its 3G network using the CDMA-2000 standard. China Unicom keeps its GSM network and offers 3G via WCDMA, a mature technology already in wide use internationally.

China Mobile, which owns over 70 percent of the cellphone market, will be using the unproven domestic technology TD-SCDMA to offer 3G services. If TD-SCDMA gets off to a rocky start, China Telecom and China Unicom could gain ground on its rival.

As mentioned, Google China has worked on mobile internet since 2007. Its headquarters launched the Android program to make internet-ready phones easier to produce.

"Many applications will be even more useful over the cellphone. For example, Beijing is often choked with traffic. For people who are driving, a real-time traffic map of the city available on cellphone will be very useful," said Lee. "Google has an application called Latitude. It

[61] Source: Baidu Press release, "Baidu Provides Wireless Search for China Telecom 3G Subscribers," May 18, 2009.

shows the location of a user's friends so that the user can message them to arrange a get-together, say. This kind of application will be more useful in a cellphone whose location is changing as a person travels than in a PC whose location is always fixed," he added.

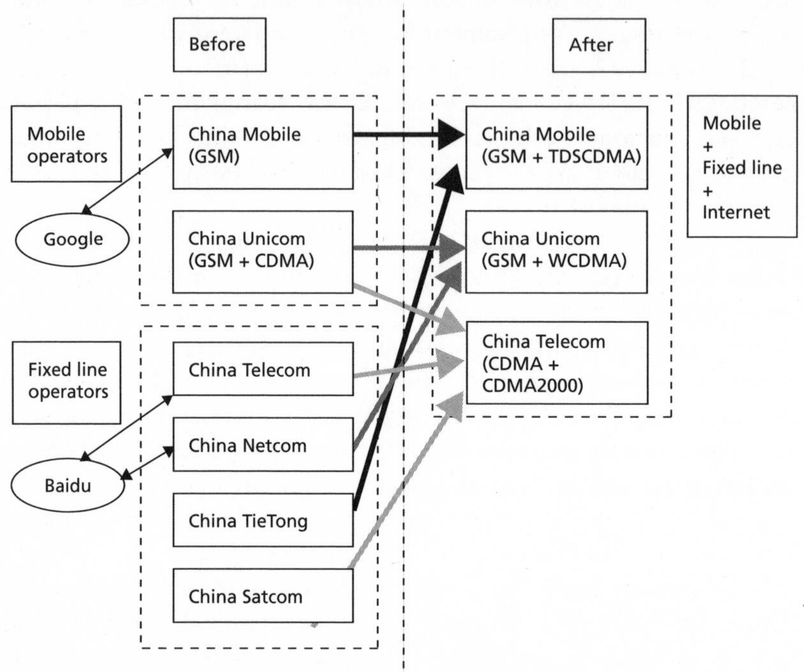

Figure 4.3: **Telecoms restructure in 2008**

Note: Under the restructuring plan, fixed line carrier China Telecommunications (China Telecom) acquired the CDMA (Code Division Multiple Access) cellphone network from China United Telecommunications (China Unicom). China Telecom also acquired China Satcom, which offers satellite-based communications services. China Unicom retained its GSM (Global System for Mobile Communication) network and merged with fixed line operator China Network Communications (China Netcom). China Mobile Communications, China's largest cellphone operator, merged with China Tietong Telecommunication, which operates a national fixed line network.[62]

Applications that use GPS and cell triangulation information to determine the person's location and show restaurants, cinemas, and other nearby points of interest are increasingly popular and numerous in America and Europe. But some industry insiders feel such Google

62 Source: Sumner Lemon, "China Announces Telecom Restructuring, Clearing Way for 3G," IDG News Service, May 25, 2008.

applications may be too sophisticated for the broad Chinese public. "In our experience, cellphone users are generally more low-end than people who use a PC to access the internet. They prefer entertainment and simple applications," said Jay Chang, CFO of Kongzhong, a leading mobile data service provider in China. In Chang's view, the ideal mobile internet applications are multiple-player games and novel downloads.

Baidu has yet to launch special cellphone applications, but some analysts believe its share of mobile traffic is larger than Google's merely on the strength of its local name recognition. Baidu has also teamed up with handset makers such as Samsung, Lenovo, Nokia and Motorola—one development is the pre-installation of a search box on the handset, making it easy for users to access Baidu's service. However, the site that attracts the most cellphone traffic belongs to neither Baidu nor Google. It is Tencent's 3G.QQ.com, the dominant online chat platform.

Lessons learned

1 Don't get mad—get successful!

One of the most important lessons foreign companies can learn from Google's China experience is how to deal with aggressive local rivals with fewer competitive scruples.

Don't just cry "unfair." Don't get mad. Keep your composure, and carefully weigh all of the strategies available to you. The first thing you'll want to do is to identify all the tactics your opponents are using to win market share. *Some will be smart—and ethical—and worth imitating.* For example, Google followed Baidu in using third-party sales agents to target small businesses in China. And after Baidu acquired the most popular directory site Hao123.com, Google bought the second most popular, 265.com, to attract internet novices.

2 As for machinations that might be considered improper or illegal in your home country, steer clear.

Google neither introduced illegal music search nor mixed search results with paid ads. And it continues to enjoy healthy profits and growth in China. (Just for the record, Baidu is not the most aggressive company in China—not even within the internet sector. Many companies have used even more questionable tactics than Baidu has. We only cite it as an example because some of its alleged lapses of judgment and ethics have come under the public spotlight.)

3 Finally, play to your strengths.

You undoubtedly have advantages over your local rivals. For example, Google has a global user network whereas Baidu is China-only. Companies in China need Google to market their products and services overseas. Google's better technology also gives it an edge on its ad platform and network sites.

Remember that as China becomes more integrated with the rest of the world, its legal system will get tougher, and customers and competitors will be faster to denounce unethical practices. Players who depend for success on their ability to walk a fine line between legality and illegality will not last.

5. Alibaba: The electric souq

In ancient times, souqs (Arabic سوق) were held outside the cities, in a location where a caravan loaded with goods would stop and merchants would display their wares for sale. They were organized for the benefit of caravans of suppliers. From this idea came Jack Ma's concept of a floating base of suppliers; a movable souq that he called Alibaba, after the character in the Arabic tales of *One Thousand and One Nights*.

Of all the Chinese internet companies, Alibaba is the most original. While others replicated successful Western models, there is no successful Western company doing what Alibaba does. Jack Ma, a diminutive ex-English teacher, became one of the most successful entrepreneurs in the country by having the simple idea of setting up an electronic message board for small businessmen in China and around the world to exchange trading information.

To grab market share, Ma allowed users to access the service for free. But while this allowed Alibaba.com to grow fast and dominate most of its competitors, the zero revenue strategy almost bankrupted him in the beginning.

The richest and happiest place on earth

In a way, Ma's story is like the American dream come true—except that the backdrop is not capitalist America, but communist China. Born in 1964, Ma grew up in a land impoverished by ten years of cultural revolution (1966–76) and decades of central planning, where government officials decided everything—what to produce and how much of it, who to sell it to and at what price.

By 1978, the country had a new leader, Deng Xiaoping. He believed there was no way the country could continue under the central planning regime. Economic reform began. China was opening up again for trade and tourism.

Ma's hometown is Hangzhou, a tourist spot for over a thousand years. It is famous for its scenic West Lake, its gardens, and temples. As a small boy, he watched as the first foreign tourist groups arrived in the country. When he was 12 years old, he became interested in learning English. Every day for the next nine years, Ma would ride his bike for 40 minutes every morning to a hotel near the city, where he offered his services as a guide to foreigners visiting Hangzhou.[63]

At first he could manage no more than "hello" and "good morning," but soon his English improved. What's more, he began to suspect that the world outside might be bigger and better than anything he had imagined. For decades, China had been a closed country. The Chinese knew no more about the outside world than foreigners knew about China.

He soon realized that what he learned from his teachers and books was different from what the foreign visitors told him. In 1985, Ma was invited by a pen pal to spend his summer vacation in Australia. He went and the experience totally changed him. Before he left, he was told that China was the richest, happiest country in the world. When Ma arrived in Australia, he thought that was totally not the case—so he started to think differently.

As bright and inquisitive as he was, in the eyes of China's educational system Ma was a failure. He could not gain admission to the elite universities. After twice failing his college entry examinations, he was finally accepted by Hangzhou Teacher's Institute, the least prestigious post-secondary institution in the city.

Nevertheless, Jack Ma began to shine. He became chairman of the student body at his own school and went on from there to be chairman of the entire city's Student Federation. After graduation, he remained at Hangzhou Teacher's Institute as a lecturer in English and international trade for five years. In 1992, the business environment was improving. He applied for lots of jobs, but again nobody seemed to want him.

A turning point came in 1995. He was hired as an interpreter for a Chinese trade delegation to America. He was dazzled when a friend introduced him to the internet, and he did not fail to notice how little data on China it contained.[64] There was no result when he did a search on "beer" and "China" in Yahoo. It was at that point Ma decided to launch a website and registered the name China Pages.

China Pages, which Ma started with several friends and about US$2,000, hosted websites for China's numerous small companies.

63 Source: Rebecca Fannin, "How I Did It: Jack Ma, Alibaba.com, The unlikely rise of China's hottest internet tycoon." *Inc. Magazine*, January 2008.

64 Source: Ken Howe, Alan T. Saracevic, Carrie Kirby, Verne Kopytoff, Ellen Lee, Steve Corder, "ALIBABA.COM: On the Record: Jack Ma," *San Francisco Chronicle*, May 7, 2006.

The tiny outfit was competing head to head with China Telecom, the country's dominant fixed line phone company and internet service provider, which was government owned. After about a year China Telecom offered Ma and his friends a buyout. It proposed forming a joint venture in which it would invest US$185,000.

It was the most money Ma had ever seen in his life. He gladly accepted the offer. But that was the last time China Telecom wanted to hear from him. Once it had control of the venture, the big company turned a deaf ear to all of Ma's suggestions. He resigned. He then received an offer to go to Beijing and run a new government group to promote e-commerce. He briefly became head of the China International Electronic Commerce Center's Infoshare division before founding his own e-commerce company.

In 1999, internet startups were all the rage. Everyone who was anyone was starting an internet company, dreaming of sugar plums and IPO riches. Ma was one of the dreamers. He bet on something he was familiar with and something he knew would be growing for a long time: trade. He gathered 18 friends and ex-colleagues in his apartment in Hangzhou. He told them about his idea—a global marketplace where buyers and sellers could find each other online. Together they raised US$60,000 and Alibaba was born.

Alibaba is easy to spell, and people everywhere associate that with "Open, Sesame," said Ma. (In the *One Thousand and One Nights*, the story of Ali Baba and the 40 Thieves tells of a poor boy who unlocks a cave full of hidden treasures using the magic words "Open, Sesame.")

Today, 17 of Ma's 18 original partners are still with him and the company. They, too, have unlocked their own treasures, while helping millions of small businessmen to trade.

Middleman kingdom

"Made in China" is a familiar label in supermarkets, electronic stores, fashion outlets, department stores, etc. But how do those shoes, toys, and TVs actually find their way onto the shelves? Traditionally, they had to pass through a long chain of intermediaries (Factories → trading companies → importers → distributors → retailers → consumers). A middleman takes a cut every time the goods change hands, which is how a pair of shoes sold by a Chinese factory for US$8–10 winds up costing US$50–100 in a Western shoe store.

Buyers always want to go up the food chain and find cheaper suppliers. Factories always want to go down the food chain and find buyers who pay better. But the opaque processes of traditional trade made it difficult for both parties to achieve their ends. Low margins have long been a problem for small factories in China. Without a way of marketing themselves globally, they are often at the mercy of a few large trading houses. The biggest problem for small businesses in China was how to find buyers for their goods, realized Ma. That was the first task that Alibaba tried to solve.

Open, Sesame

Alibaba's solution was simple: let Chinese suppliers put their information online—the products they make, their prices (optional), and their contact information. Overseas buyers can read these messages and contact the factories directly, either by email, phone, or fax. Similarly, buyers who need certain products can put their requirements online and wait for interested suppliers to contact them.

It is basically an electronic message board, but for trade (both domestic and international), rather than chitchat about the latest movies. It is also like a catalog or a yellow pages directory. But updates are instant and dynamic, and there is no central control—buyers and sellers post their information by themselves.

Figure 5.1: **Business model of Alibaba's B2B marketplace**

It has become a fantastic way for buyers to find suppliers. Just type "shoe" in the search box of Alibaba.com, and thousands of listings appear, each with the image of a shoe, a description, and the contact information of the supplier. It is also an easy way for suppliers to market themselves globally.

In 1999, some people ridiculed Alibaba's technology, which was primitive compared to that of the Silicon Valley startups that developed complex systems for managing supply chains down to the most minute details, such as California-based Ariba, which was founded in 1996 by Keith Krach. But the simple design worked. The network effect kicked in—as more suppliers put their information on Alibaba's site, more buyers used it, which attracted even more suppliers to register. Alibaba.com quickly became a popular destination on the early Chinese internet landscape.

Free market

Alibaba also had a most striking come-on—it promised not to charge users (either sellers or buyers) during its first three years of operation.

Ma thought Alibaba at that time was like a child. "You don't ask your child to go to work at the age of five. You raise him and give him a proper education so that he can land a good job and make lots of money," said Ma.[65] That was Ma's vision—let Alibaba grow and become part of the life of its users. Once users formed an inseparable bond with the trading platform, he could start charging them and the money would roll in. By not charging, Alibaba was able to grow its user base rapidly and wipe out most of its competitors, who were less well-financed and unable to survive for long without a revenue stream.

Alibaba was lucky in having deep-pocketed backers. In 1999, not long after launching the site, Ma got US$5 million from Goldman Sachs, Venture TDF and Fidelity. Softbank of Japan also threw in another US$20 million. Flush with cash, Ma set out to implement his global vision. He opened offices in San Francisco and Hong Kong. A group of highly paid American executives and engineers were hired to build the technology platform and oversee global expansion. Commercials appeared on CNBC, the international business television network, urging the world to come to Alibaba.com for Chinese trade.

Competition

There have been numerous attempts to create business-to-business (B2B) portals in the West. The most successful have been captives of either buyer or seller groups. There was nothing like Alibaba in the West, where most business-to-business companies solve problems for the benefit of large buyers or sellers; the challenge was not to find new suppliers, but to help retailers place orders with their existing suppliers more quickly and cheaply.

[65] As Jack Ma told the Hong Kong media when he visited in 1999.

When the dot.com bubble burst in 2000, many such B2B companies failed. For example, California-based Ariba, which had a market capitalization of over US$40 billion in 2000, saw its value wiped out by over 95 percent after the crash. It never recovered. Another California-based company, Commerce One, also saw its stock value tumble. It filed for bankruptcy in 2004.

China, however, had many players running on models similar to Alibaba's. One was Global Sources, a Hong Kong-based trade magazine publisher that had started to develop its web presence around the same time.

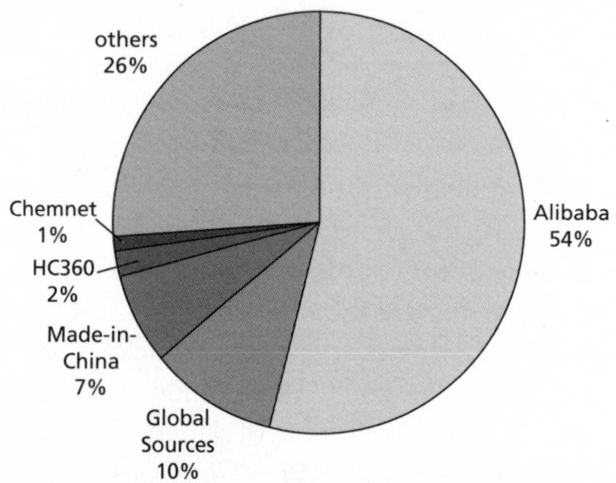

***Figure 5.2:* Market share of China's B2B operators by revenue**

Data source: iResearch, 2008, 2nd quarter

Note: This survey included only the Chinese marketplaces of Alibaba and Global Sources. If international marketplaces were also included, Global Source's market share is about a third of Alibaba. Alibaba's revenue was US$106.6 million in 2008, 2nd quarter and the online revenue of Global Sources was US$36.9 million.

CEO Merle Hinrichs, a graduate of the University of Nebraska, founded the company in Hong Kong, a busy trading port in South China, in 1971. It began by publishing a series of trade magazines called *Asian Sources*. These inches-thick catalogs were stuffed with advertisements from hundreds of factories and trading houses in Asia. They were distributed monthly to importers and traders in North America, the Middle East, and Europe. The company had everything from clothing and shoes to electronics and auto parts covered. A website, Asia Sources Online, was launched in 1995. By 1999, renamed Global Sources, the site was already a bustling e-marketplace just like Alibaba.com.[66] "Our edge is that we have the world's largest buyers, over 803,000, as our users," said Hinrichs.

In the course of publishing its magazines, the company had come to know the network of buyers and suppliers well, so it was easily able to branch into the B2B e-marketplace. Many suppliers were willing to pay yearly subscription fees of several thousand US dollars to get listed on the Global Sources site.

Global Source positions itself at the high end of the market, dealing with the largest buyers and their suppliers. The company targeted the mid- to large-sized companies as Hinrichs believed in the 80/20 rule (an example: in America the top 3,000 buyers account for more than 67 percent of total imports). Alibaba, on the other hand, welcomes anyone, even the smallest traders and factories. Most of its users are small- to medium-sized companies.

In 2004, Global Source also branched into organizing trade shows where thousands of buyers and suppliers could meet. It arranged private sourcing events for major buyers, such as Lowe's, Office Depot, Tesco, Samsung, NEC, etc. These are one-on-one meetings where buyers and suppliers can really write orders. "e-Commerce is not just a click on screen," said Hinrichs, who prefers to give traders different options— magazines, online, and face-to-face—to do business.

Global Sources became the first B2B company trading on the NASDAQ via a back-door listing in April 2000. When the internet bubble burst in 2000, its business took a serious hit, and until 2004 it was only marginally profitable. But compared to Alibaba in 2000, it was in great shape.

Catastrophe

Failure to get a listing on NASDAQ before the internet stock collapse caused Alibaba to stumble. Its no-charge policy had helped it to grab

[66] From Global Source Annual Report 2000: "We are a leading enabler of online global merchandise trade. Our business began in 1971 in Hong Kong when we launched *Asian Sources*, a magazine to serve global buyers importing products in volume from Asia. Realizing the importance of e-commerce, we commercially released the first version of Global Sources Transact, our proprietary trade management software to facilitate international transactions in 1991. We then became one of the first business-to-business online marketplaces by launching Asian Sources Online in 1995. At that time, we began repositioning our trade magazines to play a supportive, educational, and promotional role to accelerate the shift of our customers to our e-commerce services. In 1999, we expanded our scope to include global suppliers and changed the name of our online marketplace to Global Sources Online."

market share, but the lack of revenue left it with a net loss every month. By 2001, the company had only US$10 million in the bank and was spending US$2 million a month.[67] There was no choice. It had to downsize.

The highly paid American executives were let go. The offices in San Francisco were closed. Management took a voluntary salary cut. The company retreated to Ma's hometown of Hangzhou. "It was our B2C strategy—Back to China," an Alibaba employee recalled. Monthly expenses (the so-called "burn rate") were cut by three-quarters, to US$500,000.

An ex-General Electric executive, Savio Kwan, was hired to cut spending and do the layoffs. He tidied up Alibaba's operations, which had been running without much discipline. A corporate value system was introduced to give employees a sense of direction and guidance on what was and was not acceptable behavior. Traffic and users were no longer the only objectives. The new goal was to generate revenue—sustainable long-term cashflow.

That was when Alibaba started to notice the business model of its competitor, Global Sources, which in 2000 raked in US$54 million in online membership fees. Global Sources' experience showed that suppliers were willing to pay subscription fees of several thousand American dollars per year, as long as the site generated new sales. For suppliers, it was a part of their marketing, just like placing ads in trade magazines or setting up booths at trade shows.

Of course, in China, you would need an aggressive sales force to carry off the same trick. No one would be willing to turn over thousands of dollars, a considerable sum for most companies, without a sales rep egging them on. Kwan started to train a sales force, which remains a key asset for Alibaba to this day.

Alibaba successfully made the transition. As of June 2007, 71 percent of Alibaba's 4,400 staff were in sales and marketing. It had large teams in 30 cities across China and Hong Kong, over 1,900 full-time field sales employees, over 800 telephone sales employees, and more than 400 full-time customer service employees.[68]

[67] Source: Rebecca A. Fannin, *Silicon Dragon*, McGraw Hill, 2008.
[68] Source: Alibaba's IPO prospectus.

Restoration

Though buyers and suppliers could continue to enjoy free services, Alibaba introduced a premium membership called Gold Supplier for exporters in China. The subscription fee was about half what Global Sources charged its clients. Paying customers would be entitled to display a much bigger catalog on the site, and their products would be guaranteed to pop up first in response to buyer searches. Plenty of extras were thrown in to add value to the membership, for example, free photo shoots for their products, video factory tours, training courses on dealing with overseas clients, and so on.

Later Alibaba introduced two other forms of paid membership at a much lower price point (less than a hundred dollars a year), International TrustPass and China TrustPass. These members would enjoy fewer privileges than Gold Supplier members, but more than the nonpaying users. For example, their products would be shown after those of the Gold Supplier members, but before those of the nonpaying users.

By 2002, Alibaba managed to get US$3.7 million in revenue from selling memberships, mainly to suppliers in China. Alibaba broke even, and Ma heaved a sigh of relief.[69] It was a best-of-both-worlds strategy—the offer of free, basic services continued to increase user numbers, and as the B2B site grew in popularity, more suppliers were willing to sign on as premium members in order to stand out from their competitors. Aggressive sales tactics helped to speed up the process.

More investment arrived in 2004 from Softbank, Fidelity Capital, Granite Global Ventures, and Singapore's Venture TDF Pte Ltd (US$82 million).[70] This money, however, was mainly intended to support Ma's new initiative—he started an auction site, Taobao, to compete head on with eBay in China—a story we will tell in detail in the next chapter. Another boost to Alibaba's confidence and bank balance came in 2005, when Yahoo bought 40 percent of the company for US$1 billion and turned over Yahoo's China operation for Ma to run. Of this sum, US$750 million was used to pay back earlier investors. Alibaba kept US$250 million for expanding its footprint in other internet businesses. Apart from the B2B site and the auction site, Alibaba branched into online payment with Alipay and internet-based business software with Alisoft.

69 Source: Rebecca A. Fannin, *Silicon Dragon*, McGraw Hill, 2008.
70 Source: "Alibaba.com secures $82m funding," *Computer Business Review*, Feb 19, 2004.

In 2007, bolstered by strong domestic consumption and robust global trade, China recorded GDP growth of 11.4 percent, with export growth significantly outpacing GDP. China's export volume grew 23.5 percent to reach US$1,218 billion, according to government statistics. The total trading volume of China was US$2,174 billion, up 23 percent from the previous year.

	2004	2005	2006	2007
Registered users	1,165,911	1,949,741	3,115,153	4,405,557
Storefronts	142,805	292,414	514,891	697,563
Paying members				
—Gold Supplier members	6,435	12,192	18,682	27,384
—International TrustPass members	5,015	7,791	10,843	12,152

Table 5.1: **Alibaba's international marketplace**

Data source: Alibaba Annual Report 2007

	2004	2005	2006	2007
Registered users	4,840,641	9,019,214	16,649,073	23,194,402
Storefronts	497,876	1,002,768	1,557,874	2,259,283
Paying members				
—China TrustPass members	66,472	121,631	189,573	266,009

Table 5.2: **Alibaba's Chinese marketplace**

Data source: Alibaba Annual Report 2007

Alibaba's B2B site, which thrived on trade and exports, recorded US$285.3 million in revenue in 2007, up about 59 percent from the previous year, while profit increased 4.4 times to US$127.7 million.

It decided there was no point in further delaying its IPO plans. Alibaba listed its B2B site, Alibaba.com, on the Hong Kong stock exchange in November 2007. It raised US$1.5 billion, the largest internet-related stock sale since Google. Its share price nearly tripled on the first day of trading.

Economic winter

However, Alibaba's glory was short lived. By 2008, the world economy had started to tumble. Exports, which had been driving China's GDP growth since the country opened up its economy in 1978, met an unexpected downturn. Ma called it the "Economic Winter." Factories in China were badly hurt by growing costs and a sudden decline in overseas demand.

Under pressure from America, China modified its pro-export policies. Its currency, the yuan, which had been kept artificially low, appreciated 20 percent over four years (2004–08). The government also reduced tax rebates to export companies. It amended its labor laws in 2008, increasing most factories' wage costs by 10 percent.

Oil prices reached a record high of nearly US$150 per barrel in 2008 and the price of materials such as iron, copper, and plastic doubled or tripled. An electrical fan maker in South China said his costs increased by 40 percent over three years, wiping out his profit margin. At the same time, the global financial crisis started by subprime lending began to take a toll on consumer spending. Many retailers, such as the 100-year-old British department store chain Woolworths, went bankrupt. Others, such as the American electronic store Circuit City, were reducing the number of outlets and cutting their total floor space.

Demand for consumer goods dwindled worldwide, especially in America and Europe, where most Chinese exports go. Chinese exports, after shrinking for four consecutive months from November 2008, dropped by 25.7 percent from a year earlier in February 2009, the sharpest fall in at least 18 years. Imports fell 24.1 percent.

Twenty thousand factories in China's Guangdong province closed in the five-month period from October 2008 to February 2009, according to a local newspaper. Two million factory workers were laid off. Those feeling the squeeze included suppliers to companies such as Mattel Inc, the world's biggest toymaker, and the American department-store chain JC Penney Company.

Alibaba saw its growth rate for new subscriptions and renewal rate for existing subscriptions slow from the beginning of 2008. Especially hard hit was its pricey premium membership, Gold Supplier. At the same time, competitor Global Sources cut its prices significantly. Alibaba matched that by launching a baby version of Gold Supplier at about half the price. Although that encouraged more suppliers to sign up, its profit margin was hurt.

Alibaba also started to focus more on domestic trade in China and opportunities for Chinese import trade. The Chinese domestic economy was holding up quite well. The top 1,000 retailers saw their sales rise by something like 24 percent for 2008. Because its subscriptions are prepaid, the downturn did not affect Alibaba's financial performance until late 2008, but worried investors dumped its shares anyway. From a peak in November 2007, Alibaba.com's stock market value fell 90 percent in the space of a year.

Overall, Alibaba still managed well under the financial crisis, although its growth in revenue was slower and profit margin lower.[71] Net profit in 2008 grew 37 percent to US$174.8 million, although this was much less than the 362 percent growth it had had the year before.

Global expansion

As a business based on assisting trade, Alibaba.com was always destined to be a global company. It has millions of users overseas. Ma was not discouraged by his failures early this decade. Once Alibaba's foundations were firm, it was ready to take on the world again.

Country or region	Number of registered users in country or region	Percentage of total registered users
1. United States	967,991	17.2%
2. India	539,910	9.6%
3. European Union	511,021	9.1%
4. United Kingdom	323,495	5.8%
5. Canada	149,965	2.7%

***Table 5.3:* Geographic distribution of registered users (other than Mainland China) of Alibaba's international marketplace as of June 30, 2008**

Data source: Alibaba interim report 2008

Naturally, its first focus was on Asia, particularly Hong Kong, Taiwan, India, and Japan, where the concentration of suppliers is high. Since all revenue comes from suppliers (buyers use the site for a fee), opening offices in those areas would help Alibaba to sign up more paid members.

Initially, Alibaba did not worry about increasing the buyer community, as more suppliers would naturally attract more buyers. But years of exclusive focus on adding suppliers to its membership roster have caused inequality in Alibaba's marketplace, said an industry analyst. "You cannot just grow the supplier network infinitely without promoting the buyers network equally," said the analyst. "Many paid

[71] Alibaba's sales were still growing in 2008, up 53 percent to US$435.2 million, although slower than the 66 percent growth it had had a year earlier. Net profit margin decreased to 40 percent from 45 percent the year before.

members of Alibaba.com notice they have been getting fewer buyers' requests over the years."

By 2009, it seemed that the natural growth rate of buyers was no longer enough. Alibaba wanted to actively promote itself in areas where buyers were concentrated. "It's just like a party—you cannot just invite the boys," said Dick Wei, China internet analyst of JP Morgan. A US$30 million marketing campaign was devised to build awareness of the brand in America and Britain, and attract more buyers to its site. Although the extra marketing costs mean more pressure on Alibaba's profit margin, in the long run it should restore the balance of buyers and suppliers, making it a more healthy and vibrant trading platform.

Lessons learned

1 Keen powers of observation are the key to developing any good business model.

What Ma did at Alibaba.com could never have happened in the West, where the prerequisite—thousands of small factories looking for new trading partners—did not exist. On the other hand, it was quite natural for Ma to think of this idea. The regions around his hometown of Hangzhou are full of small factories making everything from buttons to television sets. Ma's academic and professional experience made him aware of the problems faced by Chinese trade, so he dreamed up a solution—a B2B platform, an electronic message board where buyers and suppliers could freely exchange information.

Global Sources had a similar inspiration from observing traders in its Hong Kong home base, who for years have been making goods in China and shipping them worldwide.

2 The network effect is an important factor (but not the only one) in success in many internet marketplaces.

Some of the principles behind the success of Alibaba.com have universal application. The B2B trading platform is a marketplace. For a marketplace to boom, the key is to have a critical mass of buyers and sellers. After that, the network effect will kick in—more buyers will attract more sellers and vice versa, and participation in the marketplace will grow exponentially.

Global Sources relied on a buyer and supplier network built up over 40 years of publishing trade magazines to achieve that critical mass. Alibaba, having no such advantages, relied on offering free services at first, plus heavy advertising and promotion. Both companies built up networks that were big enough to be useful for their users. Other players tried, but could not reach critical size quickly enough, so their users lost interest and left.

At first glance, Alibaba's initial policy of not charging users seems as effective as Global Sources' 40 years of experience in building up a customer network. But it was a very risky strategy, as shown by Alibaba's near bankruptcy in 2000. With a no-charge model, any deterioration in buyer interest or seller demand, or the financial conditions of the company, will cause it to fail.

3 Balancing the number of buyers and suppliers is key to building a robust marketplace.

The number of buyers and sellers (suppliers) must be balanced. For a long time, Alibaba put most of its effort into getting suppliers to join because when it began to charge, it only charged suppliers. The company runs advertisements in China, Hong Kong, etc., and it has a sales force to push paid membership among the Chinese suppliers.

At first, the network effect worked its charms. As the number of suppliers grew, so did the number of buyers. But eventually the growth of suppliers outstripped the natural growth of buyers, causing frustration among suppliers. To fix the problem, Alibaba launched a marketing campaign in areas where buyers are concentrated, notably America and Britain.

6. Taobao: A market for the rest of us

After Alibaba started making a profit on its main B2B site, its founder Jack Ma took aim at the potentially much bigger consumer-to-consumer (C2C) market. He picked the right moment to strike—just as eBay was buying the homegrown online auction king EachNet, whose much-loved (at least by the locals) CEO Bo Shao was about to be replaced by one of the San Francisco firm's faceless executives.

While eBay was busy consolidating EachNet into its global operation, Alibaba was plugging Taobao as a new online shopping destination. And unlike its American-owned competitor, Taobao was free! But levying listing fees and transaction fees was not the only reason eBay lost its dominance to Taobao. A key catalyst was "migration," the decision to terminate EachNet's homegrown technology platform and move all EachNet users to the eBay American platform. On the day of migration, traffic to eBay China dropped by half.

Despite the seriousness of the customer losses, Meg Whitman, then CEO of eBay, only learned about it a month later, on a visit to Shanghai. Shao recalls that Whitman was shocked and very upset. So was Shao, who by then was living in America, but had accompanied Whitman to China. Apparently, the head of eBay international at the time, who was one of the most ardent proponents of migration, did not tell Whitman about it.

Echo Bay

One of the most successful early internet business models was the online auction, pioneered by San Jose, California-based eBay.

In 1995, 28-year-old Pierre Omidyar, a French-born Iranian who had previously developed software for Apple computers, sat down to write the code that would allow people to list and bid for products and services over the internet. Originally called AuctionWeb and hosted on the same server as Omidyar's page about the ebola virus, the site began with the listing of a single broken laser pointer. It was a test rather than a serious offer to sell at auction. Omidyar, however, was shocked when the item sold for US$14.83. He contacted the winning bidder to ask if he understood that the pointer was broken—the person said he was a collector of broken laser pointers.[72]

Omidyar knew that he had created something big, a market where individuals across America could buy and sell the kind of items one would normally find at a garage sale. On the other hand, a hard-to-find baseball card might also be found at your fingertips, sometimes at very low prices—if no one else was bidding.

AuctionWeb soon took over his entire domain, www.ebay.com, short for Echo Bay, which was the name of his consulting firm at the time (the Echo Bay name had already been taken by a gold mining company, so Omidyar opted for the abbreviated eBay). eBay grew rapidly, branching out from collectibles into nearly every type of product. And unlike most early internet businesses, such as Yahoo, Amazon, etc., eBay was profitable within a year.[73]

It charges a tiny amount every time a seller lists a new item for auction and another small percentage when the item is sold. Besides auctions, it also allows users to sell items at fixed prices. Currently, fixed price items account for about half of eBay's sales.[74]

Figure 6.1: **Business model of eBay's C2C marketplace**

By the time eBay went public in 1998, it was making US$2.4 million net profit on revenue of U$47.4 million. It had 2.1 million registered users and over one million items up for sale on any given day.[75] After its rapid success, eBay had plenty of challengers. Yahoo, for example, was once a serious competitor in online auctions, along with around 300 other companies, most of whom folded during the dot.com bust. But the online auction is a business model where the "network effect" is very pronounced. People like to trade in the market with the most users: For buyers, a bigger market offers more products to choose from; for sellers it offers more potential buyers. The ability to trade quickly and with maximum choice offered by a large market is called "liquidity." The larger the network, the greater the liquidity.

72 Source: Aron Hsiao, "How did eBay start? A brief history of eBay," About.com.
73 From eBay's Annual Report 1998: it made US$148,000 net profit in 1996.
74 Source: eBay, Financial History & Metrics, Apr 22, 2009.
75 Source: eBay Annual Report 1998.

Therefore, the auction market that starts first usually gathers the most users and becomes dominant on account of this "first mover advantage." New challengers cannot easily steal users from it, even if they lower their transaction fees or charge nothing at all—no one wants to trade in a marketplace where transactions are few and far between. Being the first mover, eBay dominated the America market, and quickly expanded internationally.

By 2002, eBay's expansion plan had reached China. It acquired 33 percent of the country's dominant auction player, EachNet, for US$30 million in March 2002. It purchased the remainder for US$150 million in July 2003.

EachNet was a homegrown company whose business model was similar to eBay's. Bo Shao, a Harvard MBA who previously worked for Boston Consulting Group and Goldman Sachs, founded it in 1999 together with his partner, Haiyin Tan, with funding from venture capital firms Whitney & Co, AsiaTech Ventures Limited, and Orchid Asia Holdings. By 2003, when eBay acquired the company, EachNet had more than 2 million users and about 85 percent of the market.

Shao started charging listing and transaction fees in 2001, despite the existence of free competing sites, because he believed that as long as the site had the most buyers and made money for sellers, the sellers would be willing to pay. According to Shao, fees did not affect user loyalty. In fact, EachNet's dominance increased after it started charging.

After the acquisition, Shao retired from the daily operations of eBay China and moved to America in late 2003 with his family. eBay sent in a number of expats to run the China division, and hired a number of senior executives from other multinational corporations in China.

It thought everything would be fine. After all, EachNet (or eBay China) had an overwhelmingly dominant position and it planned to spend an extra US$100 million to improve its technology platform and promote eBay's brand in China. Any new competitors would be easy to crush. However, nothing ever goes according to plan. A new rival appeared, and eBay ultimately retreated from China four years later.

Taobao's beginnings

In 2002 Alibaba's B2B business stabilized. User numbers were growing and it started making money from selling premium memberships to Chinese exporters.

Jack Ma went to Japan for a business trip. He visited his friend and investor, Masayoshi Son, CEO of Softbank Corp, who told him that eBay might not be as mighty as it looked. Yahoo! Japan, which is controlled by Son, had beaten eBay for dominance in the Japanese auction market. Similar things could happen in China, too, if Ma seized the opportunity.

Alibaba was also afraid eBay would branch into the business-to-business market, by approaching buyers and sellers of industrial products, according to local media at the time.

On his return from Japan, Ma gathered a small team and set them to work on his "secret" project, Skunkworks style. By May 2003, their product, a website called Taobao, which means "seeking for treasure" in Chinese, had been launched. Constrained by its small budget, Taobao could not advertise on the largest online portals and major media. But the team figured out other ways to promote the site.

"They went to small websites and online forums and told people there was a new site called Taobao and there were plenty of bargains," said Porter Erisman, a former vice president for corporate affairs at Alibaba, in 2004. "What is more: it's free." Taobao levied neither listing nor transaction fees. Ma was using the free service trick again—the same one that Alibaba had used to conquer the B2B market.

By July 2003, Taobao was no longer a secret—its name had spread all over China's internet space. Sellers, having nothing to lose, listed their items with Taobao. More items for sale attracted more buyers, who in turn attracted more sellers. The network effect kicked in and Taobao's popularity grew.

eBay was in a quandary. If it adopted Taobao's tactics, eBay China would bleed to death, while Taobao could survive off the profits from Alibaba's B2B site. To back Ma for his fight against eBay in China, Softbank and other investors chipped in another US$82 million into Alibaba in 2004.[76]

80 percent

Taobao's popularity rose quickly. A year after it started, Taobao became the second most popular C2C site after EachNet, according to iResearch, a Shanghai-based market research firm. Its traffic, as measured by page views, was about half that of EachNet (or eBay China) by May 2004.

[76] Source: "Alibaba.com secures $82m funding," *Computer Business Review*, Feb 19, 2004.

Its market share continued to grow, despite eBay's heavy promotion. eBay was the top spender on online advertising. In the single month of December 2004, it spent over US$1 million on advertising, more than twice as much as Samsung, the second largest, according to iResearch.

By the fall of 2005, Taobao had eclipsed eBay as the largest online auction company in China. Although eBay still had more registered users, Taobao had 57 percent of market transaction volume compared to eBay's 34 percent, according to Analysys International.

eBay significantly cut its prices to try and compete, and in late 2005 it stopped charging altogether, but it was too little too late. Its market share dropped from 85 percent when it purchased EachNet in 2003 to about 30 percent in 2006.

After investing nearly US$300 million (US$180 million for acquiring Eachnet and US$100 million as extra budget for its China push), eBay all but threw in the towel. It folded its China operation into a joint venture with Tom Online, a leading cellphone value-added services provider in China at the end of 2006. But Tom Online could not turn this situation around, either. eBay's market share had shrunk to 7 percent by the second quarter of 2007. Taobao held 82 percent of the market.

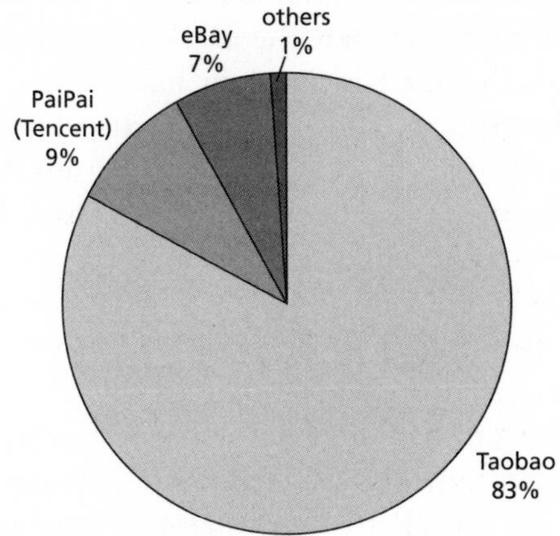

Figure 6.2: **China's C2C market**

Data source: Analysys International, 2007, 2nd quarter

Why eBay got it wrong

Many believed Taobao beat eBay by being free. But EachNet co-founder Shao held a different position. After selling the company to eBay in July 2003, he stayed on as a consultant for over a year. "At first, even with Taobao making a lot of noise, our users and traffic did not change much," said Shao. Despite having to pay fees, the larger user base of eBay China was more than enough to keep sellers coming. Similarly, most buyers stayed as there were more sellers and products offered. Latecomers have seldom posed a serious threat to the dominant online auction player. They might capture some market share, but seldom a big chunk. Latecomer Yahoo's free auction service in America had scarcely any effect on eBay's market dominance.

According to Shao, what really caused eBay to lose its dominance in China was its decision to move its technology platform from China to America. Internally, it was called "migration," which was the project to terminate EachNet's homegrown technology platform and move all EachNet users to the American eBay platform in October 2004.

Meg Whitman, then CEO of eBay, had a vision—she wanted all eBay users, wherever they were, to be able to trade with each other. She wanted a "global village." For example, users in America would be able to see products offered by users in China and bid for them.

"In fact, it was Pierre's idea. The founder of eBay noticed the first international trade two weeks after he started his AuctionWeb. So, from the very beginning, he knew the market is global," said a former eBay executive, who worked in its Asia Pacific office. Dealing with cross-border trade has an added benefit. It allows eBay's online payment division, PayPal, to get extra profit from handling foreign exchange. For example, a German buyer purchases a book from an American seller. He or she will need to change euros into US dollars to settle the bill. "Each individual transaction is tiny and the traders might not notice. But it adds up and the total can be huge," said the former eBay executive.

It was a great vision, but terrible business strategy. To implement Whitman's global vision, eBay's technology platforms in different countries had to be moved to headquarters, consolidated, and put under the control of the company's chief technology officer. The former EachNet management supported the vision, according to Shao, but felt that it was premature to migrate the EachNet users to the American platform, which was not yet flexible enough to accommodate the China-specific features that EachNet needed to compete in China. EachNet's technology team was also concerned about transmission speed issues across the Pacific. Such concerns, however, were downplayed during the eBay technology team's presentation to Whitman.

"On the exact day of the move, traffic (of eBay China) dropped by half," said Shao. What had been information flow within China had become traffic across borders and across the Pacific Ocean. However, the internet infrastructure between China and America at that time was not very good. The loading speed of eBay China's web page, one of the most important user issues, slowed dramatically.

What's more, the Chinese government by then had built its "great firewall" to block any traffic of which it disapproved. The censorship was quite tight—anything that looked suspicious would be blocked and the foreign computer server that processed the problematic information would be banned for anywhere from 24 hours to several days.

Shao claimed that many usernames and product descriptions in eBay China could get into trouble because of the "firewall." For example, beijing64 could be a problematic username because 64 could stand for the June 4th event—the student demonstration in Beijing's Tiananmen Square for democracy in China. And when the blocking occurred, not only was user beijing64 affected, but also all users accessing the same foreign computer servers.

One particularly damaging rumor that was circulating about this time suggested that eBay's rival, the Chinese company Taobao, created usernames and product descriptions on eBay China that were designed to get eBay into trouble with the government. As a result, eBay's slow and unstable services frustrated users and caused them to leave eBay China in droves. The presence of Taobao, as a better alternative, further sped up the process.

Unfortunately, this news did not reach Meg Whitman, then CEO of eBay, until a month later, said Shao. The head of eBay International at the time was a major proponent of migration and did not tell her about the crisis.

Whitman cared a great deal about China and treated eBay China as a strategic priority. Shao recalled that Whitman was shocked and upset when she found out about the problems. He said that eBay originally wanted him to talk to the head of eBay Taiwan, which had already moved its platform, before the China move took place. However, the conversation never went any further. When he eventually ran into eBay's Taiwan head after the migration, he found out eBay Taiwan had had exactly the same experience of slowing services and lost users.

Furthermore, the head of eBay Taiwan had been discouraged from talking to Shao.

The move of the technology platform to America also brought the development of eBay China to a halt. "In order for the American eBay platform to catch up with EachNet's China-specific features, development on the site was frozen for a year before the platform was moved," said Shao. For an entire year beginning in October 2003, EachNet could not develop any new features or make significant changes to existing features.

After the move, the local team lost most of its control on the site. "It took nine months to implement any major changes and nine weeks to even change a word on the website as everything had to go through the headquarters technology development team," said Shao. "This is unthinkable. Fast reaction to user demands is crucial in this market."

Taobao, meanwhile, was quickly adding new features and making its design more and more appealing to Chinese users. It added an online chat function that allowed buyers and sellers to communicate before trading. It implemented an online payment solution, Alipay. It made its page design more feminine to appeal to a growing number of female users.

Slow and unstable services and a lack of updates caused eBay China to lose users fast. Three months after the platform moved, the market share of eBay China had dropped to almost the same level as Taobao, said Shao. "After that, there was no more reason for users to stay (with eBay China)," said Shao. eBay China had fewer users and worse services than Taobao, and it charged. Six months after the move, Taobao had turned the tables on eBay China, capturing 60 percent of the market while its rival languished at 30 percent.

"Korea is the only Asian market where eBay allowed the local operation to keep their platform. It remains competitive. And now it has acquired its arch rival Gmarket[77], it is even stronger," said a former eBay executive.

But platform migration was not the only reason eBay lost many of its Asia markets, continued the former executive. "Every market has its unique situation. For example, some eBay websites could not be advertised on general portals in Asia Pacific where the portal also operated an auction business. This was the case in markets like Singapore, Taiwan, and Hong Kong." When the competition is keen, it would be difficult for such portals to advertise eBay's services on their sites.

77 Source: "EBay completes offer for Gmarket," Associated Press, June 15, 2009.

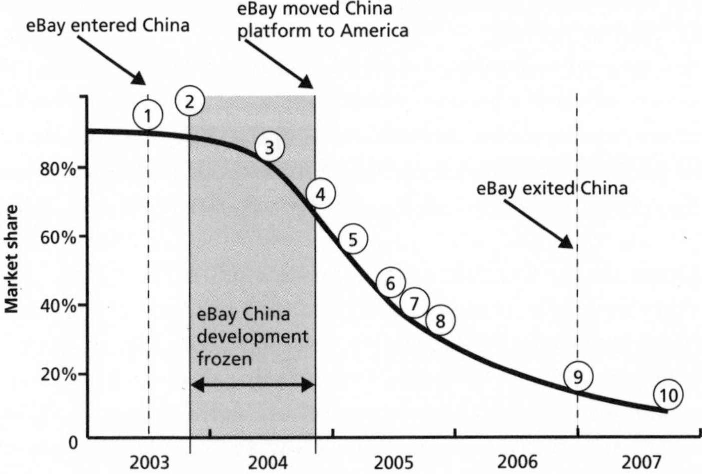

Figure 6.3: **Change of eBay's market share in China (2003–07)**

Data source: iResearch, Analysys International, Bo Shao

Notes:

1. July 2003, eBay entered China by acquiring Eachnet, 85% market share
2. October 2003, eBay froze development on Eachnet's auction platform for a year to facilitate the migration to America
3. May 2004, research firm iResearch found that Taobao's traffic reached half that of eBay China
4. October 2004, eBay China's auction platform moved to America
5. January 2005, market share of eBay China dropped to about the same level as Taobao
6. April 2005, Taobao led eBay China in market share, about 60 percent to 30 percent
7. 2005, 2nd quarter, research firm Analysys International found the transaction volume of Taobao led eBay China, 57 percent to 34 percent
8. Late 2005, eBay China cut its fees and eventually stopped charging users
9. End of 2006, eBay folded its China operation into a joint venture with Tom Online
10. 2007, 2nd quarter, Analysys International found the transaction volume of Taobao led eBay China, 82 percent to 7 percent

PayPal setback

Originally, eBay wanted to introduce its PayPal payment platform—which is used by many of its American customers—to China right after it acquired EachNet in mid 2003. But the plan was delayed for over a year because of Chinese government regulation. "PayPal allows users to transfer money between different countries. eBay asked if this was all right in China," said an industry insider who knew about the incident. "Of course, no Chinese official can ever say yes. A local player will do it first before asking. But eBay is a multinational. They always ask first," said the insider.

The Chinese government has strict controls on the flow of money into and out of the country, so when PayPal finally launched in China in mid 2005, it was with a curtailed version that only allowed for use of the Chinese RMB. However, by then Taobao had already launched its payment solution, Alipay, which was better designed for the local market. Notably, it had an escrow function, which addressed the lack of trust issue that is common among Chinese online shoppers.

The trust issue was one of the biggest problems for e-commerce in China, said Jacky Huang, China Internet Research Manager of IDC. "Should sellers ship the product first or the buyers pay first? There are always arguments. No one trusts each other," said Huang. With Alipay, buyers first send their money to the escrow account of Alibaba, which notifies the sellers to ship the products. Once the buyers receive their purchases, they notify Alibaba, which releases money from the escrow account to the sellers. What's more, Alibaba guaranteed it would compensate anyone who was cheated in the process.

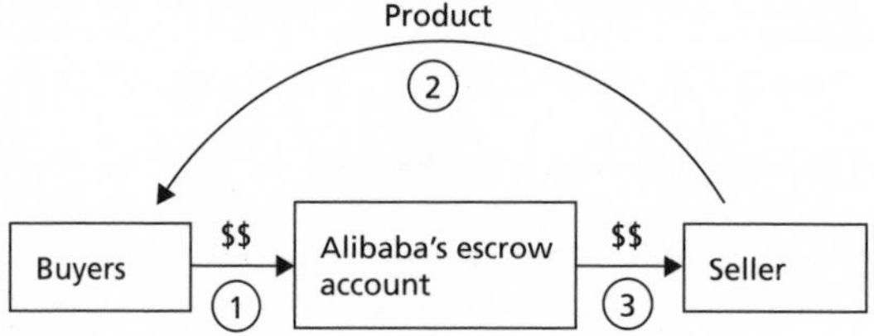

***Figure 6.4:* How it works—Alipay's escrow function**

Steps:

① Buyer transfers money into Alibaba's escrow account

② Seller ships product to buyer

③ Money transfers from Alibaba's escrow account to seller

The escrow function hit the right buttons with Chinese shoppers. Online shopping took off with Alipay and Taobao. The total transaction volume of Chinese online shopping increased close to 12 times from 2004 (a year after Taobao started) to US$7.4 billion in 2007, and was projected to reach US$53.6 billion by 2011, according to iResearch. The number of online shoppers more than doubled in the same period, reaching 55 million. Their number is projected to reach 200 million by 2011.

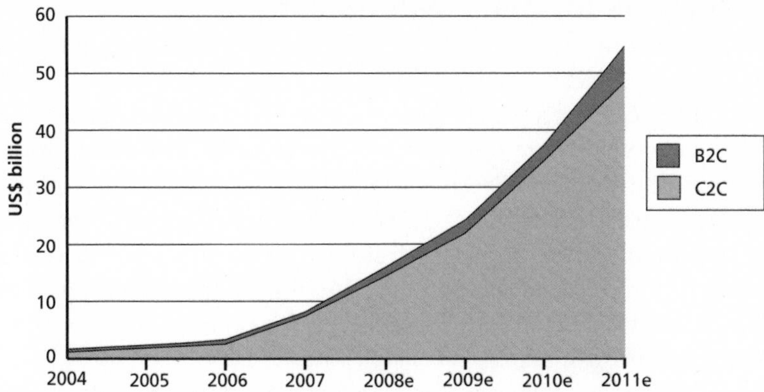

Figure 6.5: **Gross trading volume of China's online shopping market (2004–11)**

Data source: iResearch

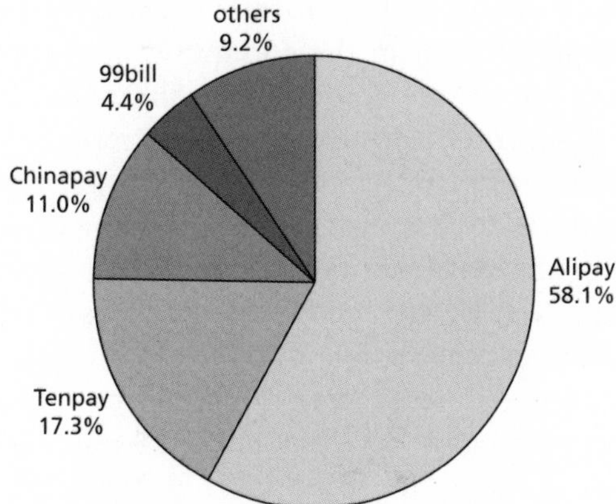

Figure 6.6: **China's online payment market share**

Data source: Analysys International, 2008, 3rd quarter

eBay China's loss of market dominance further removed the justification for using PayPal in China. "We knew about the trust issue, too," said Shao. Before being acquired by eBay, EachNet already had a beta version of a payment solution with an escrow function, called An Fu Tong. But its development was stopped to make way for PayPal in China.

Core reasons for multinationals' failures

eBay is not the only internet giant to have lost to a local rival in China. Many other American internet companies, such as Google, Yahoo, Expedia, and MySpace, have been beaten at their own game too. China's local competitors seem to be better at innovation and localization—particularly where it relates to the idiosyncrasies of the Chinese market. They are much faster at decision-making. To achieve what they want, they sometimes are not afraid to cross the line of ethical propriety, or to break the law. But why don't multinationals try as hard as their local rivals? What is stopping them from being more localized or faster in decision-making?

Shao of EachNet, believes that it all comes down to people and culture. A multinational is very different from a startup. Many decisions cannot be made locally in the multinational: instead of five people huddling in the corner of the pantry, decisions had to go through a long chain of emails and conference calls across time zones. A lot of time had to be spent educating headquarters staff about China. Information was lost in the communication process, particularly as EachNet's junior staff could not speak English well and could not make compelling arguments in a foreign language.

EachNet's original team was mostly demoted and a more polished executive team from eBay was installed. Many former EachNet staffers complained about the revolving door of expatriate management they had to work under. Nor did they enjoy having visitors from the American headquarters and other parts of the world breathing down their necks.

eBay's matrix corporate structure, which groups employees both by function (such as marketing, development, etc.) and region (America, China, Japan, etc.), makes the process even more complicated. For each decision, the local team needed to get approval from every related department at headquarters. "If marketing likes it, the finance department might not, " said a former eBay China employee. This further slowed eBay's response to user demands, not to mention Taobao's challenges.

Some of the practices of a big corporation also puzzled Shao. "I made a suggestion (to eBay China) that to reactivate users who hadn't traded with us for a long time, we should give them a special bonus the next time they trade. We might lose a small sum at first, but if the users became active again, we would soon make the money back." Everyone thought it was worth a try (at least that was Shao's impression).

On his next visit, Shao asked the eBay China team about the results of the promotion. Had it made idle users active again? No, they replied. The promotion was not designed well; many users took advantage of the bonus to trade once and then register a new username to take advantage of it again. "Then why do you keep it going?" asked Shao. They said headquarters liked it—it improved certain numbers it was tracking in its matrix. Shao was dumbfounded.

Many former EachNet employees became frustrated and left. Those who remained became less entrepreneurial than before, according to Shao. The focus was no longer on making the company successful, but on protecting one's own job and increasing one's power.

Taobao's era

After the de facto failure of eBay China, Taobao completely dominated China's consumer C2C auction market. It changed the habits of a generation of Chinese shoppers. Many female office workers browse Taobao during the lunch hour, much as they go shopping (or window shopping) in the malls. "It's fun. There are many different types of products," said Ida Chen, a recent university graduate who worked in the office of a Beijing company. "Sometimes, the product (when shipped to me) was not quite the same as it was on the website. But the price was so cheap, so I don't mind very much," said Chen. "Many of my friends are doing the same."

Not all of Taobao's users are shopaholics; others are purely driven by price and convenience. "I usually buy books online and milk powder for our new baby," said Alex Huang, a thirty-something professional working in Beijing. "The price is good and it is quite convenient. I have them deliver to my office—usually the products come within one or two days." Having the company receptionist take care of one's personal purchases seems an acceptable norm in Chinese offices. "No one is at home during office hours. The boss will understand," said Huang.

Most items are sold at a fixed price rather than by auction. Small businesses, who treat the online marketplace as an extension of their shops, sell household items, such as clothing, toys, and electronics. Apart from small individual sellers, Taobao also lined up major vendors and retailers in China to have their shops online. For example, Lenovo, the largest Chinese computer maker, is selling its products through Taobao; so are electronics firms Philips and Sony.

	Taobao	eBay
Transaction volume	US$14.62 billion[78] up 131% year on year.	US$59.7 billion; same as last year.
Number of users	98 million	86.3 million
Age (16–24)	35%	N/a
Age (25–32)	48%	N/a

***Table 6.1:* Taobao and eBay operational data (2008)**

Data source: Alibaba,[79] eBay[80]

Rank	Category	Transaction volume (US$ millions)
1	Apparel	2,307
2	Cellphones	1,564
3	Cosmetics	808
4	Household goods	805
5	Sporting goods	779
6	Personal computers and accessories	744
7	Jewelry	723
8	Laptop computers	704
9	Home appliances	552
10	Stored value cards (for cellphones)	531

***Table 6.2:* Top 10 retail items on Taobao**

Data source: Alibaba, 2008[81]

Taobao went on to improve its services and made them better for Chinese shoppers. It lined up logistic services; it started guarantee programs. The company also cracked down on counterfeiting—fake Louis Vuitton handbags, once very popular on Taobao, have disappeared. Sales of shark's fin were banned for environmental reasons.

But while it is a huge success in terms of user numbers and transaction volumes, Taobao has yet to prove itself financially. While being free was the silver bullet Taobao used to slay eBay, new competitors are using the same tactic, effectively preventing Taobao from taking advantage of its dominant position to charge users.

Tencent, which operates China's dominant online chat platform, QQ, started its auction market, Paipai, in 2006. Baidu, the top search

[78] That is, approximately 1 percent of China's total retail trade in 2008, according to statistics released by the Chinese Ministry of Commerce.

[79] Source: Alibaba press release, Feb 10, 2009.

[80] Source: eBay, Financial History & Metrics, Apr 22, 2009.

[81] Source: Alibaba press release, Feb 10, 2009.

engine in China, started Youa in 2008. Both are free. Like Alibaba, Tencent and Baidu are strong local internet companies. Since their core businesses make tons of money, it appears they can afford to keep their auction sites free forever.

"They did not start their auction markets for money. They did so just to keep Alibaba in check," said an industry analyst. "They did not want Alibaba to be too successful and start going after their core businesses."

Although Tencent's Paipai and Baidu's Youa were small, Taobao dared not risk its hard-won market share by charging user fees. So it figured out another way to charge—selling keywords, much like Google does. Sellers at Taobao can bid for keywords. Buyers searching on certain keywords see the results as well as the related ads. Sellers are not charged unless buyers click on their ads.

Ma said Taobao broke even on advertising revenue in August 2008. But how profitable Taobao will be in the long run remains uncertain. Alipay is free for Taobao users, but it charges a fee to third parties who use its payment solution. Many online game companies and online stores use Alipay as one of their online payment methods. In August 2007, Alipay launched an online payment solution to allow merchants worldwide to sell directly to consumers in China. Today, it cooperates with over 300 global retail brands from Japan, South Korea, Southeast Asia, Europe, America, and Australia, and supports transactions in 12 major foreign currencies.

	Alipay	PayPal
Number of users	150 million: up 50% from six months earlier	70.4 million: up 23% from a year earlier, up 12% from six months earlier
Daily transactions	4 million	2.4 million
Total transactions per year	n/a	888.6 million: up 24% year on year
Daily payment volume	US$103 million (peak)	US$164 million (average)
Total payment volume per year	n/a	US$60.1 billion: up 26% year on year

***Table 6.3:* Alipay and PayPal operational data**

Data source: Alibaba (Feb 2009),[82] eBay (December 2008)[83]

[82] Source: Alibaba press release, Apr 1, 2009.
[83] Source: eBay, Financial History & Metrics, Apr 22, 2009.

In adapting eBay's C2C model to China, Taobao implemented several changes, which made it the dominant player. But as discussed above, a significant part of eBay's failure in China was its own fault.

	ebay	Taobao	Reason for change
Revenue	Listing and transaction fees	Advertising—sellers bid for keywords	Keen competition in China market—every player offers their services for free
Payment	PayPal—online payment only	Alipay—online payment with escrow function	The lack of trust issue with Chinese online shoppers
Page Design	Neutral	Feminine	More female online shoppers in China

Table 6.4: **Differences in eBay's and Taobao's models**

eBay's Chinese dilemma—profitability or market share?

To sum up eBay's experience in China, a former eBay Asia Pacific executive said, "In the online auction business, if the market has a situation where companies do not charge sellers to list items on the site, and are using a free model to gain market share, then it is difficult for companies to run a profitable operation. Revenue will have to come from advertising or other value added services. From a global perspective, if, for the foreseeable future, you have a market where companies are not charging fees, you may ask yourself if you want to put investments in other markets around the world where there is a better chance of making a good return on the investment. So you can find a partner who will operate the business in a local market (for example, China) and they can justify the investment from other areas of their business. A business like eBay, which is global, can earn money from the local market via cross-border trade. If, over time, the local market has ways to charge users to list items on the site, then there may be more reason to increase investments in the local market."

That explains why eBay struck a deal with Tom Online in China to give it the domestic market to run. Tom was a leading mobile data services provider at the time, making lots of money from wireless services, and it could keep the auction market running even if there were not sufficient revenue from the operation.

Meanwhile, eBay kept its profitable international business. Today, many Chinese traders are active in eBay's American, British, German, and Australian markets. They sell everything from electronics and clothes, to car parts and accessories.

"One of the most creative shops I've seen sells body parts of cars online. If your car gets hit in America and has damage to part of its bodywork, you can order the part online. Just specify the brand and model of the car and the part you want. It will ship the part from its shop in Guangzhou [a city in Southern China]. Then you can go to any auto shop nearby to have the new part installed on your car. And the price is quite cheap," said the executive.

Many Chinese are also buying overseas from eBay. "One of the biggest items is the stamp. And when we broke down the category, the largest portions are Chinese stamps, which originally come from China," said the executive. Why don't Chinese buy the stamps locally? "It turned out that there is an authorized Chinese stamp organization in San Francisco. The buyers would rather pay 10–20 times more to buy stamps from America than from the local Chinese market, as they believe that what they are buying is authorized and legitimate."

Despite the retreat of eBay from the domestic market, it is doing well on cross-border trade to and from China. Even better: it can charge these traders. "In terms of market share, yes, we lost to Taobao. But in terms of profitability, I am not very sure. We were doing pretty well," said the executive.

Nonetheless, without a strong domestic market to funnel users to its international market, the growth of Chinese trade on eBay is restricted. In terms of gross trading volume, Chinese trade is still less than 5 percent of the overall eBay market, according to the executive, despite China having the largest number of internet users in the world.

Lessons learned

1 How much should you localize?

When a multinational arrives in a new market, it must decide how much it wants to adapt its original model to local tastes.

Many Asian centers have a small internet population (e.g., Hong Kong, Singapore) which makes developing new features for local markets expensive. So most American internet companies just moved in with their existing models. Their only major concession to local needs was to change the language of the web page. They usually have a small office for sales and marketing and rely on headquarters for everything else.

This could have worked, because most local markets were too small to support their own internet alternatives. Hong Kong, a city of seven million people, is a typical example. Its few internet startups were wiped out when the bubble burst in 2000. Most people in Hong Kong use Google, Yahoo, eBay, Facebook, and whatever else is popular in America. One of the few local internet firms that remain is JobsDB.com, a recruitment site similar to Monster.com.

China is very different. Its internet population is over 338 million,[84] the largest in the world. It can support its own local internet firms, with unique business models that suit local tastes. In fact, before the multinationals came in, the market was already packed with local rivals competing vigorously among themselves. The structure of the multinationals' divisions in other Asia cities—small offices totally controlled by headquarters—does not apply to China.

However, many American internet companies made the mistake of underestimating the size and complexity of the China market. They tried to force too many of their own ways on their China divisions.

At eBay China, the local team had to face an aggressive rival, Taobao, with their hands tied. eBay China's technology platform was moved to America. Every decision had to go through headquarters. This made little sense, as eBay China was already a full-blown operation. By trying too hard to consolidate its operations at headquarters, eBay quickly lost its dominance in China.

2 If it ain't broke, don't fix it. Keep it going and spend your resources on other projects that generate profit.

The online retailer Amazon shared a similar fate. It bought Joyo, then China's largest online bookstore, for US$75 million in 2004. After the takeover, Joyo ceded its dominance in China to local rival Dangdang. The Amazon headquarters wanted to implement its successful American formula in the newly acquired China division—it was a "long tail" policy: give customers a large catalog, so that even if just one copy of each title is sold, it amounts to a lot of books.

Steve Kessel, senior vice president, worldwide digital media of Amazon, said if he has 100,000 books that sell one copy every other

[84] Source: CNNIC, end of June 2009.

year, then in ten years he would have sold more of these, together, than he would have of the latest Harry Potter.[85] But Joyo, in fact, had built its dominance by offering a few hot items that it sold in large quantities, according to Chen Nian, who ran Joyo at the time of takeover. "In China, the profit margin of an online book store is very thin. We depended on getting deep discounts on certain hot items from vendors through volume sales," said Chen.

After the change of business model eliminated the bargains on hot items, Joyo slipped to second place. According to Analysys International, Dangdang topped the Chinese business-to-consumer (B2C) market with an 18 percent market share in the third quarter of 2007, while Joyo lagged behind with 14 percent.

Chen left Joyo and founded another online retailer in China—Vancl sells men's shirts online under its own brand. It became very successful and achieved sales of over US$25 million just one year after it was founded (2007). (We will discuss Chen's story and the development of China's online retail sector on our book's website: *www.redwiredrevolution.com*.)

Sometimes, American headquarters may be educating its China team too much, when the education should be done the other way around. They might have better results in China if they listened to their local staff more. These people might not have a PhD from MIT or an MBA from Harvard (not everyone is Bo Shao). Sometimes they might not even speak English well. But they know about the local market: what works and what does not.

eBay's China team could have warned its headquarters and stopped them from moving the platform prematurely. eBay's China team had raised concerns about transmission speed issues across the Pacific Ocean. Such concerns, however, were downplayed during eBay technology team's presentation to eBay's then CEO, Meg Whitman.

[85] Source: Gary Wolf, "The Great Library of Amazonia," *Wired*, Dec 2003.

7. Tencent: I seek you

Instant messaging services such as Microsoft Windows Live Messager, Yahoo Messager, and so forth, are typically not attractive businesses, as they can only generate minuscule revenues from online advertising. In China, the situation is completely different. Instant messaging services or online chat are not only popular, but hugely profitable. In fact, the dominant online chat provider, Tencent, has become the largest internet company in China by revenue and profit.

Online advertising is a small portion of Tencent's revenue. Most of the company's revenue comes from "internet valued added services," such as avatars (icons representing users' identities), virtual pets, and online games. It was able to capitalize on its users—hundreds of millions of teenagers—by selling them something extra on top of a free basic service. Its founder Ma Huateng, or Pony Ma, saw online chat differently—it was not a tool for office workers, but a community for young kids.

How R U?

Instant messaging predates the internet, first appearing on multiuser operating systems in the mid 1960s. These were initially used as notification systems for services like printing, but were quickly repurposed to allow users logged in to the same machine to talk to each other. This has always been an incredibly popular service, allowing people to communicate with their friends instantly over the network, with their own unique collection of abbreviations and clichés. It killed many hours of teenagers' time, which they were supposed to spend on finishing their school projects.

In 1996, the Israeli company Mirabilis made a breakthrough that allowed online chatting to spread out to a wider community. The five founders at Mirabilis built a program that could work on Microsoft Windows—the most popular computer operating system in the world. Mirabilis also designed a nice interface, so that people who didn't know a single computer command could figure out how to talk to their friends and add new friends to their contacts list.

The program, called ICQ, became an instant hit. Millions of people used ICQ, a homophone for the phrase "I seek you," to stay in contact with their friends. It was such a successful service that AOL, the leading ISP in America, acquired Mirabilis for US$407 million in 1998, even before it could figure how to profit from the business.

Other major internet companies also launched their competing online chat programs. Yahoo developed Yahoo Messenger and Microsoft had Windows Live Messenger. By 2005, Google also launched a similar service, called Google Talk. Many computer users automatically connected to their online chat platform when switching on their computers. It is a highly "sticky" application—a program people use every day.

However, the question of how to profit from online chat had always been a difficult one. To most players, such as Yahoo, Microsoft, and Google, online chat services were just something they provided to increase the loyalty or stickiness of their users. They sold some advertisements on it—but the amount was small in comparison with advertising on portals or search engines.

In China, the situation was completely different. Online chat or instant messaging services were not only popular, but hugely profitable. In fact, the dominant online chat provider, Tencent, was also the largest internet company in China by revenue and profit.

Online advertising was a small portion of Tencent revenue. As mentioned earlier, most of the company's revenue comes from internet valued added services. It was able to leverage on its hundreds of millions of teenage users—selling them something extra on top of a free basic service—because its founder Ma Huateng, or Pony Ma, saw online chat differently—it was not a tool but a community. Once the crowd had gathered on its online chat platform, QQ, Ma would take the opportunity to dazzle them with different tricks and try to sell them different things.

Through Ma's effort, QQ has become China's largest "online park," said Richard Ji, managing director of Morgan Stanley, who is in charge of the firm's equity research on China's internet and media sector.

Building the online park

Born in 1972, Ma's résumé did not look as impressive as those of many of the founders of early Chinese internet startups. He did not come from a top university—he graduated from Shenzhen University with a degree in computer science. He did not go abroad. After graduation, he joined a local firm, China Motion, as a software engineer, but never held a high position in the firm. Before he founded Tencent with a group of friends in 1998, he was in charge of research and development for internet paging system development at China Motion.

His lack of pedigree caused a venture capitalist to not even bother to meet with him when Ma was asking for investment in the early days. "I called up a friend working in the telecom industry. He said Ma was just a junior staff," said the venture capitalist. Ma and his team were doing all manner of IT projects for other companies in the early days—email systems, interactive programs for paging companies, and so on.

Tencent's online chat platform QQ was first implemented as a prototype or a demo for its instant messaging program, which Ma hoped to sell to other companies. But he failed to get any offers.[86] Ma and his team ended up having to run the service themselves. It was first named Online ICQ, but changed to QQ to avoid the violation of the trademark of American-based online chat service ICQ.

In retrospect, Ma thought they were lucky that they didn't get an offer. The competitors that won bids got the money and stopped further development on their projects. Being one of the first in China, QQ became popular among young internet users very quickly—it had tens of thousands of users and the number was increasing fast. By 2000, in almost every internet café, the penguin logo of QQ was on computer screens. Teenagers were thrilled by the experience of chatting with others, friends or strangers, online.

"QQ focuses on the user's experience. Other guys had good ideas, but Ma and his team implemented them," said Alvin Liu, CEO of A8 and an early investor in Tencent. But its popularity created a serious problem. The cost of the bandwidth and computer servers to support QQ also increased fast—it quickly used up the initial investment and started eating into the profit of the small startup. Ma had to find some serious investors soon.

Luckily, the internet boom was at its all-time height in the late 1990s. With AOL's acquisition of ICQ for US$407 million as a precedent, Ma argued a similar service in China should be worth

[86] Source: Zhang Tao , "Ma Hateng: Spot crisis early on, you still have chance to win," *Shanghai Security Post*, November 6, 2008.

something as well. He finally convinced IDG and PCCW—each chipped in US$1.1 million for a 20 percent stake in the company in early 2000. IDG is a venture capital firm active in China that invested in many early internet startups. PCCW was the internet venture of Richard Li, son of Hong Kong tycoon Li Ka Shing, and it became the territory's dominant telecom operator after it acquired Hong Kong Telecom.

But by mid 2001, PCCW was longer in the mood for expansion after the dot.com bubble burst and its IPO funds had been depleted. It hoped to sell its stake in Tencent. IDG also tried to find other investors. They seemingly looked everywhere and contacted everyone who might have an interest in the company. Even the country's two major portals, Sina and Sohu, were asked to look at Tencent. But no one was interested—as how to profit from an online chat service, no matter how popular, was still uncertain and "cash was king" in those troubled times.

Finally, Naspers Limited, a media group based in South Africa, was willing to make a bet on QQ and Ma's team. It bought PCCW's share for US$12.6 million, plus part of IDG's share (12.8 percent) and some of the early founders' stakes (13.5 percent) for a further US$19.4 million. Before Tencent issued an IPO in 2004 in Hong Kong, Naspers made another round of investment, buying up half of IDG's remaining shares and increasing its stake to 50 percent. (The other 50 percent belonged to Ma and his team.)

"It was the most successful deal foreigners have ever made in China's internet sector," said Fritz Demopoulos, CEO and founder of Qunar, a Chinese search engine for travel information. By August 2009, Tencent had grown into a business worth over US$27 billion, making it the largest among Chinese internet companies in terms of market capitalization. Naspers still owns 35 percent of the company, and its shares are valued at over US$9.45 billion. In comparison, Baidu, the largest Chinese search engine, was worth only US$12 billion, less than half the value of Tencent.

Talking up profits

In the early 2000s, however, there seemed to be no easy answer to the question of how to profit from instant messaging. Online advertising was clearly not the way to go—it was badly hurt after the dot.com bust in 2000. Even the leading portals, Sina and Sohu, were losing money and very few advertisers wanted to try QQ. Ma tried launching a paid premium service, but the response was poor initially.

In 2000, a new opportunity emerged when China Mobile and China Unicom, the country's two cellphone operators, opened their platform for third parties to provide data services. Ma thought QQ users on the move might want to keep chatting with their friends online. Mobile QQ was launched in mid 2000—charging users a tiny monthly fee of RMB5 or US$0.6. The service was a hit and Tencent started to see its first significant revenue stream.

While the QQ platform was of no interest to advertisers, Ma soon found out it was a powerful tool for marketing its own services to its large number of highly loyal members, many of whom logged in every day. Besides Mobile QQ, he started to promote other mobile data services, such as picture and ringtone downloads, news, stock, and financial information, etc.

The mobile data services allowed Tencent to achieve profitability in 2001, when it was making US$1.2 million profit out of sales of US$5.9 million.[87] Ma tried to apply the mobile data service concept to the internet—if users were willing to pay small amounts to download pictures to their phones, would they also be willing to pay for getting new avatars for their QQ accounts? The answer was yes.

The "internet value added services" concept worked. QQ users paid a small sum to get avatars, adopt online pets, have an extra chat room, and for many other small, extra services. With these initial successes, Ma realized online chat was not just a communication tool, but it was also a powerful key to forming a large and loyal community. The network effect was strong in online chat because once a person joined QQ, he or she would ask friends to join as well, who in turn asked their friends. And many if not all of them logged on to the service almost every day.

If Ma could keep these people happy and logged on to his platform for long enough, he would also have the opportunity to sell them something. A ringtone this time, a picture download the next. They might not be able to pay a lot, as most QQ members were students or low paid workers, but the aggregated amount could be huge.

This became a fundamental strategy for Tencent's future development. It kept adding new services—dating, email, alumni club, portals,

87 Source: Tencent's IPO prospectus.

auction, search, online games, blogs, etc. Some were for keeping users happy, others were for making money, and some were for both. It kept its costs down by developing most services itself and using its online chat platform for promotion.

Some of the trials were not very successful, for example, its search engine Soso and its online auction platform Paipai. Both had a small market share and made no money for Tencent. But others became extreme successful. Its online game, Dungeon and Fighter, became a hit in China, with over 1.6 million players at its peak hours in March 2009. Its online portal QQ.com has become one of the most popular in China and its blog service, Qzone, is also one of the most successful in China.

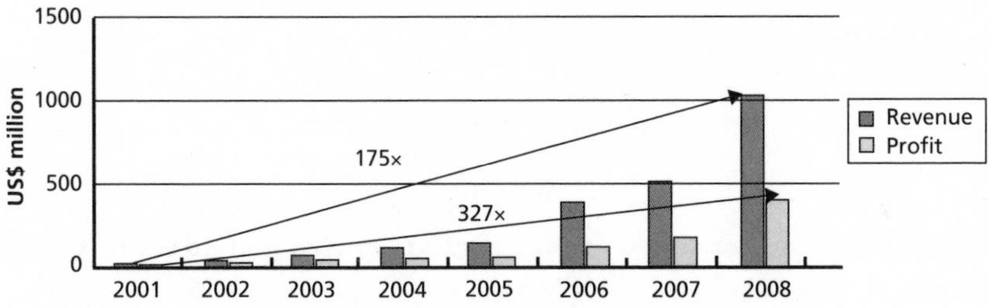

Figure 7.1: **Revenue and profit of Tencent (2001–08)**

Data source: Tencent

One uncharitable charge leveled at Tencent was that it was opportunistic. Tencent's headquarters are in Shenzhen, in southern China, away from most of the other Chinese internet companies. But it maintains a research and development center in Shanghai, where many internet firms are based. An executive of a major Chinese internet company once said this was a "copy center," where Tencent spied on others and duplicated whatever was hot.

Nevertheless, its revenue and profit grew fast. Revenue increased 175 times from 2001 to 2008, while profit multiplied by 327 times during the same period.

A dearth of competition

No other players threaten QQ's position as the dominant online chat service in China. It has close to 80 percent market share, according to Beijing-based research firm Analysys International. It's believed that 70 percent of Chinese internet users log on to QQ every day, to chat with friends, colleagues, or business partners. Many people print their QQ numbers on their business cards as a way of contacting them.

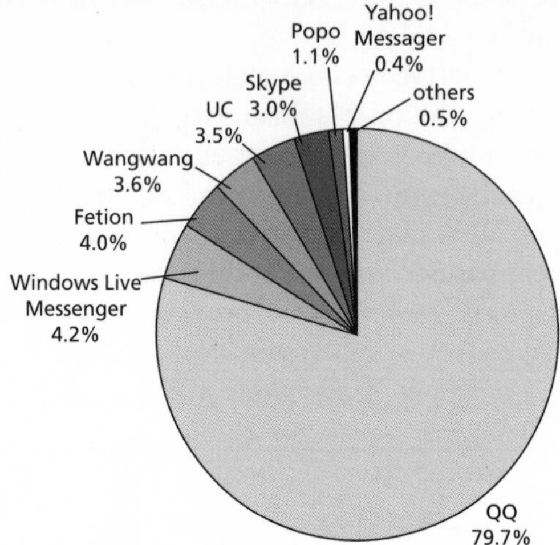

***Figure** 7.2:* **Market share of online chat service providers in China**

Data source: Analysys International (2008, 1st quarter)

Microsoft's Windows Live Messenger is used by some office workers—about 4 percent. Other local rivals, such as Alibaba's WangWang, have some market share, but it is tiny. The network effect partly explains QQ's dominance.

Being one of the first online chat services, QQ benefited from a positive network effect, a virtuous cycle—the more people there are on one online chat platform, the more chances a newcomer would join the platform. They would seldom move to another platform because inviting all their friends in their contact lists to a new platform could be very troublesome, as many QQ users have over a hundred friends in their contact list.

But the major reasons for QQ's dominance and its tremendous financial success were that Ma had two ideas that were different from his competitors. He targeted low-end rather than high-end users, and he considered online chat as a community, not a tool.

Kids' stuff

Most other players perceived online chat or instant messaging services as a tool for communication. They targeted high-end, white-collar workers, thinking they had a lot of spending power to pay for premium services and that advertisers would love them. This, however, represents only a small group of people in China. Also, they are focused on their jobs—anything extra would be seen as annoying or a distraction. Instead, Ma saw online chatting as a community. Users come and kill time with each other. QQ has traditionally been popular among school kids and factory workers—China's low-end users. These users have plenty of time on their hands and come online looking for fun. Therefore, when QQ started offering them many different attractions they stayed longer in the community and even paid for some of the services. Ma turned out to be right, and his ideas applied broadly to the majority of Chinese internet users—young people looking for fun. He built QQ into the largest online playground for them and the most profitable internet company in China.

By 2008, Tencent made US$403.8 million in profit, out of sales of US$1.04 billion. Sixty-nine percent was from internet value added services. Another 20 percent was from mobile data services, and 12 percent from online advertising.

Tencent's profitability was sustained even during the economic downturn. As a low-cost entertainment alternative for youth, Tencent business was hardly affected when the financial crisis driven by subprime lending hit America and the rest of world in 2008. Tencent's profit grew 79 percent to US$403.0 million in 2008, accelerated from the 47.5 percent growth rate it had had a year earlier. Other internet players, such as Alibaba's B2B market and Ctrip's online travel services, were hurt.[88]

	2008
Total registered online chat user accounts	891.9 million
Active user accounts	376.6 million[89]
Peak simultaneous online chat users	49.7 million
Peak simultaneous online users of QQ Game portal (for mini casual games only)	4.7 million
Internet value added services paying subscriptions	31.4 million
Mobile data service paying subscriptions	14.7 million

Table 7.1: **Key operational data for Tencent**

Data source: Tencent

[88] Alibaba's net profit in 2008 grew 37 percent to US$174.8 million, much slower than the 362 percent growth it had had the year before. Ctrip's profit grew 23 percent to US$52.5 million in 2008, a slowdown from the 74 percent growth rate it had had a year earlier.

[89] That's more than the total number of internet users in China. CNNIC estimated that there were 298 million internet users in China at the end of 2008.

Tencent and the pretenders

Tencent's QQ was perhaps the most successful transfer of a Western internet business model to China because it completely outperformed its precedents. No other online chat service was as profitable. Most of them earned an insignificant amount out of online advertising, which hardly covered their costs. To most other players, such as Yahoo, Microsoft, and Google, online chat was just something they provided to increase the stickiness of their users. Their major income source was their core businesses, such as an online portal, software, or search engines. Therefore, they did not invest a lot of time and effort in trying to profit from their online chat platforms.

Tencent's QQ was different. It was Tencent's core business and Ma had to make it profitable. With a trial-and-error approach, Ma succeeded. He also used the QQ platform as a springboard into many other businesses, for example online games, which provided new income streams to Tencent.

The idea of treating online chat as a community for kids, not a tool for adults, also explained QQ's difference from rival services, such as Microsoft's Windows Live Messenger. QQ's interface is much more noisy than that of Windows Live Messenger, because Ma thought its users come to kill time, rather than get business done. It turned out to be a very valuable proposition, and Tencent became the largest Chinese internet company in terms of revenue and profit.

	Revenue (US$ million)	Profit (US$ million)	Core businesses
Tencent	1037.4	403.8	Online chat
Shanda	522.2	182.7	Online games
Baidu	468.8	153.6	Search engine
Netease	436.2	234.0	Online games
Alibaba	435.2	174.8	Business to business marketplace
Sohu	429.1	158.6	Online portal and online games
Sina	369.6	88.8	Online portal
The9	264.2	51.1	Online games
Giant	233.3	162.9	Online games
Ctrip	232.8	65.1	Online travel

***Table 7.2:* Revenue and profit of major Chinese internet companies (2008)**

Data source: individual companies

Lessons learned

1 Chinese internet users = young people looking for fun (c. 2009).

A major reason for Tencent's success was because China has a large number of young people looking for cheap entertainment over the internet. Sports facilities are few and poor in China, while traveling, dining, and shopping are not regular activities.

QQ offered the right package. The basic service was free and for a tiny amount they could buy themselves or their friends something special, whether it was a ringtone, a new avatar, an online pet, or magic power in their favorite online games.

About 70 percent of China's internet-using population is younger than 30 years old, according to Morgan Stanley. They look for entertainment and companionship online, especially when most of them are the only child in their families.

Tencent's QQ is their perfect playground, allowing them to look for friends and fun.

In fact, out of China's ten largest internet companies by revenue, six offer online gaming as their major business (see Table 7.3). Tencent also derives a significant part of its revenue from online games. The rest of Tencent's paid services are mostly entertainment related, such as, avatars, ringtone, etc.

On the other hand, 70 percent of the American internet population were more than 30 years old, said Morgan Stanley. The major concern of middle-aged people is looking for information to help them solve problems in real life. "Which bank offers the cheapest mortage?" "Where can I find travel information for Thailand?" "What are the latest cancer treatments," and so on.

Therefore, online portals, such as Yahoo, which help people to find information, were among the first stars of the American internet business. Their roles were later replaced by more effective search engines such as Google, which became the most profitable internet business.

Only recently, Web 2.0 services, such as MySpace and YouTube, which are targeting young people looking for entertainment and companionship, have become popular in the West. However, these services' long-term profitability has not been clearly proven yet.

8. Shanda: Pay now, enjoy later

When Chen Tianqiao founded Shanda, the first major online game company in China, its games were licensed in Korea, where MMORPG, or Massive Multiplayer Online Role-Playing Games, had been going strong for several years.

The real problem that Shanda solved, which allowed it to list on NASDAQ about three years after launching its first game, was how to collect money from millions of players. Credit cards were scarce in China, as were forms of electronic payment. Most transactions were done in cash. And their solution was simple, but very much adapted to the business and social realities in China—prepaid cards bearing an access code and password and sold through hundreds of thousands of retail outlets. Chen also created a computer program to sell prepaid cards virtually in internet cafés, the main venue for online games in China.

Fantasy and reality in online gaming

People have been playing games on personal computers for as long as PCs have existed. Whether they crave the excitement of "killing" their enemies or the quiet contentment of creating a city building by building, people spend thousands of hours playing computer games.

As technology has evolved, game design has become intricate, and graphics and sound effects have had more impact. Special devices were invented for the purpose of playing games, such as Nintendo's Wii, Microsoft's Xbox and Sony's PlayStation. These consoles are generally sold at a small profit margin; the companies make their real money by selling games separately to users. Whether designed for PCs or consoles, games are generally sold as packaged software, with a one-time license fee built into the price. Apart from the three mentioned above, major game developers include American-based Electronic Arts, France's Ubisoft Entertainment and Japan's Konami Corporation. As the internet grew, game developers began taking advantage of the new medium to let users play together virtually. Today, most games can be played online as well as individually.

MMORPG

The technologies that have really pushed the limits and allowed thousands of players to interact in a virtual world are the MMORPG, or Massive Multiplayer Online Role-Playing Games. Everyone can take on an imagined role—a witch, a knight, a thief, a king, or a queen—and embark on a journey to meet new friends, kill monsters, forge alliances, destroy enemies, or get married. The game will never end until you cancel your account. A central computer server keeps track of all these assumed roles and lets thousands of users play and dream in the virtual world. In general, MMORPG users pay a subscription fee to log on to the central server and play with others.

The most successful MMORPG in the West is World of Warcraft, which is the extension of Warcraft: Orcs & Humans, a real-time strategy game developed by American-based Blizzard Entertainment in 1994. More than 11 million people subscribed to it in 2008. But still the popularity of MMORPG is low in the West when compared with other PC games and console games.

The situation in Korea is different. Online games, particularly the MMORPG, are the most popular form of digital entertainment. Korea led the world in broadband penetration, reaching 70 percent in 2003[90] (American broadband penetration was about 36 percent in 2003[91]). High broadband penetration and government support allowed online games to develop in Korea early on. A vast network of internet cafés also helped to establish the online game culture in the country. Most Korean gamers go to the country's over 20,000 internet cafés to play online.

Enter the dragon

In China, piracy is such a huge problem that the licensing model does not work. Lots of people play pirated PC and console games. Put a game online, however, and you can defeat the pirates by charging subscription fees—there is no way to log on to the central server and play in the virtual world without paying the fee. This would seem to be the only way for game companies to see a return on their investment.

90 Source: Ministry of Information and Communication of Korea, May 2003.
91 Source: Nielsen NetRatings, May 2003.

Getting paid is a big problem in China though[92]. Early in the new millennium, most transactions in China were still done in cash. So how could a game company efficiently collect small sums from millions of users scattered all over China?

The problem was eventually solved by Shanda's founder, Chen Tianqiao—prepaid cards are sold through corner stores in China. Chen also created an e-sale system to allow prepaid cards to be bought online in internet cafés.

Chen's innovations unlocked the magic of online games in China. Millions of teenagers and young adults have been bewitched as a result, spending their weekends in endless virtual battles online. It also made many super rich, including Chen, who floated his company on the NASDAQ stock market in 2004, less than three years after he launched his first game, Legend of Mir 2.

In revenue terms, online gaming is the largest sector in China's internet industry. Six of China's ten largest internet companies, in terms of revenue, run online games as a major part of their business. In 2008, total online game revenue reached US$2.69 billion in China, according to IDC. Total online advertising revenue was estimated to be US$1.93 billion only, of which paid search accounted for US$627.2 million and display ad US$515.6 million.

Shanda rising

Born in 1973, Chen graduated from one of the most prominent schools in China—Fudan University in Shanghai. Afterward, he joined Shanghai Lujiazui Group, a government body that oversees property development in the Pudong area of Shanghai, now the country's financial and commercial hub—Shanghai Stock Exchange was set up in Pudong. Chen worked as a manager at Shanghai Lujiazui Group from 1994 to 1998 before joining a local investment management firm, Kinghing Trust & Investment.[93]

By 1999, the internet boom had reached its height. Together with his brother, Chen Danian, Chen and his wife Luo Qianqian founded Shanda Networking in Shanghai in December 1999. The company's goal was to develop a Chinese-language online community around

[92] China holds the dubious distinction of being, on average, the slowest paying country on Earth, tied with Italy for an average accounts receivable turnover of 253 days.

[93] Source: Shanda IPO prospectus: Our Corporate History and Structure, Management.

cartoons, which teenagers adored. An early player in China's internet industry, CDC Corporation (formerly known as China.com) invested US$3 million in the startup in 2000.

When the dot.com bubble burst the next year, their startup was strapped for cash. Most of the seed money had been spent. Revenue from online advertising never materialized. With about 100 staff, it was running at a monthly loss and CDC Corporation was getting ready to pull the plug on new investment. With less than US$1 million remaining, Chen made a bet in mid 2001. He spent most of the sum on an upfront fee to license a newly developed online game from Korea's Wemade Entertainment.[94] The game, Legend of Mir 2, was a sequel to a game that had never been particularly popular. Chen obtained the operating rights for Mir 2 in China from Wemade's distributor, Actoz Soft, another Korean company. To run the game, he rented computer servers from data centers run by telecom operators.

He also managed to line up Ubisoft to distribute the game for him. The French company was one of the first foreign game companies to enter China, where it was selling its games (in CD form) in many computer software shops. In 2001, online games were just emerging in China, and this is how they were sold in the main. Shanda's game, Mir 2, was launched in November 2001. In the first three days of operation, it recorded 3,000 to 5,000 users, according to a former Shanda executive, but three months after launch it had 300,000 active users.

It was without doubt a huge success. With every user paying on average RMB30, or US$3.75 a month, Chen was estimated to be making over US$1 million a month. After deducting 20 percent for distribution costs and another 20–30 percent for computer server, bandwidth, and other operational costs, he should be left with a net profit of over US$500,000 a month, according to an industry expert.

Prepaid cards and the e-sale system

With such volumes, Chen decided he did not need Ubisoft any more. He started his own distribution network for the game in 2002. He was not content with reaching software stores alone. He wanted maximum

[94] Wemade was not even the largest game company in Korea. NCsoft was the largest, and its game Lineage was the most popular then, with 100,000 people playing together at peak hours in Korea in December 2000.

coverage throughout the country. Prepaid cards for telephone services (cellphone and long-distance calls) are popular in China. The small paper cards, each bearing an access code and a password, are available in many retail outlets—convenience stores, newsstands etc. There are even specialty stores that sell nothing but telecom cards. And they can be found in almost every street and on every corner.

The distribution system is well organized—telecom companies sell the prepaid cards (at a discount to face value) to large regional distributors, which in turn sell to subdistributors that supply local stores. Chen thought this would be a good channel and started to contact major regional distributors about selling Shanda's prepaid cards.

But, another problem arose—how to match the inventory of prepaid cards with user demand in different locations, so that all would have just enough cards and none would be overstocked?

As Korea's experience showed, internet cafés were a great place for people to play online games. Before the arrival of Mir 2, most users in internet cafés in China had played pirated PC games. Chen wanted to change that. Shanda developed a special computer program, called the e-sale system, which allowed internet café owners to buy virtual prepaid cards from Shanda and sell them to their customers. Since they were taking a cut, the café owners encouraged their customers to play Shanda's Mir 2. They paid the café owner in cash and got the access code and password electronically.

The café owners settle their bills with Shanda's distributor in the area in cash. All parties are connected electronically through the system and the transactions are done instantly. With the e-sale system, Shanda can see how much each internet café is selling. This helps it figure out how popular the game is in each area and distribute its physical prepaid cards accordingly. By tapping into the internet cafés with the e-sale system, Shanda solved not just the payment issue, but also the problem of how to promote the game. Sales through internet cafés were as much as 80 percent of Shanda's revenues in the early days, said a former executive of Shanda.

By 2004, Shanda had built a nationwide distribution network that reached over 317,000 retail points of sale throughout the country, of which over 40 percent were internet cafés. Fifty-four percent of Shanda's revenue came from the e-sales channel and 42 percent from other retail outlets. As broadband penetration rose and online payment developed in China, more and more players began to use online solutions such as Alipay to recharge their game accounts. Shanda also embraced online payment, as it became popular. Currently, Shanda derives about a quarter of its revenue from direct online payment. The e-sale channel from internet cafés still accounts for over half of its revenue, and over 20 percent comes from selling prepaid cards in other retail outlets.

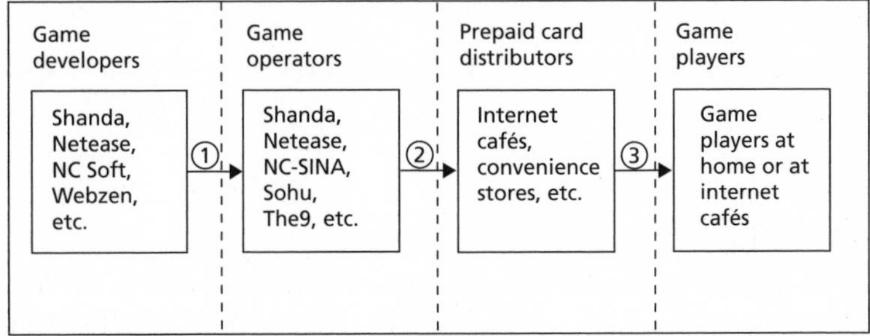

***Figure 8.1:* Online game supply chain**

Data source: J. P. Morgan

Note:

① Licensing agreement with upfront fee and revenue sharing

② Prepaid card through online system or physical prepaid card. Distributor discounts of 15–30 percent

③ Prepaid card

Internet cafés

Internet cafés played a vital role in the development of the internet in China. For many people, especially the poorer classes, they are where computers and the online world are first encountered. Just over 42 percent of the country's 298 million internet users went online in internet cafés, according to a survey carried out by CNNIC in 2008. But going online is not the only thing people can do in an internet café. The computers are installed with many pirated PC games. Users can also watch movies and TV dramas (also pirated) on the computer screens.

An internet café is like a local bar, but for a younger generation. They are where kids and teenagers go to escape the prying eyes of their parents. Many young lovers use the cafés as a trysting place. And there are drinks and snacks for sale to those who spend long hours in front of the screen. The prices are low, less than RMB2 or 30 American cents an hour. Kids can easily pay with their pocket money.

Internet cafés have provided the perfect atmosphere for kids to immerse themselves in the virtual world. Friends who hang out together in the cafés easily become teammates in the game world—sharing their experiences and teaming up to kill major game monsters or accomplish other difficult tasks. The most avid players are usually the technical staff in the internet cafés, so that they are able to help out anyone who needs it. Once one person in an internet café starts playing a certain game, it soon spreads to others. And the internet café owners encourage the trend, since they take a cut of the sales of online game prepaid cards.

Critical success factors

Solving the payment issue and reaching out to internet cafés were not the only factors behind Shanda's huge success with Mir 2. By 2001, most Chinese internet users were browsing news or chatting with others online. They were ready for something more entertaining. Online games were the perfect next step. "It is like online chat plus PC game," said Wu Kai, an executive of the Shanghai-based online game company 9you.

The first two or three online games to arrive in China never became mainstream; their designs were still immature. But Mir 2 turned out to be a really good game, something that may not have been self-evident when Chen first licensed it. For users, the graphic design was nice. The game play was easy to understand and the characters were easy to control. Another important point, which has helped to ensure Mir 2's popularity, is the game "economy"—the fantasy world's counterpart to the real world's economic system. An online game's economic system decides things like:

- the price of a weapon;
- how many experience points and gold coins a player gets for killing a certain monster;
- how quickly a player's weapon will wear out;
- how many points a player needs to achieve promotion to a new status.

These seemingly trivial questions, in their own complicated way, decide the fairness of a game. If they are not designed well, players will soon find the game unfair and lose interest.

From the operators' point of view, Mir 2 does not have many bugs. Its servers are stable and easy for Shanda to maintain. Wemade, the Korean developer, cooperated in the development of the Chinese version.

Another factor in Shanda's success was the fact that the Chinese fixed line telecom operators, China Telecom and China Netcom, were pushing broadband services at the same time. If people are just browsing news or chatting online, a dial-up connection is fast enough. But online games need a faster connection, hence the need for an upgrade to broadband services.

Shanda prepared a large number of co-promotions with the fixed line operators. The fixed line operator in Sichuan province was especially helpful, putting all of its promotional muscle behind Shanda by, for example, printing game advertisements on its bills to customers. "At one point, one-third of Shanda's users were from Sichuan," said a former Shanda executive.

By June 2002, seven months after Mir 2 first launched in China, the game had 400,000 people playing together during peak hours and on average 300,000 people playing at any given time. Shanda was estimated to be making US$3.45 million in revenue a month—the most among Chinese internet companies.[95] The leading online portal, Sina, was making about US$3.24 million a month in the same period from online advertising and mobile data services.[96]

In 2003 Shanda developed a sequel to Mir 2, called Woool. In 2004, the two games made a total revenue of US$165 million and Shanda made a net profit of US$53 million.

Chen floated his company on NASDAQ in May 2004, raising about US$150 million. He became an instant billionaire. Forbes estimated he was worth US$1 billion in 2004, the tenth richest person in China.

Gaming comes of age

As Shanda proved how lucrative online games could be in China, many competitors tried to emulate its success. They printed their prepaid cards to sell in retail outlets. They created their own electronic systems for sales in internet cafés, like Shanda's e-sale system. Many distributors began to sell prepaid cards for the new entrants as well as Shanda.

95 From Shanda IPO prospectus: "revenue for year ended Dec 31, 2002 was RMB 344.5 million or US$41.5 million."

96 From Sina annual report 2002: "revenue for year ended Dec 31, 2002 was US$38.9 million."

Once payment issues were resolved, online games grew rapidly. From virtually nothing in 2001, online game revenues reached US$110 million in 2002 and US$159 million in 2003, according to IDC. (By comparison China's total movie box office receipts were approximately US$117 million in 2002—China's movie industry was hurt by rampant piracy, too.)

One of the most successful players was Netease, founded by William Ding. Born in 1971, Ding graduated from the University of Electronic Science and Technology in China with a Bachelor of Science degree in engineering. He worked as a technical engineer for China Telecom and as a technical support engineer for the American-based database software company Sybase in China before founding Netease in 1999.

Before branching into online games, Netease was the third largest online portal in China, as well as the largest free email provider. Its experience in building email and other web applications made Ding confident about his company's technology development capability. He did not want to license a game from Korea, like Shanda had. Instead he wanted to develop his own game.

His first attempt, Western Journey Online, a game based on the Chinese classic novel *Journey to the West*, did not make it big. But the sequel Western Journey II became a huge success after its launch in 2003. Besides its familiar Chinese theme, people fell in love with its kinder, gentler nature. Western Journey II stresses cooperation with other players more than murder and mayhem. The lesser degree of intensity also allows players to socialize more while playing. Making new friends is very appealing to Chinese teenagers, few of whom have siblings due to the country's one child policy.

Ding launched an improved version, Fantasy Westward Journey, the next year. He also changed the design to make it more cartoon-like. Fantasy attracted many female users because of its cuter graphics and rather peaceful nature. Boys who were keen to meet girls flocked to Fantasy as well. It soon became the most popular online game in China—a title it has yet to relinquish. With constant updates, Fantasy has kept its fans loyal for over five years. In August 2008, during peak hours, 2.3 million people were playing the game together. Despite having many other businesses, Netease was predominantly an online game company, making close to 90 percent of its revenue from games.[97]

[97] Netease is also the country's largest provider of free email and the third largest online portal.

Many competitors continued to license games from overseas, as game development was still immature in China. In the early days, licensed games, especially those from Korea, accounted for the majority of online games in China. Licensing games, however, has its own risks, as Shanda soon found out.

The dark side of licensing

Shanda made a lot of money from Mir 2. Understandably, its game developer Wemade expected—indeed demanded—a larger share of royalties. "It thought Shanda's success was mainly because its game is good—which is partly true," said a former Shanda executive.

Shanda signed the deal with Wemade's distributor Actoz, which owned about 40 percent of Wemade, in mid 2001. The three-year contract was confidential, but Shanda essentially promised to give 20 percent of Mir 2 sales as a royalty to Actoz, which would pass on 5 percent to Wemade. Wemade thought that was unfair and demanded a bigger share.

Shanda refused to cave in. This made Wemade so furious that it walked out on its part of the contract, declining to help Shanda update Mir 2 in China. Online games depend on constant updates to keep up player interest. Wemade's boycott also meant that Shanda could not count on it for technical support if the game had bugs.

Shanda had no choice but to start maintaining the game itself via "reverse engineering," said the executive. It hired a group of developers who hacked into the game, remedied its bugs and developed new features in response to player demand. New maps and new monsters were added. Some of the game rules were also changed. "That is why Shanda's Mir 2 is very different from the Korean version. It has many China-specific features. For example, one of its weapons is the 'dragon-slaying blade,' which was made famous by traditional Chinese martial arts novels," said the executive.

Incredibly, this worked. Shanda kept its players happy despite losing support from the game developer. In mid 2002, Shanda stopped paying royalties on Mir 2. When Wemade was ready to launch a new version of the game, Legend of Mir 3, it refused to give the game to Shanda. Instead, it licensed Mir 3 to another Chinese game operator.

Afraid of losing players to Mir 3, Shanda went on to develop its own sequel to the game and called it Woool, or World of Legend in

Chinese. Although Woool is different from Mir 3, Shanda after years of operation knew what players liked, so Woool became a hit game, too, after its launch in late 2003. Less charitably, competitors have speculated that Woool may have become successful partly because Shanda may have encouraged Mir 2 players to switch to the new product.

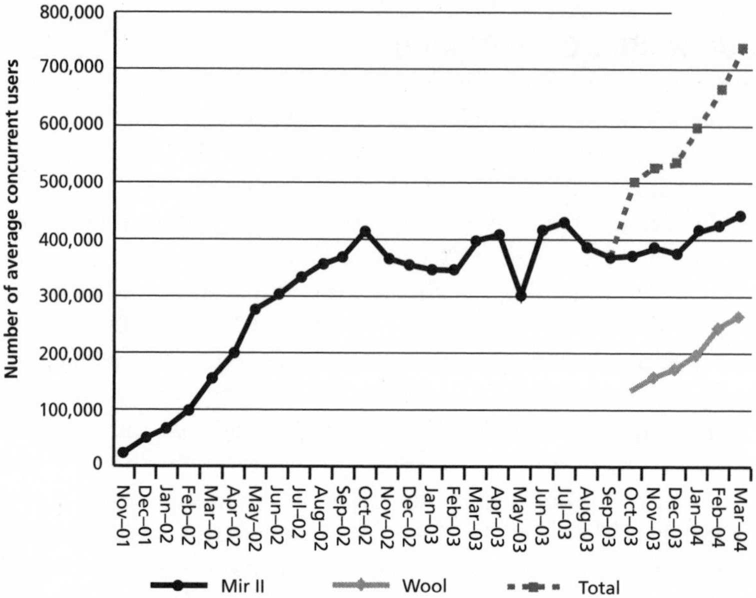

***Figure 8.2:* Average number of concurrent users of Shanda's games (2001–04)**

Data source: Shanda

Actoz, Wemade, and Shanda had been engaged in a series of lawsuits since 2003. If Actoz and Wemade won, Shanda might lose the rights to Mir 2 in China. Woool was also at risk of being banned after Wemade accused Shanda of using its intellectual property to develop the game. Together the two games accounted for the majority of Shanda's revenue. Moreover, Shanda risked having to pay a huge sum to compensate Wemade and Actoz for their losses.

Over the years, Shanda had renegotiated with Actoz and Wemade for operational rights of Mir 2 and Woool in China and to pay various amounts to the two parties. In 2004–05, Shanda bought a 29 percent controlling stake in Actoz for US$91.7 million, then another 9 percent for US$14.4 million in the open market. But Wemade, despite being partly owned by Actoz, kept up its legal pursuit.

The incident was not fully resolved until mid 2007. According to a former Shanda executive, the Chinese firm paid Wemade a sum roughly equal to what it was claiming in royalties on Mir 2 as the upfront fee for licensing a new Wemade game, Changchun. Wemade used the money to buy back Actoz's stake in the company. A side effect of the incident was that Shanda lost the operating rights to World of Warcraft (WoW), a highly anticipated game, to another local rival, Shanghai-based The9.

"Our discussions with Blizzard, WoW's developer, were going well at the beginning. But by the end of 2004, our lawsuits with the Korean companies made Blizzard think we were dishonest. And it chose our rival, The9," said the former Shanda executive.

China, WoW!

The9 was cofounded by Zhu Jun, a Shanghai Jiao Tong University graduate. He was working on his own IT firm, Flagholder New Technology, from 1997 to 1999 before founding The9 in late 1999.

The9 was even more aggressive than Shanda in licensing games. It was willing to make huge down payments and pay high royalties to the game developers in the hope of landing a mega hit. The first game Zhu licensed to run in China was MU from Korean developer Webzen. The three-dimensional MMORPG was a hit in Korea, and Zhu paid a huge upfront fee to obtain the rights for China. He also gave a large share of sales to Webzen as a royalty.[98]

But MU was a flop after its launch in early 2003. Many local Chinese set up their own computer servers, called private servers, to run the game. These servers stole a lot of players from The9. Also, some players had developed a cheating program for MU, leaving other players frus-

98 From The9 Annual Report 2004: "9Webzen, a joint venture between us and Webzen, has the exclusive license to operate MU in China. We hold a 51 percent interest in 9Webzen and are entitled to 51 percent of the dividends distributed by 9Webzen. We account for our interest in 9Webzen using the equity method since Webzen has the right to participate in certain decisions to be made in the ordinary course of business of 9Webzen. Under the MU license agreement, 9Webzen is required to pay royalties to Webzen equal to 20 percent of the after-tax sales revenue derived from operating MU in China. In addition, 9Webzen Shanghai is obligated to meet a minimum MU sales revenue target of at least US$1.4 million per quarter. If 9Webzen Shanghai fails to meet 70 percent of the minimum MU revenue target for two consecutive quarters, Webzen shall have the right to license MU to third parties. If 9Webzen Shanghai fails to meet its minimum revenue target for more than two years, Webzen may terminate the license."

trated. "If Webzen or The9 had had more operational experience, they would have been able to fix the problem of private servers and cheating programs," said an analyst.

So when The9 bid what was then a gigantic sum again for the American game World of Warcraft, using most of the money it had raised on the NASDAQ stock market, industry watchers thought Zhu had lost his mind. Over US$80.3 million was promised for marketing and loyalty for the next four years.[99] It was a huge bet for Zhu—if World of Warcraft had flopped, The9 would have been bankrupt.

There were worries that the Western science fiction background of the game might not take with Chinese players, who so far had tended to prefer games based on Eastern cultural artifacts. Other skeptics noted that running the 3D game would require high-performance computers that most internet cafés in China did not own.

But World of Warcraft became an incredible success. In just a few hours after the game's beta testing started in the early hours of April 26, 2005, the first two data centers in China, hosting close to 100 servers, were full. During peak times, it was so popular that 2,000 players were queuing on each server for their turns to try the game. Three days later, Blizzard and The9 opened a third data center. In less than one hour, all of these new servers were full as well.

The overwhelming appeal of World of Warcraft had shocked the whole of China. During peak hours of the game's beta testing in April 2005, half a million players logged on to its servers to play. One month after it formally launched in June 2005, the total number of paying players reached 1.5 million. The second month, it reached 2 million. "Many people in China were playing its [pirated] PC game before the online version entered China. They are familiar with its theme and like the game," said Bryan Yuan, an analyst from market researcher IDC.

[99] From The9 Annual Report 2004: "C9I, a joint venture between us and China Interactive, has an exclusive license to localize and operate WoW in China. Currently, GameNow and China Interactive own 68.9 and 31.1 percent of C9I, respectively. Pursuant to the WoW license agreement with VUG, we are obligated to pay royalties equal to 22 percent of the face value of WoW prepaid cards and online points sold by us by making recoupable advances against royalty payments in an aggregate amount of approximately US$51.3 million over a four-year period commencing from the commercial launch. We paid VUG an initial non-refundable license fee of US$3.0 million in 2004 and the first year minimum royalty guarantee of US$13.0 million in 2005. We are also obligated to commit no less than approximately US$13.0 million in the marketing and promotion of WoW in China during the term of the license agreement. As security for each advance payment, C9I is obligated to procure a standby letter of credit prior to each relevant period."

World of Warcraft also has superior graphic design and game play—making it the game of choice for sophisticated game players, especially those who prefer hard-core fighting games, according to Yuan.

Its marketing campaign with Coca-Cola was also very successful. Besides TV and other media advertising, a Warcraft character was printed on every Coke can at the time the game was launched in mid 2005. "It is a clever idea to promote the game, as Coke is widely available in internet cafés," said Oliver He, a vice president from The9. The marketing synergy between The9 and Coca-Cola was incredible, said He. Coke got a cool "spokesperson" for its product. The9 got to promote World of Warcraft everywhere, and most importantly in the internet cafés, where online game players gathered.

In the third quarter of 2005, 2.5 million players registered with World of Warcraft. On average, 240,000 were playing the game at any given time. During peak hours, 467,000 players were playing the game.

Zhu's huge bet paid off. The9 was rich. Its quarterly revenue jumped 20 times from the same period in the previous year to US$22.8 million and it turned a profit of US$4.7 million, from a loss of US$2.8 million a year earlier. World of Warcraft stole a lot of players from Shanda's games, which had already been losing ground to Netease. Shanda saw its first significant slide in revenue and profit in the fall of 2005.

In the next chapter we will talk in detail about how Shanda decided to face the new challenge and, in the end, raise the popularity of online games in China to another level.

Lessons learned

1 Better technology alone won't ensure success.

Chen's solution to the payment issue in China was hardly advanced in terms of technology. Shanda's prepaid cards are printed paper cards distributed physically by retailer networks. Its e-sale system is hardly proprietary either. Every other game company has been able to develop their own to facilitate sales in internet cafés, afterward.

In fact, one venture capitalist said that his company had looked into investing in Shanda in its early stages. "But, there is no core technology in the firm," said the venture capitalist, "and our mandate was to invest in technology firms in China." He certainly missed out on a great deal. Shanda later raised US$40 million from SAIF Partners and went for a successful IPO on NASDAQ in 2004.

Despite being low-tech, Chen's idea worked and it allowed online games to develop in China early on (in 2002), before online payment became popular in China (after 2005). Other examples also showed that the best solution might require no technology at all. For example, Ctrip uses promoters to market its travel services in train stations and airports.

Baidu's overwhelming lead over Google (60 to 30 percent) shows that those with inferior technology can win in China by having more customized solutions to the local market. Baidu's applications, such as MP3 search, virtual forum—Postbar (Tiebar), community drive knowledge base—Baidu Know (Zhidao), are hardly advanced in technology. But they made Baidu popular in China, particular among young people looking for entertainment and companionship.

2 A local partner can be very useful in entering China's market. But be careful.

Although Wemade's Mir 2 was a good quality game, for Mir 2 to succeed in China, Shanda had to put in a lot of effort. Issues the firm had to solve included payment, working with internet cafés, partnering with fixed line operators, dealing with private servers and cheating programs. These are difficult if not impossible for a foreign company to do in China.

Partnering with local operators seemed the way to go for many foreign game companies. As long as their games are good, they have no problem finding local partners under favorable terms, as Blizzard found out from its experience with World of Warcraft.

But there are hazards, too. Is the local partner honest about the quantity of product sold, sales commission to local distributors, and so on? Local partners could start to produce copycats of your products, if they become successful in the market. Shanda made Woool, its own sequel to Mir2, out of despair. But other game companies have tried to make clones of games they licensed, just for higher profit.

9. Shanda: Freebirds reign

After World of Warcraft launched in China, it stole many users from Shanda, which suffered its first significant slide in revenue and profit in late 2005.

Shanda did not sit still. In December 2005, to everyone's surprise, Shanda declared that its three most popular games would be free—players would only be charged if they wanted better game weapons or costumes. Most people in the industry saw this as an act of pure desperation. But again, they were wrong. Shanda's offer brought in enough new players to restore the firm's revenue to previous levels within a year.

Soon, free games became the dominant trend. New companies launched many fresh titles. The entrants included Giant Interactive, founded by Shi Yuzhu, a legendary figure in his own right. Giant's first game, ZT Online, was the second in China to have more than a million users playing at the same time. The self-developed game was not atypical in terms of technology or game play, but the free game tactic and Shi's marketing genius made it work.

An army of 2,000 promoters marched into every internet café in China campaigning for new players to join ZT Online.

The phoenix

Blizzard's World of Warcraft conquered China, just as it had dominated the rest of the world. Game players flocked to join the new game, which offers true three-dimensional adventures and tons of excitement from better graphics and more thrilling story lines.

Shanda's games, Mir 2 and Woool, were in their fifth and third year of operation by late 2005. The games were the first love of many players in China, but customers started to become bored with the outdated graphics and technical details. Many switched to World of Warcraft.

Netease's games, Western Journey II and Fantasy Westward Journey, were less affected because they appealed to a different group—players who preferred socializing to killing.

By late 2005, six months after World of Warcraft entered China, Shanda suffered its first substantial decline in revenue and profit. Fourth quarter revenue dropped 28 percent from the previous quarter and 16 percent from a year earlier. It made a huge loss (US$66.8 million). Part of the loss was caused by a one-time impairment charge (US$64.6 million) for its investment in Actoz. But, even excluding this, Shanda's profitability dropped a great deal. It had made a profit of US$32.4 million in the previous quarter and US$28 million a year earlier.

In December 2005, Chen Tianqiao, Shanda's CEO, made a decision that shocked the whole industry. He announced that all three of Shanda's major games, Mir 2, Woool, and Magical Land, could be played for free, with users only paying for improved weapons or outfits.

Sales of the three games accounted for an estimated 70 percent of Shanda's revenue at the time. Imagine abandoning all of that while continuing to pay for the servers and bandwidth costs, as well as staff for operating the games. Could sales of virtual weapons and other game items really make up for lost subscription fees? At that time no free MMORPG had turned out to be as profitable as a paid game. Most people in the industry saw this as a ploy to keep Shanda's game players from switching to its rivals.

But again, Chen's bet paid off. It took a tough nine to 12 months for Shanda to adjust to the new model. The firm had to figure out the tricks for selling magic powders and virtual weapons to the game players—what would make them pay? Shanda found that it attracted enough new players for it to regain its old levels of revenue and profit.

"Shanda's games are old favorites for many game players in China. Once they became free, some players returned. And new players started to try these games as they are classic in the industry," said a former Shanda executive. "Some of our players can reach levels they could never attain before, because they are able to buy weapons and upgrade easily under the new model."

Revenue rebounded 41 percent from the lowest level of US$42.6 million in the first quarter of 2006 to US$60.3 million in the fourth quarter. Profit also recovered to US$30.8 million in the fourth quarter, not much different from Shanda's earnings before World of Warcraft stole its business. It earned US$32.3 million in the third quarter of 2005.

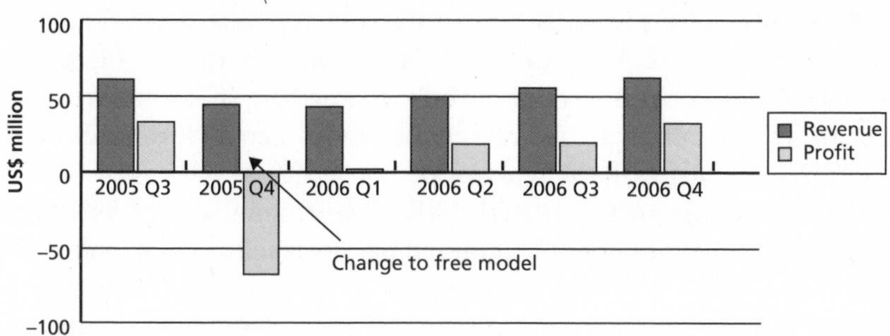

Figure 9.1: **Shanda's revenue and profit before and after the change to the free model**

Data source: Shanda

"The year 2006 was a landmark year for our company. We implemented a new business model and proved once again Shanda is a leading force in the online game market in China," said Chen.

By the end of 2006, Shanda's games had a total of 4.7 million paying accounts, 80 million active accounts and 500 million registered accounts. China's internet population was just 137 million in 2006, according to the government-backed researcher CNNIC.

2B free

Shanda's success in profiting by giving away the game was not a total surprise. Korea, which led China in online game development by a few years, had seen a steady growth in the popularity of free online games.

Before Shanda's change in business model, one of the Korean games licensed for China sales also found that selling game items could be more profitable than charging a subscription. The Korean game was called Audition. It was not a MMORPG, but a dancing simulation game, where players controlled their characters to dance to music. Players danced together and the best one won. Very soon the focus was no longer on who won, but on who wore the best outfit.

"The default clothing of the characters is rather plain. But players can buy from a wide selection of dresses, T-shirts, trousers, shoes, or even evening gowns and wedding dresses," said Wu Kai, an executive with 9you, the Chinese company that licensed the game from Korean developer T3.

Those who have played Second Life, a virtual world developed by US-based Linden Lab, would understand the experience. Many buy extensive wardrobes for their virtual characters, so as to live their dreams or stand out from the rest of the crowd. People love to show off in cyberspace, just as in the real world.

Audition was popular—in mid 2005, a few months after its official launch, the game's number of registered players reached 30 million. At its peak hours, 300,000 were playing together at the same time. But it did not become a money-spinner until it switched to an item-based model. Liu Hongbin, a venture capitalist who invested in 9you, said the game was much more profitable after it switched to an item-based model. The reason was that some rich players were also enjoying online games. In fact, game players were not only limited to kids and teenagers, but included young adults who had started to earn a living on their own. Many owners of small businesses also enjoyed the pastime, as did some professionals.

Although 43.4 percent of online game players were students, 8.1 percent worked in management, according to a survey done by IDC in 2007. Of the players, 17.9 percent earned more than RMB2,000 (about US$300) a month (the middle-income group in China) and 1.5 percent brought in more than RMB10,000 (US$1,500) a month (high income group in China), while 25.7 percent had a bachelors degree.

Income (RMB per month)	Percentage
Below 500	18.8
501–1,000	12.3
1,001–1,500	16.8
1,501–2,000	11.6
2,001–3,000	8.5
3,001–5,000	5.6
5,001–10,000	2.3
Above 10,000	1.5
None	22.6

Occupation	Percentage
Government	3.9
Management	8.1
Production	8.6
Public service	4.0
Business/Services	9.8
IT/Information	8.9
Education/Media	2.6
Student	43.4
Unemployed	6.1
Others	4.7

***Table 9.1:* Income and occupation distribution of China's online game users (2007)**

Data source: IDC

"More and more game players switched from the status of 'no money and plenty of time' to 'have money but no time,'" said an industry expert explaining the popularity of free games.

People were paying for gold farmers and cheats.[100] These suggested that some game players, if they could, would pay to cheat. Free games in effect allowed rich players to cheat openly—they can buy better weapons, upgrade their characters faster, become super warriors and kings and queens in the virtual world. For many, such accomplishments (although just in a virtual world) were reward enough for them to spend a lot of money.

"Shanda's Mir 2 and Woool were some of the oldest games. They attracted a group of fairly wealthy, but not very sophisticated, players. World of Warcraft did not suit their taste as it seems too complicated. Many of them are factory owners in small cities in China. They loved Mir 2 and Woool as they have played these game for a long time," said a former Shanda executive, "For them, spending a few thousand Renminbi a month is not a problem."

Average spending of paid users in Shanda's games gradually increased to RMB50–60 (US$7–9) per month, more than the average of RMB30 (US$4.50) it earned when it charged subscription fees to all users.

Awaken the giant

Another pioneer in free games was Giant Interactive, founded by Shi Yuzhu. Born in 1962, Shi studied mathematics in Zhejiang University, one of leading colleges in China and made his first fortune by developing Chinese software in the 1980s. Then, in a bout of megalomania not uncommon in entrepreneurs, he tried to build the tallest mansion in China in 1998, and nearly went bankrupt. Zhuhai Giant, Shi's company at the time, ceased operations with significant outstanding debts and claims for repayment.

Nonetheless, Shi made a comeback selling health boosters for the elderly. The product was called Nao Baijin (脑白金) or Brain Platinum in Chinese. The medicine is supposed to make the elderly sleep better and live healthier. His marketing strategies were enormously successful—huge primetime TV advertising and thousands of sales

100 Gold farming is a general term for a MMORPG activity in which a player attempts to acquire (or "farm") items of value that are sold to create stocks of in-game currency ("gold"), usually by exploiting repetitive elements of the game's mechanics. Once a gold farmer or workshop has created a stockpile of currency, they will try to sell it. Gold farming is often used with two other separate in-game cheats: power leveling and the creation and selling of high-level character accounts.

agents who covered every city and town encouraged millions to line up for Shi's products, especially as gifts for their elderly parents.

"Shi studied mathematics and before he started his own businesses, he worked as a statistician. He knows how to do market research and how to interpret the results. Many of his successes in business were due to his understanding of consumer psychology from doing detailed market research. Also, his organization of the sales network was superb," said Jacky Huang, China Internet Research Manager of IDC.

Shi said he was a devoted online game player—spending a lot of time and money on Shanda's games. By 2004–05, the serial entrepreneur and self-made millionaire was ready to turn his hobby into a new venture. He recruited a team of developers from Shanda and started developing a new game, ZT Online.

By the time he had entered online gaming, the market was already packed with strong players—Shanda, Netease, The9, and so on. And his game ZT Online offered nothing special—no fancy graphics or extraordinary story line. But he had a relatively new tactic under his belt: his game would be free to all players—they would only be charged if they wanted better game weapons or costumes.

The game started open beta testing in August 2005 and was officially launched in January 2006. Shi used the same promotion tactics for ZT Online as he did with his health boosters. From his earlier days with Brain Platinum, Shi had built a nationwide marketing network. This time he was using it to sell his online game.

A 2,000-strong troop of promoters was sent to internet cafés in every city and every town to encourage players to join the new game. The nationwide distribution network consisted of over 270 distributors and reached over 116,500 retail outlets. Some 530 liaison offices were set up countrywide to organize the effort. And indeed, the campaign was very well organized.

Each city was divided into different regions. Each region was divided into smaller areas. And each area would be taken care of by one promoter. "Every day, our promoters pack materials, such as posters and souvenirs of the game, into their backpacks and go to the internet cafés within their area," said Eric He, chief financial officer of Giant. "By offering some incentives, the promoters would ask internet café owners to show the game's posters in their premises and install ZT Online on their machines. They would also talk to individual users in the cafés, and encourage them to join ZT Online," said He.

The promoters would also register the IP address of the internet café so Giant's central server would know how many game players were registered in each area and how much they were spending. These figures would be used to evaluate the performance of each promoter and determine whether he or she received a bonus.

Shi's promotion worked very well. By May 2007, a year and half after its official launch, ZT Online had more than one million players in its peak hour. There was only one other game that could achieve that at the time—Netease's Fantasy Westward Journey.

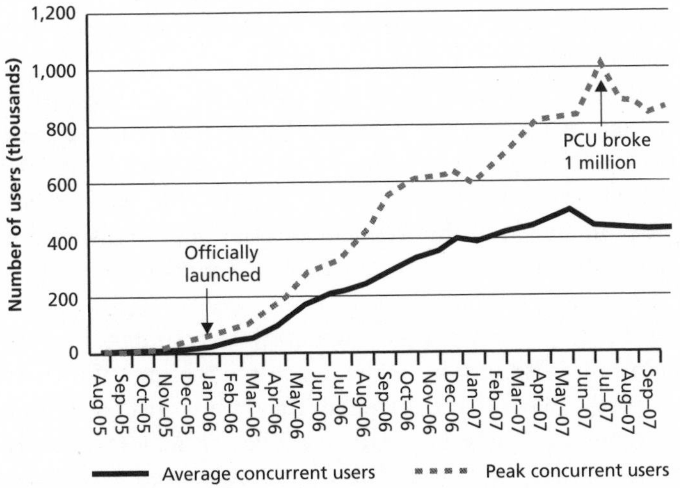

Figure 9.2: **Number of users for ZT Online (Aug 2005–Sep 2007)**

Data source: Giant

The business model ultimately proved itself, and free games soon became the dominant trend. New companies such as Beijing Perfect World launched many new titles. Major internet companies such as Tencent and Sohu also branched into the online game business. Online game popularity in China reached new heights after the free model became the trend. "The item-based model is helpful in attracting numerous new users to join in the game world. It has become the new force for the development of China's online game industry," said Bryan Yuan, an analyst from market researcher IDC.

The revenue from China's online gaming market surged 61.5 percent in 2007 to US$1.39 billion from a year earlier, said IDC. Most of the new games launched in 2007 adopted the item-based model.

The revenue from such games accounted for 67 percent of the total market income.

The dark side of free

ZT Online was the ultimate "cash is king" game. Players could do very well very quickly if they paid. Zhi's team also figured out plenty of tricks to make people spend more. Innovations included virtual treasure boxes, which may contain in-game items worth more than the cost of the box itself, and allowing players to hire in-game "substitute players" which let them raise their characters' experience levels without actually playing.

This allowed ZT Online to enjoy one of highest rate of sales per paying user among games in China. People, on average, spent RMB90–100 (or US$13–14) per month, compared with RMB50–60 (or US$7–9) on Shanda's games. But, on the flip side, players could easily become tired of the frequent promotions—treasure boxes one day, substitute players the other, beauty contest the next, and so on.

Also, being able to pay their way to superhero status might be a thrill for rich players, but it is not fair for the less affluent ones. "Why would poorer users keep playing the game if they were just slaughtered continuously by others," asked an industry follower. Moreover, as rich players were quickly able to accomplish what they wanted—to be super warriors, kings, or queens—they soon lost interest. "They experience everything the game can offer in one to two years. If this was a time-based game, it might take three to four years or even longer to become a top warrior," said Yuan of IDC.

If the interests of paying and non-paying users are not balanced, they soon lose interest. And if the game tempts users too often with promotions, they will become exhausted. The life cycle of a game can be greatly shortened if the game companies try too hard to gain cash quickly, as Giant experienced.

ZT Online pushed its moneymaking tricks to the limit in mid 2008. Although it lifted the game's peak concurrent users to new heights—2.1 million were playing together in its peak hours in April 2008—the glory was short lived. Users felt frustrated and started to complain.

Shi began to reformulate his games. Excessive promotions were cut back in ZT Online. The game started to emphasize daily consumption items rather than promotional items. He also launched a new version, called ZT Online Classic Edition, which is geared toward recapturing former ZT Online gamers who prefer game play without any promotional items, much like the structure of ZT Online in 2006.

The impact was felt immediately. In the third quarter, the average number of users dropped 12 percent from the previous quarter to about 543,000, and only 1.5 million were playing the game during peak hours. Paying users dropped 47 percent from the previous quarter. Average spending fell 12 percent. ZT Online's popularity gradually recovered afterwards.

"The Free model has changed the focus of development of online games. Companies are no longer focused on designing better story lines to keep players interested in the games for a long time. They just concentrate on devising more promotions to keep players spending money in the game. It could harm the industry in the long run," said Clement Song, a former Microsoft Xbox developer.

Let 100 flowers bloom

The online game industry was fully developed in China by 2006–07. There were all kinds of games targeting different users. The game player tally reached 49 million in 2008, accounting for about 16 percent of the total internet population and 30 percent of broadband users. IDC forecasts that eight to ten million new game players will appear each year in the next five years.

Even as free games became mainstream, the time-based model did not completely fade away. Researcher IDC believes that the time-based and item charge models will coexist in the long run.[101]

In fact, there were players who loved the fairness that time-based games offered. "The best players are those who have spent the most time playing the game, the most skillful and dedicated," said Yuan of IDC, "Even a nobody in the real world can be a super hero in the game

[101] From IDC China Gaming 2008–12 Forecast and Analysis: "The item-based business model has become the mainstream while time-based games will co-exist for a long time. The item-based model is helpful in attracting numerous new users to join in the game world. It has become the new force for the development of China's online game industry. Most of the new games launched in 2007 adopt the item-based model, while the revenue from such games in 2007 occupied 67 percent of the total market income. Even as item-based games become the mainstream, this does not mean that the time-based model will completely fade away. IDC believes that the time-based and item-charge models will co-exist in the long run."

if they make the effort. That is what attracted many to play online games in the beginning."

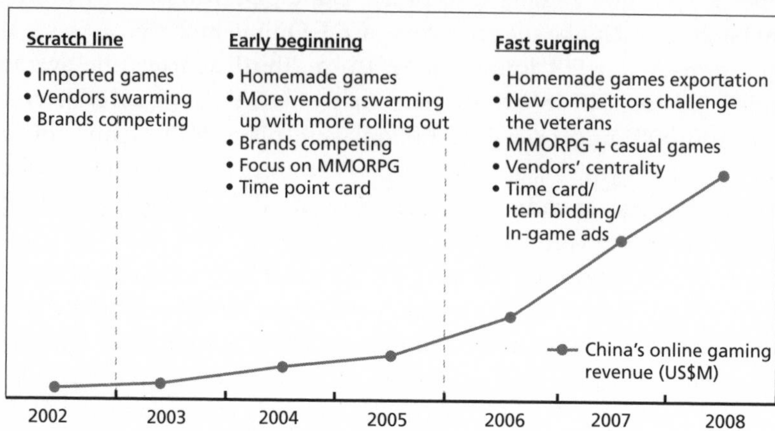

***Figure 9.3:* China's online gaming road map**

Data source: IDC

Moreover, many of the hit time-based games, such as World of Warcraft or Fantasy Western Journey, are old-time classics. Over the years, they have cultivated a loyal group of long-term fans and kept them interested by continuously upgrading the games. "There a lot of friends in the game and your teammates need you. That is what keeps many players staying with a game for years," said Yuan.

While Shi's ZT Online was the ultimate "cash is king" game, time-based World of Warcraft is the ultimate fair game for those willing to make the effort. It appeals especially to sophisticated players, who demand excellent graphics, control, and game play. In terms of technology, World of Warcraft, which took Blizzard four to five years to develop, is the best in the market. No other company can offer similar products. World of Warcraft user numbers have continued to grow since it entered China in mid 2005. By mid 2008, it had more than one million users playing the game in its peak hours. On average, 449,000 players were playing simultaneously in 2008.

Shanda continued to license and develop new games. It had more than 20 games running at the end of 2008. But most revenue still comes from its two early hits, Mir 2 and Woool. The two games have kept a group of rather affluent long-term fans, who prefer the relatively simple game play.

Netease's Fantasy Westward Journey appeals to peaceful types, who are less interested in warfare, but more interested in socializing with others in the game. The game's cute graphics attracted many girl players, and hence boys followed. There are many copycats of Fantasy Western Journey among Chinese games. But it kept its popularity and the title of top online game in China—2.3 million users playing at the same time during peak hours in August 2008.

Game	Operator	Developer	Nature	Popularity
Fantasy Westward Journey	Netease	Self-developed	Paid game, MMORPG, Chinese myth	2.3 million peak concurrent users
ZT Online	Giant	Self-developed	Free game, MMORPG, Chinese martial art	1.5 million peak concurrent users
World of Warcraft	The9	US-based Blizzard	Paid game, MMORPG, western myth	1 million peak concurrent users
Audition	9you	Korea-based T3	Free game, dancing simulation, modern	800,000 peak concurrent users
TLBB	Sohu	Self-developed	Free game, MMORPG, chinese martial art	800,000 peak concurrent users
Dungeon and Fighter	Tencent	Korea-based Neople	Free Game, side-scrolling online fighting game	1.6 million peak concurrent users
Mir 2 and Woool	Shanda	Korea-based Wemade	Free game MMORPG, ancient myth	Not available

***Table 9.2:* Top Chinese online games**

Data source: individual companies

The ultimate female game in China is the dancing simulation Audition, where players compete more with their outfits than their skills on the virtual dance floor. Weddings and virtual gifts are also big in Audition. More than half of the game players are girls, the highest proportion among all Chinese games, mainly the 14–26 age group, according to Wu Kai, an executive of 9you, operator of Audition in China. The game had 800,000 players at its peak hours in 2007. Overall, female players remain the minority in online games, accounting for only 12.9 percent of users according to a survey done by IDC in 2007.

The latest hit in 2008 was leading online portal Sohu's self-developed game Tian Long Ba Bu (TLBB). It is based on a classical Chinese martial-arts novel written by Louis Cha, or better known as Jin Yong. It had 800,000 players at its peak hours in March 2009.

And Dungeon and Fighter, a side-scrolling online fighting game licensed from Korea by dominant instant message operator Tencent, also became a hit. It had more than 1.6 million players at its peak hours in March 2009. Online casual games—such as car racing, basketball, and card games—are popular in China, too. Tencent's online casual games platform had over 4 million users playing at the same time in 2008.

"Many overseas developers asked me what kinds of game could be popular in China. I told them any types could, as long as the game is good," said Oliver He, a vice president of The9. Besides licensing World of Warcraft from Blizzard, The9 has also licensed the hit sport game FIFA Online 2 from Electronic Arts with plans to launch it in 2009.

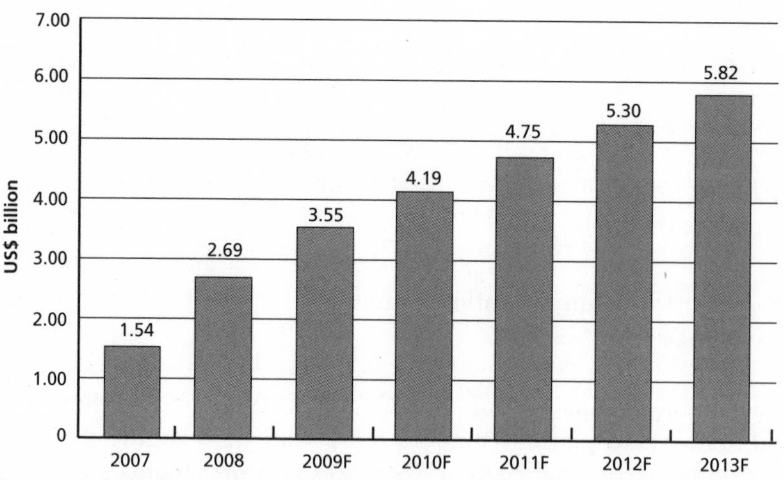

***Figure 9.4:* Online game market size (2007–13)**

Data source: IDC

The majority of hit online games in China were MMORPG, based on Chinese martial art fiction or myths; other types also found their niche in China.

IDC expected that revenue from China's online gaming market would grow from US$2.69 billion in 2008 to US$5.82 billion in 2013.

Homemade games

Another trend in the industry is the surge of popularity in games developed domestically. Starting from Netease's Westward Journey II, many homemade games have become mega hits in China, including Netease's Fantasy Westward Journey, Giant's ZT Online, and Sohu's TLBB.

"Ten year ago, game development in China was in a very bad shape. Piracy was a big problem for PC games. Since no one was making money, no one was willing to invest," said He of The9. "As the online game market becomes proven, many companies are willing to invest in the research and development of games."

There were 126 online game developers in China in 2007. In total they hired more than 21,000 people, up 51 percent from 2006, said IDC. Apart from the above-mentioned game companies, leading developers in China also include Perfect World and Kingsoft in Beijing, as well as Net Dragon in the southern coastal city, Fuzhou. They have yet to come up with mega hits, but they have established large development teams and have launched some relatively successful games.

Perfect World previously engaged in developing educational software. It specialized in three-dimensional games based on Chinese myths and martial arts fictional stories. Kingsoft still develops desktop applications and antivirus software, but the bulk of its income today is from online gaming.

The development capability of Chinese companies has already matched that of the Korean firms that started a few years earlier. However, it was still inferior to the level of top Western games, such as World of Warcraft, according to He of The9. The initial cost for developing a MMORPG is usually somewhere between RMB3 million to RMB30 million, although some products can cost over RMB50 million. "In the West, it's about the same numbers but in US dollars," said Clement Song, a former developer for Microsoft Xbox. (That means development cost is usually seven times more in America.)

Their technology might not be top-notch, but domestically developed games were loved by many Chinese players because of cultural familiarity and fast upgrades. From a humble beginning, homemade games gradually showed strong competitive advantages in the market. They accounted for 65.1 percent of online game revenue in 2007, said IDC. Of the 76 new online games launched in 2007, 53 were developed domestically.

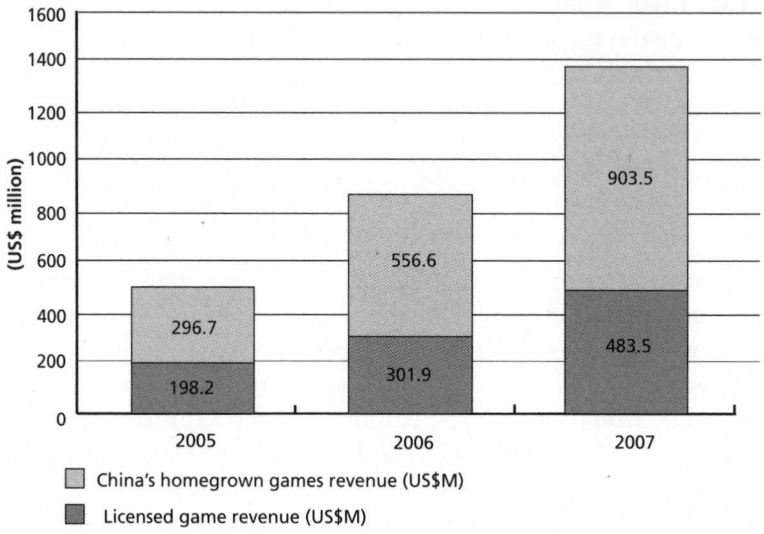

***Figure 9.5:* China's homegrown games revenue (2005–07)**
Data source: IDC

For operators, developing one's own game could be cheaper than licensing one from overseas. Licensing a major hit from overseas could be very expensive as The9's experience with World of Warcraft showed. The9's net profit margin was about 20 percent in 2008, much lower than that of Netease (53 percent) and Giant (70 percent), which depend on their self-developed games for the bulk of revenue.

Also, if a game was self-developed, the operator has more control over the game for new upgrades or other modifications, according to Yuan. Most importantly, licensing games has a major pitfall—operators could be at the mercy of the developers if the games became very successful.

Shanda had its dispute with the Korean developers when the game Mir 2 became popular. Shanghai-based 9you also met a similar fate with its hit dancing game, Audition. The game's Korean developer T3 and its distributor Yedang fought with 9you over loyalty issues in 2007. The dispute finally resolved after 9you promised a more generous revenue sharing scheme, but it caused 9you and T3's parent company G10 to abandon their initial public offering plans in 2007.

The9, which depended on Blizzard's World of Warcraft for over 90 percent of its revenue, was constantly under pressure. Investors worried about The9's relations with the game's developer Blizzard, and wondered if it could renew its contract with Blizzard on favorable terms. In April 2009, The9 finally lost its right to operate World of Warcraft in China. Blizzard gave it to Netease. The share price of The9 dropped 25 percent on the day of the announcement.

"The9's fate will depend on whether its other games—FIFA, Hellgate, Audition 2 could be successful," said Dick Wei, China internet analyst of J.P. Morgan.

Game dynamics

Online games are relatively cheap to develop in China. A former Shanda executive estimated that it took a ten-person team one year to develop a small MMORPG, which could reach about 20,000 to 30,000 average concurrent users and generate sales of over RMB1 million (or US$140,000) a year.

Of course, major hits such as Fastasy Westward Journey will need a team of over a hundred developers for two to three years. But, if it succeeds, the payoff can be huge. "If a game could reach 100,000 average concurrent users, it can survive. If it reached 200,000, it starts to be profitable. If it reached over 300,000, it will be hugely profitable," said Yuan.

Profits from a successful game, such as Shanda's Mir 2 and Giant's ZT Online, were enough to take a company from nothing to IPO. Sohu spun off its game division, Changyou, in a separate listing on NASDAQ in 2009, after TLBB became a hit game.

Nevertheless, before a game was launched, it was hard to predict how popular it would be. Track records did not count in this industry. After the success of Fantasy Westward Journey and Westward Journey II, Netease failed to produce a new hit. The games it developed subsequently, Datang and Tianxi, were flops. Giant's new game, Giant Online, was much less popular than its first, ZT Online. Before the launch of Sohu's TLBB, no one expected it would become a hit, similar to Tencent's Dungeon and Fighter.

Even licensed games have similar problems. Popularity in other markets does not guarantee popularity in China. MU was popular in Korea, but it was a flop in China as its operator The9 found out. The9's next trial, World of Warcraft, on the other hand was a mega hit in China.

The industry was full of companies depending on one or two games for most of their revenue. To produce the next hit game, some game developers, such as Netease and Giant, put all their efforts into a few major projects. Anything less than a mega hit was considered a failure. Others, such as Perfect World and Net Dragon, spread their resources over many projects. As long as everyone has achieved some degree of success, the aggregated total will be enough.

As a rule of thumb, industry experts estimate a MMORPG has a life span of four years. A successful game will experience strong growth in the number of users in the first 18 months after it is launched, little or no growth in the next 18 months, and a decline, likely significant, in the number of users after 36 months of commercial operation.

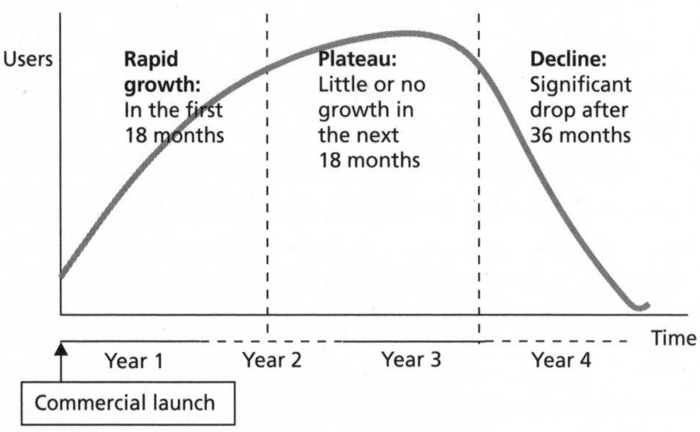

Figure 9.6: **Life cycle of a MMORPG**

But many hit games in China have a life span much longer than the four-year estimate. The very first hit title, Shanda's Mir 2, was still running after eight years of operation. China's number one game, Netease's Fantasy Westward Journey, was in its sixth year. They extend their life span by constant updates. Community bonding between players is another factor. "Players formed a community of their own after playing the same game for a long time. They no long play solely for the game itself, but to stay with their friends," said Yuan of IDC.

By 2008, some game companies in China started to explore the possibility of combining online games with online communities. Shi of Giant bought 25 percent of 51.com, a leading online community in China for US$51 million in 2008. 51.com is like MySpace in China, appealing to youngsters who like to write blogs and make friends online.

"We are positioning Giant at the forefront of the trend toward increasing convergence between online games and social networking communities," said Shi. In his opinion, the combination can broaden Giant's player base, expand its community-building opportunities, reinforce user stickiness, and extend the life cycles of its games.

For 51.com, introducing games to its community can help it to generate revenue. Although the online community has lots of users and traffic, there are not many ways of generating cash. The online advertising on social networking sites is still immature.

From import to export

After Chinese game companies mastered the skill of developing their own games, they started to export.

Most of them exported their games to nearby regions, such as Taiwan, Vietnam, and Hong Kong, where the culture and internet development are similar to that in China. They used the same licensing model as the Korean and US game developers. In general, Chinese games can get US$50,000 to US$300,000 in upfront fees, plus at least 20 percent net revenue as an ongoing royalty, according to Kevin Wang, chief financial officer of Beijing-based Kingsoft. "I think, in the long run, China can be a supplier of online games in nearby countries and regions," said Wang, "many of which are too small to support their own game developing companies."

Chen's story, becoming rich by licensing an online game to run, is being repeated in other Asian countries. Kingsoft's game, JX Online, became the first hit game in Vietnam in 2005, much like the surge of Wemade's Mir 2 in China in 2001. JX Online, a MMORPG about Chinese martial arts, had more than 200,000 users playing at the same time during its peak hours. It made its Vietnamese operator, Vinagame, rich—a similar experience to Shanda's in China. Kingsoft also licensed its games to such places as Taiwan, Malaysia, Singapore, and Thailand.

Another Beijing-based company, Perfect World, has its games licensed to 13 countries and regions, including Japan, Korea, and Russian-speaking countries. It had US$27.3 million in overseas sales in 2008, up from US$9.7 million a year earlier. Some Chinese game developers have tried to tap the American and European market. Perfect World set up an American subsidiary to access potential in North America in 2008. Tencent bought the small American operator, Outspark, to test the water.

Fuzhou-based Net Dragon operates its own game in the American and European market. In 2003 it launched an English version of its game Conquer Online, a MMORPG set in a mythical China.[102] By 2007, there were over half a million overseas users playing three of NetDragon's games, in English, Spanish, French, Japanese, and Portuguese. It set up servers in America and its games are open to players all over the world—so far 35 percent have come from North America, 30 percent from Europe, and the rest from Africa, the Middle East, and Asia.

But game players in America and Europe are accustomed to playing PC and console games—which usually are more advanced, and have better graphics and smoother movement. Even the top online game World of Warcraft was small in comparison with hit PC and console games.

"Online games appeal to a different group of players. Console games are about people playing against machines, while online games are more about people playing with other people," said Liu Dejian, chairman of Net Dragon, "A lot of time, what you do in online games is make friends and chat with them, etc. It is just in the game, there is a common goal, for example, killing a monster together."

So far, the overseas market for Chinese games is still small. IDC estimated the total value of Chinese game exports to be US$55 million in 2007—12 companies exported a total of 28 games worldwide. In comparison, overseas sales of Korean online games reached US$200 million per year, based on some estimates.

The key obstacle to the popularity of Chinese games in the West was cultural, according to Liu of Net Dragon. Many games were based on Chinese myths and martial-art fiction, which foreign players might not understand or appreciate.

[102] The first game NetDragon launched overseas was an English version of Monster and Me in 2003, but it was not very successful. Conquer Online is the second game it launched overseas and is much more popular.

For mainstream Americans to appreciate online games, Liu of Net Dragon believed a game set in the background of Western culture might create a breakthrough. "What we need might be content such as Superman or Spiderman," said Liu, "If an ice-breaker can be found, sales from the Western market could easily reach five times the existing level."

Net Dragon is cooperating with Disney to develop an online game in China, Disney Fantasy Online, based on Disney's characters. It has also partnered with Electronic Arts to develop Dungeon Keeper Online, based on the famous EA Dungeon Keeper series. In addition, it is working with Time Warner's Cartoon Network to use some of its characters in games, something Liu hopes would help them to break into the American mainstream market one day. Net Dragon made US$21.6 million from overseas markets in 2008, 25 percent of its total revenue.

Gold farming

A by-product of the online game industry is the emergence of gold farmers. These are people who play online games for profit. Usually, they repeat mundane actions over and over in order to collect in-game currency and items, for example, killing an important monster repeatedly to maximize gains, sometimes by using an automatic program.

Gold farming started very early on. At some point in the late 1980s, in-game items (such as gold coins, gems, swords, or magic powder) began to be sold for money. Full commercialization of gold farming began in 1997 due to the launch of Ultima Online as the first true MMORPG, and the launch of eBay.

By 2001, entrepreneurs in America and Korea saw the opportunity to make more money from gold farming by hiring players working in low-cost locations, especially China. One brokerage in particular, IGE, was hugely successful, earning millions of dollars per month and dominating the market. Soon, lots of new brokerages, each with their own web portals and customer relationship teams, were set up, mainly taking advantage of cheap labor in developing countries.

But as gold farming activities expanded, regular players felt the results were unfair. Game companies, in particular Blizzard, started to take action against the gold farmers. They banned accounts and took legal action. eBay was persuaded to stop listing online game currency and items. Games were redesigned to make gold farming and trading much harder.

The size of the gray market is hard to estimate. Some researchers believed there were 400,000 gold farmers worldwide and the global trade was worth more than US$1 billion a year in late 2008.[103] A more daring estimate suggested there were more than a million gold farmers in China alone, with the trade worth over US$10 billion a year.[104] There are also reports of gold farming in developing countries including the Philippines, Indonesia, Mexico, and Vietnam.

Yuan of IDC said gold farmers were still a minority among Chinese game players, and accounted for only a few percentage points. There were more than 40 million game players in China in 2007 and the impact on games in China was limited. "Most of [the gold farmers] play games overseas, such as World of Warcraft in America, because they are able to earn more," said Yuan.

Moreover, as the majority of games in China switched to item-based models, there were far fewer opportunities left for gold farmers. Players could buy the gold coins and other game items they wanted directly from the official game operators. An entrepreneur who once ran a gold farming shop said he shut it down after free games became the trend. "It became very difficult for us to turn a profit. The game company is selling items directly to the players," he said.

Social impact

The social impact of online games in China cannot be underestimated. Many parents complain about their children's new addiction. The local press reported an incident where a child died after playing a game continuously for several days.

In response, the government ordered game operators to install anti-addiction systems in their games in mid 2007. Players under 18 will earn lower game scores after playing more than three hours a day, and no score at all if playing more than five hours. The policy had a minor impact on game companies in China as many game players are young adults. Determined children and teenagers were easily able to find their parent's ID documents and register under their names.

[103] Source: Richard Heeks, Current Analysis and Future Research Agenda on "Gold Farming": *Real-World Production in Developing Countries for the Virtual Economies of Online Games*, Development Informatics Group, Institute for Development Policy and Management, University of Manchester, 2008.

[104] Nick Ryan, "Gold Trading Exposed: The Sellers," *Eurogamer*, Mar 25, 2009.

Age	Percentage
Below 10	0.2
10–12	1.3
12–14	2.8
14–16	4.7
16–18	13.7
19–22	37.2
23–25	21.5
26–30	12.7
31–35	4.1
36–40	1.2
40–50	0.6
Above 50	0.1

***Table 9.3:* Age distribution of online game players in China (2007)**

Data source: IDC

There were also thefts and crimes involving online games, such as stealing a player's account and all its weapons.

Studies were conducted by local scholars seeking to determine whether virtual marriages in the games had any impact on a child's view about society. Players meet, date, marry, and divorce quickly in a game. It is not unusual for the first line of a male character to a female character (that could be played by a man in real life) to be, "Do you want to be my girlfriend?" Many game players go through several marriages a year. Dating multiple persons at the same time was also common for those enjoying the virtual romance.

Despite the negative impact online games might exert on society, the Chinese government on the whole supports the industry. "If they ban online games, what will all the kids and youth do with their spare time? If they are not at the internet cafés or their homes playing games, they might be on the streets drinking or picking a fight. There could be all sort of social problems—alcohol, drugs, prostitution, etc.," said an industry insider. "There are not many recreational facilities in China for poorer kids. Online games provide a low-cost entertainment for many."

Also, the industry was supporting a large workforce—over 21,000 in 2007. Many are technology developers, the kind the government likes to see more of in the country. It also supported many profitable domestic companies. In general, the Chinese government is biased toward local companies. It has given financial incentive to many local game companies to support their research and development.

Using censorship, the government has a rather tight rein on what games are allowed to be launched in China, and again, priority is given to locally developed games. It banned World of Warcraft for showing a skeleton after a character had been killed—deemed too bloody and unsuitable for the country's young minds.

Lessons learned

1 Study the bottom of the pyramid.

The success of online game companies in China proved that serving low-end internet users in China could be a very profitable business. Although this group, consisting of mainly students and young workers, cannot pay large amounts, their number is huge and they lack entertainment alternatives. Therefore as long as the price is low, they are willing to try many new services. Besides online games, mobile data services (e.g., ringtones) and online chat service QQ also benefit from serving this group.

Besides, the financial crisis has very little impact on those providing a low-cost entertainment alternative—as a student or an unemployed factory worker can still easily pay RMB50–100 a month. Tencent, operator of QQ, and the online games companies in China have been doing very well during the economic downturn that started in 2008.

2 Import to get up to speed quickly; export to grow the market.

The first online games in China were imported, licensed from foreign companies. But once the market was proven, Chinese companies started to develop their own. And when they became successful in the domestic market, they started to export.

This mirrored many other industries in China. The country used to depend on foreign telecoms equipment entirely. But gradually it developed its own telecom equipment manufacturers. Shenzhen-based Huawei Technologies started as a small distributor of imported PBX products. It later developed and marketed its own PBX. Huawei's products were first deployed only in small cities and rural areas. It eventually gained a market share and made its way into major cities. Other Huawei products probably had the same history for their adoption, against the competition of the then-dominant foreign telecom equipment manufacturers.

Today, Huawei is a key player in the world's telecom market, with more than 75 percent of its sales from overseas. British Telecom used it as a preferred supplier for its 21CN network. It targeted US$30 billion in overseas sales in 2009 and has become a threat to foreign players, such as Alcatel-Lucent, Nortel, Ericsson, and Cisco.

Chinese internet companies have yet to exert the same power in the world. Most of their businesses are predominantly domestic. But their potential should not be underestimated, especially in nearby regions, where the culture and internet development are similar to that in China.

10. The mobile internet revolution

As China's internet market grew, so its wireless data sector developed. More than 640 million people have cellphones in China, and the cellphone operators open their platforms for third parties to provide mobile data services such as ringtone downloads and games.

Before China's internet was large enough to attract advertisers, mobile data services formed a key part of revenue for such companies as Tencent, Sina, and Sohu. Besides the basics, many creative ideas have flourished—the most obvious example being the use of SMS (or short messaging services) voting to decide the winner of a nationwide singing contest, *Super Girl*. The television show was similar to *American Idol*. Young contestants (all girls) engaged in rounds of competition against each other; in each episode, two had to go. SMS votes from the television audience made the decision.

This competition (in 2005) drew the largest audiences in Chinese TV history. The winner received more than 3.5 million votes in the final contest. It was a huge success for the TV station that organized the show, and raked in massive rewards for the firm that ran the SMS voting platform—Linktone.

The 640 million user question

Apart from having the largest internet market in the world, China also has the biggest cellphone market. By the end of 2008, its cellphone user tally had reached more than 640 million.[105] The salient question was how to access and monetize that 640 million-strong network. The sector is highly regulated and run by government-owned cellphone operators. China Mobile and its smaller rival China Unicom had the exclusive right to provide cellphone services to the country's 1.3 billion people.[106]

[105] As of the end of 2008, there were 641.23 million cellphone subscribers in China, according to China's Ministry of Industry and Information Technology.

[106] In 2009, the government restructured its telecoms sector and a new player, China Telecom, which is also government owned, became the country's third cellphone operator.

Mobile data services such as SMS have been available in China since 1992, but until third-party companies became involved, the services were limited to simple messages sent between cellphone users, as an alternative form of communication. In 2000, the cellphone operators hoped to provide some extra data services to their customers. But the questions were, what to provide and how?

"The cellphone operators did not know what to do with [mobile data] services. So they let third-party companies design new services and provide them to their customers," said J.P. Gan, managing director of Qiming Venture Partners, a venture capital firm active in China. Gan was also a former chief financial officer of the leading third-party mobile data service provider, Kongzhong.

The evolution of the market for cellphone services in China followed the industry development experienced in Japan and Korea, where cellphone operators have provided platforms for third-party service providers to offer mobile data services to their customers. China Mobile launched its Monternet platform for mobile data services in November 2000 and China Unicom launched its Uni-Info platform in May 2001, using a business model similar to the model used in Japan and Korea.

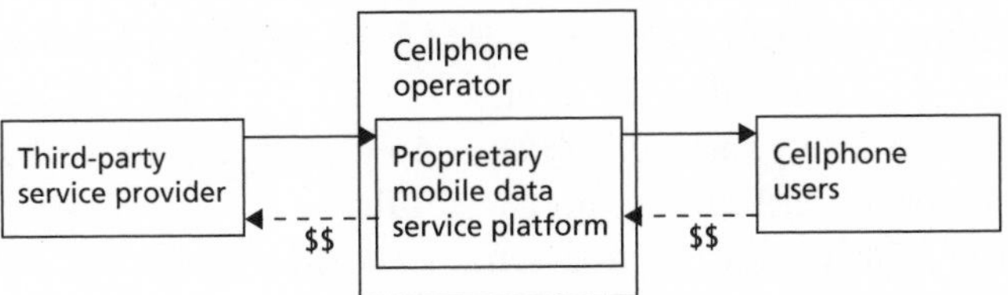

***Figure 10.1:* Business model of mobile data services in China**

The earliest third-party service providers were companies providing technology solutions to the cellphone operators. For example, Kongzhong was a company specializing in Wireless Application Protocol (WAP) technology. It helped China Mobile to develop its WAP platform. When China Mobile wanted to introduce mobile data services, Kongzhong became one of its first partners.

Similarly, Hurray was a spin-off from UT Starcom, a NASDAQ-listed company that manufactures telecommunications equipment in China. UT Starcom helped to build China Unicom's WAP technology platform and its subsidiary Hurray became a close partner for China Unicom's mobile data services.

Linktone can trace its roots to Intrinsic Technology, a wireless data software developer in China. It worked closely with China Mobile in formulating its wireless data services business strategy, which ultimately culminated in the launch of the operator's Monternet platform.[107] They designed some simple services, such as ringtone downloads, icon and screensaver downloads, Chinese and Western horoscopes, jokes, news, fan clubs, mobile games, and so on. Charges were taken monthly or per-use. China Mobile and China Unicom would collect the fees in their telephone bills and pay the service providers their share at the end of each month.

Initially, both cellphone operators encouraged the development of third-party service providers. The terms were very attractive. China Mobile gave 85 percent of total revenue from the mobile data services to their providers. China Unicom gave a similar proportion, but the actual amount was based on the volume of services.

Besides payment collection and service distribution, the operators also help the third-party companies to promote their services, for example, allowing them to send bulk SMS messages to their users.

Despite being simple, mobile data services attracted many young people looking for fun and hoping to make their cellphones special. Moreover, the charges were low—RMB1–2 (US$0.12–0.24) for a screensaver or ringtone download and RMB6–20 (US$0.72–2.42) for a WAP-based monthly service.[108] They could easily afford it.[109] It was a kind of low-cost entertainment for the youth.

The initial trials were very successful. Providing mobile data services became a hugely profitable business almost overnight. Entrepreneurs

[107] From Linktone IPO prospectus: "As one of the original participants in the wireless value-added services market, we have developed well-established relationships with China Mobile and China Unicom. In particular, we worked closely with China Mobile in formulating its wireless value-added services business strategy that ultimately culminated in the launch of its Monternet™ platform."

[108] From Linktone IPO prospectus: "As described in '—Critical Accounting Policies—Revenue and Cost of Services Recognition,' we generate revenues primarily from service fees paid by mobile phone users who use our services through China Mobile and China Unicom. Our wireless value-added services fees are charged on a monthly subscription or per use basis. Fees for our SMS-based services currently range from RMB0.1 ($0.01) to RMB2.0 ($0.24) per message and from RMB3.0 ($0.36) to RMB10.0 ($1.21) for subscription service. Fees for MMS, WAP and JAVA services currently range from RMB2.0 ($0.24) to RMB5.0 ($0.60) per message and from RMB6.0 ($0.72) to RMB20.0 ($2.42) per month for subscription service. Fees for audio-related services range from RMB1.0 ($0.01) to RMB5.0 ($0.60) per audio content download."

[109] Average spending on basic mobile services was RMB115 (U$14) per month in 2002, according to China Mobile's annual report.

spotting the opportunities rushed in. The two cellphone operators did not put up any entry barriers, essentially granting anyone a license to be a third-party provider to their mobile data platforms. These third-party companies were also called wireless value-added services providers, as they provided extra services on top of the cellphone operators' platforms.

In 2002, about one year after launching Monternet, 57 million people—or half of China Mobile's 117 million users—subscribed to some form of mobile data services, twice the number that had done so a year earlier.[110]

The mobile boom

The booming mobile data sector did not go unnoticed by early internet players.

China's internet sector was hit badly as the dot.com bubble burst in the early 2000s. Instead of the high growth that early startups had hoped for, online advertising was shrinking. All the leading portals—Sina, Sohu, and Netease—were making losses. Internet companies mastered the know-how of mobile data services quickly and started to branch into the new business, as this could be their only chance to become profitable.

Netease was the first of the major portals to offer mobile data services. By the end of 2002, sales of mobile services reached US$18.5 million or 70 percent of Netease's revenue. That year, it made a profit of US$16.3 million, turning around from a loss of US$28.2 million a year earlier. Soon Sina and Sohu followed. Sina entered the market in a big way by acquiring one of the top mobile data service providers, MeMeStar, in January 2003.

Tencent, which operated the dominant online chat platform QQ, also started its mobile services division. Beyond the basics, its key service is to provide PC-to-cellphone instant chat, so that QQ user's on the move could stay in contact with their friends online. Tencent also

110 From China Mobile Annual Report 2002: "As at the end of 2002, the Group's subscriber base reached 117.676 million, representing an increase of 29.9 percent from 2001. The aggregate subscriber usage volume reached 260.09 billion minutes, representing an increase of 24.6 percent. from 2001. The number of mobile data services users reached 57.733 million, representing an increase of 114.3 percent from 2001. SMS usage volume reached 40.41 billion messages, representing a 4.6-fold increase from 2001, and revenue from new businesses increased by 143.4 percent from 2001."

used the cellphone platform as a way for users to buy its virtual currency Q coins and pay premium service fees. Collecting a tiny amount (RMB5–10 or US$0.72–1.44) from hundreds and thousands of users could have been painful and tedious work. Now, China Mobile and China Unicom can do this for Tencent through their payment channels and hand over a lump sum at the end of each month.

Tom Online,[111] an early internet player in China, also embraced the change. It was founded in October 1999 as a joint venture between Hong Kong Tycoon Li Kai-shing's Hutchison Whampoa and Cheung Kong Holdings, and was distinguished by its controversial purchase of the Tom.com name for US$3 million, the largest sum yet paid by a Chinese company for an internet domain. Tom.com's attraction was the shortness of the name, and the domain was initially set up as an online portal. In 2003 Tom acquired Beijing Lei Ting Wu Ji Network Technology, a firm specializing in wireless interactive voice response (IVR)—a service that lets cellphone users call a number to listen to prerecorded messages, such as weather information, stock prices, astrology, jokes, songs, short stories, and various entertainment topics. After acquiring Lei Ting Wu Ji, Tom widened the focus to include other mobile data services, such as ringtone downloads. Tom Online was once the country's largest mobile data service provider.

Players in the mobile data sector were not limited to those with an internet background. Some independent players also became very successful. Apart from the three mentioned earlier (Kongzhong, Hurray, and Linktone), A8, which focuses on music, was also very successful. "Initially, the cellphone operators let us try any kind of new business and helped us to promote our services in any way we liked," said Alvin Liu, founder and CEO of A8.

The years 2001 to 2004 marked the golden era of China's mobile data services. The sector was growing fast and each company enjoyed high growth and healthy profitability. During the peak, there were nearly 2,000 third-party providers for mobile data services, of which about 300 had national coverage, according to industry expert Jin Hui. (The rest had operations in one or several provinces.)

Kongzhong's revenue grew from nothing when it started in May 2002 to US$48.0 million in 2004, with a profit of US$20.4 million. It

[111] Tom belonged to Hutchison Whampoa Limited, a conglomerate owned by Hong Kong Tycoon Li Ka-shing. Rumours in Hong Kong suggested that Tom's founder Solina Chau was Li's girlfriend. Hutchison's businesses ranged from telecom operators to container ports and supermarkets.

was listed on NASDAQ in July 2004, only two years after it was founded. Linktone and Hurray enjoyed similar growth and profitability. They were also listed on NASDAQ in 2004–05.

Super Girl 2005

Besides the basic services, many other creative ideas have flourished—the most obvious example being *Super Girl*.

The nationwide singing contest was open to all girls in the country. There were mini contests in each province, and the best performers would be selected to enter the next phase—the television show, which was broadcast every week to a national audience.

The contest in 2005 was the second *Super Girl* that the show's organizer—Hunan Satellite TV station—had arranged. "The first contest in 2004 was not very successful. But by the second one, the singing contest had a new sponsor, Mengniu," said a Linktone executive.

China Mengniu Dairy Company was one of the leading dairy product manufacturers in China. It was promoting a new Yogurt-based drink targeted at teenagers, and the project's marketing manager Sun Jun thought *Super Girl* would be an ideal channel to promote the drink. The show targeted the same age group (14–18 years old) and had a fresh and fun image, the kind Mengniu wanted to associate with its new drink.

With the marketing budget for the Yogurt drink, Mengniu launched a massive TV advertising campaign promoting the beverage alongside the singing contest. It hired one of the runner-ups of *Super Girl 2004* as the star of the commercial and spokesperson for the drink.

"A lot of new elements were added once Mengniu was involved in the project," said the Linktone executive. "The television crew showed the behind-the-scenes stories of the girls—their friends and families, their growing-up stories, the friendships among them, etc." These elements are common to all reality shows in the West. But, it gave the Chinese audience a new perspective on singing competitions. The weekly drama (the tears, the thanks, and more tears) ensured many people gathered around their TV screens every week, eager to see which girls would stay for the next round and who would be eliminated.

To increase audience involvement with the competition, Mengniu and Hunan Satellite TV station decided they would let the television audience make the final decision. Which contestants were staying or leaving was decided by the television audience voting by SMS. Linktone was chosen to provide the SMS voting platform for the show. It also provided music downloads, ringtones, and news alerts for the contest.

Little did the organizers know that some of the contestants had gradually built a loyal group of fans among the audience since the contest began in March 2005. The fans' support for their idols could be very passionate.

"These are the contestants' friends and family, and their fans," said the Linktone executive. The fan groups went onto the streets—asking passers-by to vote for the contestants they supported or to donate money for casting votes for them. Every cellphone number could only cast 20 votes each time. So the fans would ask people if they could borrow their cellphones and vote for the contestant they supported, said the executive. They also raised money to buy new cellphone cards to cast votes. A rumor circulated that some of the rich fans of the contestants would spend hundreds of thousands of RMB on cellphone cards and use dedicated equipment to send SMS votes in massive numbers, so as to support their idols.

More than two million votes were being cast in each episode by the time the competition had reached the last ten contestants. In the final round, seven to eight million votes were cast—a stunning result that was beyond everyone's expectations. The winner, Li Yuchun, a girl from Sichuan, received more than 3.5 million votes. The first runner-up had in excess of 3.2 million and the second had more than 1.3 million.

"SMS voting alone brought RMB30 million (US$3.67 million) to the television station, even more than the advertising revenue of the show." Advertising revenue for the show totaled RMB20 million (US$2.44 million); Mengmiu sponsored another RMB14 million (US$1.71 million).

Linktone's revenue went up 54 percent to US$20.5 million in the third quarter of 2005 compared to a year earlier, partly because it shared about 25 percent of the SMS voting income from the *Super Girl* contest. Soon many television programs in China had the SMS voting element, as a way of increasing audience involvement and revenue. The following year, the government-backed China Central Television (CCTV) also launched a similar singing competition, with SMS voting for its audience.

"The television audience in China has never had the chance to influence the result of a TV show. They were excited," said the Linktone executive.

Success was short-lived. "The government banned SMS voting after the third *Super Girl* contest. The media criticized that the youth was blindly worshiping their idols. Parents were complaining their children spent too much money on SMS voting for their idols," said the executive. Instead, judges and the audience at the live show would decide the fate of contestants.

Meanwhile, after its tremendous success in 2005, the popularity of *Super Girl* faded away. Besides competition from other singing contests, such as the one organized by CCTV, the novelty of reality shows had worn off. Some industry insiders suspected the unique mix of contestants of *Super Girl 2005* was the real drive for its incredible success.

"The four girls who won the contest have unique personalities and really stood out in the 2005 contest. Li Yuchun has a cool boyish look—very different from the traditional beautiful Chinese women, which is typified by another contestant, Jane Zhang. Contestant He Jie is a modern girl with lots of energy. Zhou Bichang, on the other hand, is boyish like Li, but cute," said a music program producer, "they appealed to different groups of fans." The four took the first four places in the 2005 Super Girl contest. "In the following years, the contestants were less impressive and created less controversy among them," said the producer.

Light as a song

While SMS voting for TV shows only lasted one or two seasons, another creation made a more permanent mark on China's music industry—internet songs. The piracy problem in China made it difficult for singers to sell CDs of their songs. Selling through the internet, as Apple did with its iTunes store, did not work in China either, as the online world was full of pirated MP3 files, free for download by anyone who was interested.

The internet was a powerful tool, however, if a musician or singer was seeking fame rather than profit. In 2004, 26-year-old Chinese singer Yang Chengang posted "Mice Love Rice," a song he had composed a few years earlier, online for people to freely download. Yang was a nobody at the time, but people were attracted by the song's catchy lyrics and tone. The love song grew popular quickly over the internet, partly due to Baidu's MP3 search engine, which helped spread music files around. Students downloaded it and listened to it in their dorms. Teenagers listened to it in the internet cafes.

By November 2004, the song had been downloaded 200,000 times a day in Baidu's MP3 search engine.[112] Yang became an instant celebrity. A record company tracked him down and signed him up as a contract singer, paying a handsome fee. But the next question was how to make money from a song which was already freely available on the internet. The answer was as a cellphone ringtone. As a song became popular, people wanted to download it as a ringtone for their cellphones, or set it as their ring-back tone. The record company signed deals with mobile data service providers, which in turn provided the ringtone and ring-back tone of "Mice Love Rice" to users of both China Mobile and China Unicom.

During its peak, the song recorded more than five million ringtone downloads in a month, whereas a bestselling CD in China usually sells no more than one million copies, according to a report by Wallace Cheung, research analyst of Credit Suisse.

After Yang's success, other composers and singers also tried the same thing—using the internet to promote their songs and then profiting through ringtone downloads. Soon, more internet songs and internet singers became popular. Internet songs became a new music source for the mobile data service providers, complementary to those offered by the leading record companies, such as Warner Music, Sony BMG, Universal Music, and EMI.

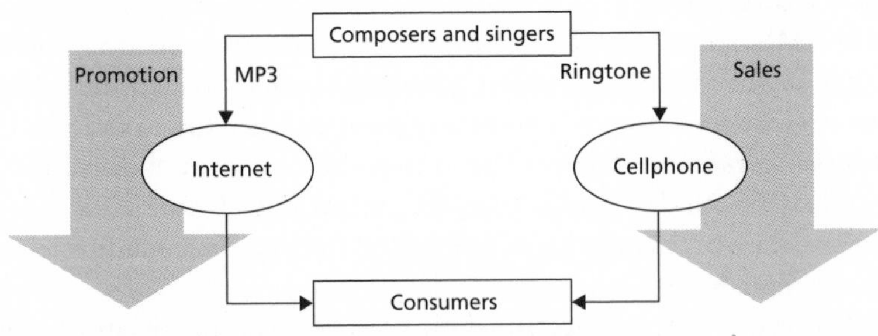

Figure 10.2: **Business model of internet music**

Note: Composers and singers distribute songs over the internet free of charge, and earn their money through ringtone downloads.

By early 2009, internet songs accounted for about half the ringtones downloaded in China, said a former Sina executive from its wireless

[112] Source: "Story Behind The Mouse Loves The Rice Song," blog, Aug 22, 2005.

division. "Many of the pop songs from top singers, such as Jay Chou, are not suitable for making ringtones, as their music is too fancy. In contrast, many internet songs have simple catchy tunes—easy to convert to a ringtone and the general public in China like them," said the executive.

Moreover, most internet singers are willing to take a lower royalty fee than the major record companies. Therefore, mobile data service providers prefer to promote ringtones made from internet songs.

Some companies took the internet song phenomenon to the next stage by building their business around it. Founded in 2000, A8 started to focus on music alone from 2004. It was one of the largest providers of mobile music services.

A8—the "electronic music" company

"In 2004, we transformed ourselves [from a general mobile data service provider] into an 'electronic music' company," said Liu, CEO of A8. The company started a dedicated website to collect songs from young composers and singers. The songs are listed in a billboard on the site for people to download and comment on. "If it was popular and if we thought it had potential, we would sign up the singer/composer through our record label subsidiary," said Liu.

A8 would then access the full potential of the song and promote it to the appropriate market segment via different channels. "Some songs are more suitable for students, while others are more suitable for factory workers," said Liu. "In this stage, we use more than just the internet for promotion. All kinds of mass media are used—radio, TV, newspapers, and magazines."

In 2005, Liu paid about US$2,400 for the copyright of one song he had received via the A8.com website. He then spent US$190,000 promoting the song. It eventually recorded 20 million cellphone downloads that year. By 2008, four years after A8 changed direction, songs sourced from its music website accounted for close to 40 percent of all its cellphone music revenue.

On average, A8 can license and promote several hundred songs sourced from its website, many more than a typical, medium-sized record company, which can only promote 10–20 songs a year. Additionally, considering that the public had already listened to a song and provided their feedback through the internet, A8 could better assess the potential of the song before paying for its copyright and allocating a budget for promotion. "A traditional record company can only make its bet blindly and sign up a singer before the song is launched into the market," said Mr Liu.

Trouble in mind

As the mobile data sector boomed and more and more players entered the market, competition grew keen. Marketing and content costs ate into the profit margins of mobile data service providers. Most of them saw their profit margins decline after 2004.

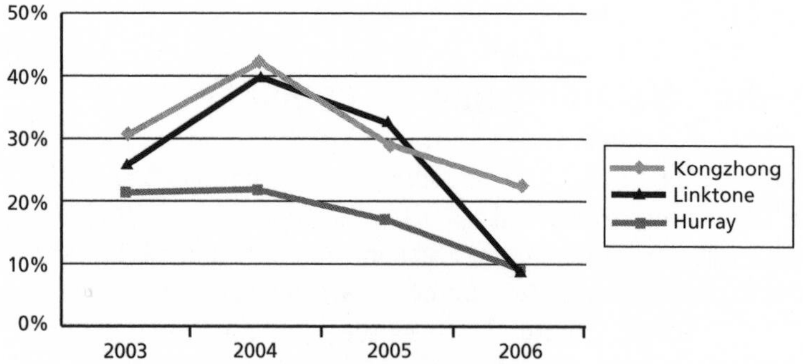

Figure 10.3: **Net profit margin of third-party mobile data service**

Data source: individual companies

To boost profits, some companies started to exploit loopholes in cellphone operators' platforms. They would make their services very difficult for users to cancel, or charge users even if they did not want the services. Other sharp practices included not paying copyright to the music companies, or paying less than they should.

Bribery was not unusual in the sector. "In order to build good relations with local staff of cellphone operators, many of the players would send expensive gifts or cash to them," said a former Sina executive from its wireless division. "This is one of the dirtiest sectors among China's technology industries," bemoaned one venture capitalist who had invested in a few mobile data service providers. "Many dirty tricks are employed to increase user numbers and enlarge sales." Adding insult to injury, cellphone operators were no longer as generous as they had been.

"Initially, it was just three companies, including us. The cellphone operators let us try any new businesses and help us to promote our services in any way we liked," said Liu of A8, "Now, for every kind of business, we have to convince the operator why it should choose us, but not the other hundred more players."

As mobile data services became a huge business worth tens of billion of US dollars a year, the cellphone operators changed their attitude toward third-party data service providers—the operators were no longer welcoming new business. In fact, since 2004, they have gradually tightened control over the services offered by third-party providers. They have started their own competing services and gradually reduced the share revenue paid to the third parties.

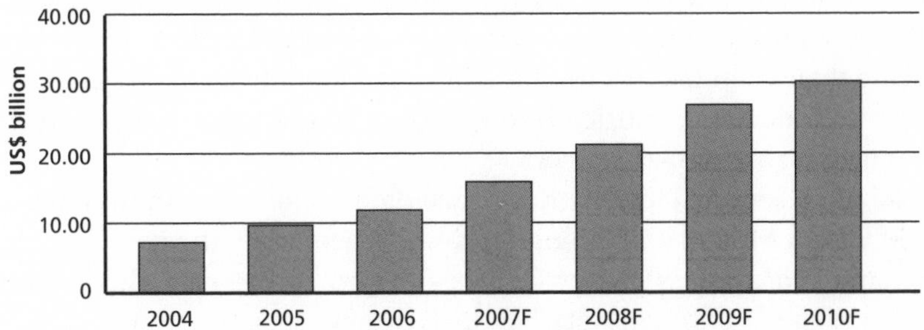

Figure 10.4: **Market size of third-party mobile data services (2004–10F)**

Data source: iResearch

For example, China Mobile and China Unicom started to limit the third-party service providers' facility to send bulk SMS messages (often regarded as spam) to users in order to promote their services.

To control the rampant sexual content in some mobile data services, the operators punished many third-party providers for crossing decency lines during 2003–04. Such punishments included censoring content, delays in fee payments, fining the third-party providers, and suspending their services on the cellphone operators' networks.

In 2006, China Unicom reduced the share of revenue it paid to third-party providers in certain provinces from 70 percent to 60 percent.[113] They also started to raise the licensing requirement for

113 From Hurray 2007 annual report: "In 2006, China Unicom entered into new contracts in certain provinces with service providers in which it changed the share percentages it retained for customer payments. For example, where prior to 2006, service providers would receive 70 percent of a payment from a customer purchase and China Unicom would retain 30 percent, China Unicom changed the share percentage of customer payments that service providers may retain to 40 percent in 2006."

third-party service providers—many small players were squeezed out. By 2009, the total number of third-party service providers was reduced to about 1,000 from close to 2,000 during the peak era in 2004. Those with national coverage were down to about 100 from 300 in 2004, according to industry expert Jin Hui.

China Mobile started to contact major record companies directly and offer its own ringtone business. In July 2006, it launched a music download service called M.Music, partnering with Universal Music Group, Sony BMG, EMI, and Warner Music. Music was the largest driver for mobile data services, as young people regularly downloaded different songs as ringtones for their phones. They also continually set different music as their ring-back tone—the sound callers hear when ringing their cellphones. The company got a lot of business from third-party providers, as music accounted for more than half of their revenue, said an industry expert.

The most serious blow to the mobile data sector came in mid 2006, when China Mobile and China Unicom, urged on by the government, implemented a series of new policies to protect users' rights—a list known as the "11 golden rules" in the industry.

The new policy made double confirmation a requirement for users subscribing to any new mobile data services. It also automatically canceled services that had been inactive for a long time. New billing reminders are needed for monthly subscribers. And positive user confirmations are needed for conversion of per-message subscriptions to monthly subscriptions.

"The new policies made user acquisition and retention difficult," said Wang Leilei, who was then Tom Online's chief executive.

	2003	2004	2005	2006	2007	2008
Kongzhong						
–Revenue	7.8	47.96	77.8	106.8	74	96.7
–Profit	2.4	20.40	22.2	24.7	0.33	-20.66
Linktone						
–Revenue	16.6	50.30	73.6	79.8	49.7	67
–Profit	3.6	11.10	12.4	6.8	–16.4	–16.5
Hurray						
–Revenue	17.8	43.20	56.1	68.7	60.5	54
–Profit	4.5	17.20	18.6	5.8	–42	–12

Table 10.1: **Revenue and profit of third-party cellphone service providers (in US$ million)**

Data source: individual companies

"Since China Mobile opened its Monternet platform to third parties, the [mobile data] sector has flourished. The high margin attracted many players," said a venture capital investor, "but soon China Mobile learned they could operate some of the services themselves, for example, ringtones. They started to be harsh on the third parties. Now, many of them are making losses."

The third generation

By 2009, China had started to roll out its long-anticipated 3G services. "I have heard the operators talking about 3G for the last 10 years," said Gan of Qiming. The country had also restructured its telecoms sector by introducing one more player, China Telecom. It acquired China Unicom's CDMA network and would develop the new 3G network based on CDMA-2000.

China Unicom kept its GSM network and would develop a network using WCDMA, the most widely used 3G standard. The dominant China Mobile, which has a GSM network at the moment, would develop its 3G network based on the homegrown TD-SCDMA technology.

To many mobile data services providers, this could mean new opportunities. Kongzhong anticipated that mobile data services run on 3G could be big starting in 2011, and it started developing new applications. "In the 2G era, the most successful [mobile data] services are entertainment related. We expected the same trend would continue in the 3G era," said Jay Chang, chief financial officer of Kongzhong. It was developing MMORPG-like mobile games. "Our recent game Tian Jie Online recorded US$700,000 in revenue per quarter," said Mr Chang in early 2009. Kongzhong was also working on mobile community services, similar to YouTube, on the cellphone.

Many industry experts thought the 3G era would mean explosive growth of mobile internet, as the higher bandwidth made surfing the web with cellphones easier. Some internet players are developing specific services for cellphone users. For example, Google has been developing its mobile search since 2007; mobile map was also a key focus of its development. Google is the mobile search partner for China Mobile. However, Chang of Kongzhong thought the mobile internet world might not be as big as many people had anticipated.

"At first, as costs of the phone and the monthly fees are high, most people using 3G services would be high-end users. They would use their cellphones to access the internet. But as time goes by, and prices of phones and monthly fees decline, 3G would be affordable to mainstream cellphone users. They are much younger and less affluent than regular internet users. Surfing the internet might not be their main focus," said Chang. He anticipated an initial convergence of the cellphone and internet worlds and a divergence of the two in the longer run.

Waves of innovation

The most important question for entrepreneurs and investors is whether 3G is going to be another boom–bust cycle for mobile data services. The answer is yes, and no. "As the cellphone operators don't know what sort of 3G data services would be popular, they will probably give third-party service providers a free hand initially," said a venture capital investor.

This could lead to another boom in the mobile data sector, as new players enter the market and new 3G services flourish. But, as soon as the cellphone operators understand the business, they might tighten their control again and start running their own competing services, just as in the 2G era, according to the venture capitalist. "In that case, it would be another blow to the sector," he added.

But, having said that, the venture capital investor was not certain whether cellphone operators could be as dominating as before—controlling the life and death of third-party mobile data services providers. "In the 3G era, the cellphone and internet worlds will merge. And no one controls the internet, not even the cellphone operators." Rather than relying on cellphone operators' proprietary platforms, mobile data services providers can also access cellphone users through an alternative means—the internet. "People are accessing WAP sites with their phones in the 2.5G environment," noted one industry expert, Jin Hui.

WAP sites are websites written specifically for use on cellphones. "Many WAP sites offer free downloads of ringtones, pictures, and so on. Users do not necessarily use the paid services offered in China Mobile's proprietary Monternet platform," said Jin. Kongzhong's WAP site, Kong.net, had 1.5 to two million visitors per day in early 2009. It was the third or fourth most popular WAP site in China. The most popular one is online chat giant Tencent's 3G.QQ.com. The other popular ones include 3G.net and Sina's WAP site.

CNNIC said that of the more than 640 million cellphone users in China by the end of 2008, about 117.6 million users have used cellphone devices to access the internet in the past six months—more than double the number of a year earlier. The report said that about 34 percent of China's mobile internet users were active users, accessing the internet with their cellphones every day.

With the higher bandwidth of 3G, WAP sites and other forms of mobile internet could become more even more popular. But, how to profit from mobile internet remains uncertain. Mobile advertising could be an income source, but it was still in its infancy in early 2009, and might take more than five years to develop into something big—just as with online advertising when the internet started to grow in China in the early 2000s.

If they are offering paid services through the internet, the service providers have to solve the payment collection problem. (They cannot charge their users through their telephone bills, as cellphone operators are not involved.) Although online payment was becoming popular in China, it was still at an early stage. The most popular service, Alipay, said it had more than 150 million users in early 2009, but that was only 23 percent of China's cellphone users.

Some industry insiders were not too worried about the payment issue. Prepaid cards distributed through retail outlets, like those offered by online game companies, could be another means for payment collection, suggested Liu of A8.

Lessons learned

1 Don't think about actually selling digital content on the internet in China; instead, use the internet to *promote* what you want to sell.

With rampant piracy, selling a song over the internet, as Apple does with its iTunes store, is almost impossible in China. But using the internet for promotion of a song worked like a charm, as the internet song phenomenon showed. Before "Mice Love Rice," composer and singer Yang Chengang was a poor musician that no one had heard of. But after he simply gave up his copyright and let people freely download the song over the internet, the tune became extremely popular.

The most amusing part of the story is that Baidu's MP3 search engine, which was hated by many record companies as it spread piracy, became a powerful tool for Yang to promote his song. In a few months, every youth in the country had heard of the song. This kind of publicity would cost Yang millions of dollars if he had promoted his song in the traditional way—through advertising and media events. Ultimately, the way to profit from the song was through cellphones—ringtone downloads and ring-back tones—where piracy was much less a problem.

The same model should work in other parts of the world where piracy is rampant—*instead of fighting piracy over the internet, simply use the internet as a channel for free promotion and profit via other means, for example, cellphone ringtones and ring-back tones, live concerts, etc.*

In fact, the online game sector works in a similar way. The games software is free to download over the internet—free digital content. Users only pay if they want to play with thousands of other users—paying for service.

2 Caution! Government policies and market conditions are subject to change.

The boom and bust cycle of the mobile data sector was mainly driven by the changing policies of cellphone operators. Initially, they wanted to encourage third-party participation and terms were very generous. A whole generation of new companies flourished. But, starting 2004, the cellphone operators wanted to tighten control and took part of the mobile data business in-house. (To be fair, some of the cellphone operators' control measures were necessary, as the abuse of users' rights was common.)

This led the sector to collapse. The fate of third-party mobile data service providers changed overnight. Many have been running at a loss since mid 2006.

Although China is becoming more and more open in its economic system, many businesses in China still depend on government policies to a large extent. *Investors should beware of businesses that are booming only because of favorable government policies or market conditions, because such policies or conditions might change in a few years, leaving the businesses nursing losses.*

3 Think different! Make your products unique for the Chinese market.

A key reason for third-party companies' vulnerability to cellphone operators' changing policies was that product differentiation among the various players was low. Everyone was doing the same thing, and keen competition drove up costs and pushed down profit margins. In addition, cellphone operators soon found out they could run some of the services themselves, for example, by providing ringtone downloads.

Realizing the problem, A8 has chosen to specialize in music since 2004 and developed a music website to source its own songs—effectively becoming a music company. Another exception was Tencent. "Its QQ online chat platform is a power tool for marketing its mobile data services," said industry expert Jin. Moreover, many of the mobile data services it provided were related specifically to QQ, for example, mobile chat, payment of premium QQ services, buying virtual currency Q coins, etc.

A8 and Tencent were some of the very few companies that could maintain revenue growth in their mobile data services after cellphone operators implemented user protection policies in mid 2006.

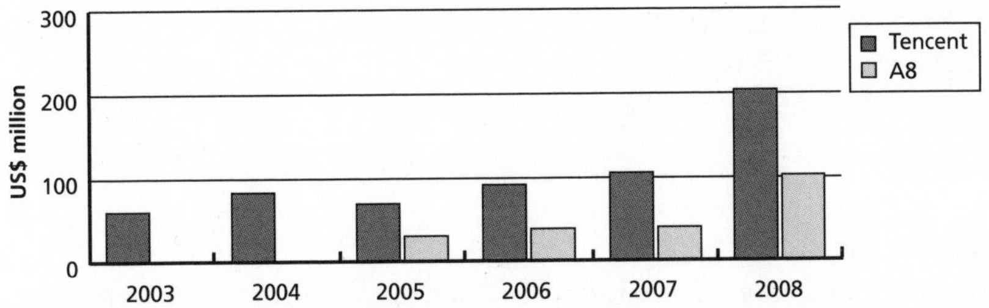

***Figure 10.5:* Tencent's and A8's mobile data services revenue**

Data source: Tencent (2003–08), A8 (2005–08)

"Service providers who have unique resources can still survive, but those without anything special can be easily squeezed out," said Jin.

Competition in China is keen for products or services that trade in a commodity-like fashion—if there is no unique edge, it is hard to maintain high profitability for the long run.

11. Youku: Waltzing with the State

When Victor Koo built Youku, his version of YouTube, he decided to focus not on homemade videos, but on professional content such as TV shows and movies.

He was able to do so because the TV and film industry in China is highly fragmented. With close to 300 TV stations and over 1,000 production houses, finding partners is not difficult. Because most of Youku's content was from the mainstream media, advertisers were reassured. Brand advertising accounts for most of Youku's revenue, whereas most of American-based YouTube's ads come via Google's AdSense network.

Chinese entrepreneurs also made their own tweaks to social networking sites. Xiaonei and 51.com, the Chinese answers to Facebook and MySpace respectively, realized that merging social networking sites with online games could be a formula for success.

Web 2.0

In 2005, O'Reilly MediaLive VP Dale Dougherty coined the term "Web 2.0." Applications that emerged from the new trend generate content that is actively distributed, managed and analyzed. Its most compelling applications to date have focused on creating dynamic social networks like Facebook and Wikipedia.

Dougherty's concept was that "Web 2.0 = social networking + management of user created social content." Social networking is a way of embracing the collective tribal power of social groups—whatever their origin—to create new content. Management and consolidation—called a "mashup" in Web 2.0 parlance—of the content can create automatic updates that keep users coming back to the site. Dougherty cites DoubleClick, created in 1998 and now owned by Google, as the prototypical Web 2.0 "mashup" service. DoubleClick served up banner ads seamlessly constructed from multiple websites.

Beyond this, Web 2.0's definition has always remained a bit amorphous on the World Wide Web.[114] Most of its core technologies were already available. Rather the term referred to cumulative changes in the ways that end-users utilized the Web—to support dialogs, not monologs; to pull people together socially; to start conversations. The internet was no longer just a one-way channel for broadcasting information, following the concept of the original online portals. It became a two-way medium that let people express their own ideas through text, pictures, and videos, while getting feedback from others.

One of the earliest Web 2.0 applications was the "blog," (the word is a prosodic truncation of Weblog) which allows people to publish their writing online. The popular service Blogger was created by San Francisco-based Pyra Labs in 1999 and bought by Google in 2003. Many people use it to write about their daily lives and express their opinions. Others use it to facilitate discussion on matters ranging from politics and technology development, to who won the poker game last night. People are curious by nature and they love to peek into other people's lives. Getting feedback from friends and strangers on your newest work is exciting, too, so much so that it gives you the appetite for more.

The Flickr blog focuses on sharing photos. It was developed by Ludicorp, a Vancouver-based company, and launched in February 2004. It has a loyal army of followers among photography buffs.

As network capacity increased and bandwidth limitations eased, video sharing became popular. YouTube was founded in early 2005 by three former employees of PayPal, Chad Hurley, Steve Chen, and Jawed Karim. They received a US$11.5 million investment from Sequoia Capital to set up the operation. The first YouTube video was uploaded on April 23, 2005. (Entitled "Me at the Zoo," it shows Karim at the San Diego Zoo. It can still be viewed on the site.)

The service quickly became a hit with youngsters who wanted to share movie and TV clips, and music videos, as well as their own short amateur videos. Google bought YouTube for US$1.65 billion in November 2006, before it even turned profitable.

Besides content sharing, the new Web 2.0 applications also allow users to simply keep in touch. Facebook is a social networking website started by Mark Zuckerberg, Dustin Moskovitz, and Chris Hughes in

[114] The term was first used by Dale Dougherty and Craig Cline, and became notable after the O'Reilly Media Web 2.0 conference in 2004.

October 2003, when they were students at Harvard University. Initially limited to Harvard students, membership was quickly expanded to other colleges in the Boston area, the Ivy League, and Stanford University. Now it can be used by anyone aged 13 or over, whether they are students or not.

Facebook users can join networks organized by city, workplace, school, and region to connect and interact. People can also add friends and send them messages, and update their personal profiles to notify friends about themselves. The website had more than 200 million active users worldwide as of January 2009.[115]

MySpace, started by Los Angeles-based internet marketing company Intermix in August 2003, is a similar social networking site. Many musicians, both the famous and the unknown, have used it to promote their songs and themselves. It was sold to Rupert Murdoch's News Corporation for US$580 million in July 2005.

As popular as Web 2.0 applications have become, especially among 20- and 30-somethings, Web 2.0 business models have yet to prove themselves. Revenue comes from advertising, but for bandwidth-intensive applications such as video sharing, it is doubtful whether advertising income is enough to cover the cost of bandwidth and servers. Moreover, advertisers are not sure how to use the new channels. Unlike the professional content of the traditional media, the response to user-generated content, with its broad range of topics and variable quality, is hard to predict. "Will my ad show next to something embarrassing?"—this is the kind of question advertisers constantly ask themselves. The advertising on YouTube and MySpace mostly comes from Google's AdSense network. Brand advertisements from major corporations are still relatively few on the Web 2.0 sites.

This means lower rates for ads. For example, Facebook had 200 million users and the company was predicted to generate US$500 million in ad sales in 2009. In comparison, the *New York Times'* digital arm, which includes NYTimes.com, Boston.com, and About.com, had just 50.8 million unique visitors each month, but raked in US$352 million in revenues in 2008.[116]

The case is different in China. When Victor Koo founded Youku, he chose to focus on professional content, such as TV programs and movies, instead of user-generated content. Advertisers, therefore, had

[115] Source: http://www.facebook.com/press/info.php?statistics
[116] Source: Evan Hessel, "Making Facebook Pay", *Forbes.com*, Jul 6, 2009.

no qualms about using the Youku platform. Brand advertising has always been its main source of revenue.

Chinese entrepreneurs additionally modified the social networking formula. Xiaonei and 51.com, the Chinese answers to Facebook and MySpace, decided to merge social networking with online gaming.

Mashup in Beijing

Mirroring developments in the West, the first Web 2.0 applications to become popular in China were the blogs. Sites such as Bokee.com and Blogcn.com were the first to encourage the Chinese to express their views online in large numbers.

Bokee.com was founded by Fang Xingdong, a renowned IT analyst in China, in 2002 in Beijing. It later received over US$10 million investment from venture capital firms. Blogcn, founded in Hangzhou by Hu Zhiguang in 2002, also got US$10 million in venture capital funding.

Blogs quickly caught on. People loved how the new channels let them express anonymously the opinions or feelings that they were embarrassed to express openly. Though the government limits discussion of politics and other sensitive issues online, it otherwise leaves the bloggers alone. Even before blogs became popular, the country's online population was already used to discussing different topics in cyber forums and chat rooms. Blogs were an extension of that tradition, according to Jacky Huang, China Internet Research Manager of IDC.

Recognizing the opportunity, major internet companies such as Sina, Sohu, Baidu, Tencent, and Netease rushed in. Sina's and Sohu's blogs focus on celebrities, such as movie stars and famous athletes. Others cater for average people looking for fun and friends. With higher brand recognition and more resources, they quickly surpassed the popularity of early players such as Bokee and Blogcn.

By 2008, 162 million people (about half of the country's online population) had their own blogs. About a third, 105 million, frequently update their content, according to government-backed researcher CNNIC. Blogs make up a large part of online portal traffic. In 2007, according to a survey sponsored by Baidu, Tencent's QQ.com derived 23.9 percent of its traffic from blog services division Qzone. The figure was 18.2 percent for Netease's 163.com and 11.4 percent for Sina. The same survey found that Tencent's Qzone generated the most traffic among blogs. The blogs of Baidu, Sina, Sohu, and Netease were all among the top ten. Social networking sites were also popular. 51.com and Xiaonei.com, the Chinese answers to MySpace and Facebook, ranked second and third in the survey.

Rank	Site	Remark
1	Tencent Qzone	Blog provided by dominant online chat player
2	51.com	Social network site targeting grass roots internet users
3	Xiaonei.com	Social networking site for university alumni
4	Baidu Space	Blog provided by dominant search engine player
5	Sina Blog	Celebrity blog provided by leading online portal
6	Netease Blog	Blog provided by dominant email provider
7	Sohu Blog	Celebrity blog provided by leading online portal
8	IPart.cn	Blog focused on dating
9	Microsoft Windows Live Space	Blog provided by Microsoft
10	360quan.com	Social networking site
11	Bokee	Blog
12	MySpace	US-based social networking site

Table 11.1: **Top blogging and social networking sites in China—ranked by traffic**

Data source: Baidu and Searchlab.com.cn (2007)

Social networking sites

Facebook-like social networking sites started to get popular in China in 2005.

Beijing-based Xiaonei was founded by students at Tsinghua University and Tingjing University[117] in December 2005. Serial entrepreneur Joe Chen bought it in October 2006, and built it into the largest alumni site for university students in China.

Chen was born in 1970 in Wuhan, an industrial city in the heart of China. In 1989 his family moved to America, where Chen studied physics at the University of Delaware and went on to earn a masters degree in mechanical design theory from the Massachusetts Institute of Technology. After working briefly at a factory that made "cherry pickers" for utility company trucks, he went to Stanford University to study for an MBA.[118] Upon graduation in 1999, he founded his first

[117] Wang Xing, Wang Huiwen, Lai Binqiang, and Tang Yang.

[118] Source: Rebecca A. Fannin, *Silicon Dragon*, McGraw Hill, 2008.

startup, ChinaRen, a community site for Chinese university students, together with his schoolmates Nick Yang and Zhou Yunfan, who studied for a masters degree in electronic engineering at Stanford.

"My first venture was ChinaRen. I sometimes call it the Web 1.0 version of Facebook," said Chen. He realized early on that the majority of China's internet users would be young people, but that they were underserved by the existing internet companies due to their perceived low economic value. With a cool, Silicon Valley-type image, ChinaRen was branded *the* online destination for young Chinese students. It cleverly chose to be "patriotic" in its image, too, so as to appeal to the Chinese government and thus ensure a safe passage for mass marketing in China. ChinaRen became one of the most popular Chinese internet sites in the early 2000s.

After the internet bubble burst in 2000, ChinaRen was sold to Sohu, the second-largest online portal in China, for US$33 million. After a brief spell at Sohu, Chen went back to America, where he made an ill-fated effort to start an optical networking company. With the industry reeling from the bursting of the bubble and the aftermath of the 9/11 terrorist attacks,[119] his timing could not have been worse.

Chen returned to China to set up another company, Oak Pacific, in November 2002. He tried all kinds of internet businesses. In 2004, he acquired Mop.com and developed it into an online community focused on entertainment. The next year, he bought DoNews, a tech blogging site. After raising US$48 million in investment from venture capital firms,[120] he was easily able to fund these acquisitions and develop their business.

In 2006, he returned to his ongoing obsession, community sites for university students, by acquiring Xiaonei. "College life has had a strong influence on me. I have always had good intuition about what kind of internet products appeal to college students," said Chen. "When I saw Facebook, I thought this model would take off. That is why I started doing the same thing."

ChinaRen is a kind of cyber forum where old school friends can leave messages for each other. Each class has its own bulletin board for discussion. In contrast, Facebook is arranged around individuals, with links to their friends and affiliated groups. "This is a more effi-

[119] Source: Bruce Einhorn, "China Web 2.0: Joe Chen Wants it All", *BusinessWeek*, Mar 21, 2007.

[120] They included Silicon Valley's Doll Capital Management and Greenwich, Connecticut-based General Atlantic.

cient way of organizing information," Chen said. "And it is stickier." (In 2009, half of Facebook's 200 million users worldwide were visiting the site daily.[121])

Xiaonei's initial experience was much like Facebook's. It became popular among students from the top universities in China and, with a lot of promotion, both in cyberspace and on campus, spread out to embrace all of the country's post-secondary institutions. Chen further extended the coverage to take in high school students and white-collar workers.

His drive to be China's Web 2.0 king got another boost in April 2008 when Japan's Softbank paid US$96 million for a 14 percent stake in his firm, Oak Pacific. (Softbank also took out an option that would allow it to raise its stake to 40 percent by investing a further US$288 million within a year.) At the conclusion of that round of funding, Chen had raised US$430 million, larger than the average IPO on NASDAQ.[122]

By 2009, Xiaonei claimed to have 40 million registered members, of whom 22 million were daily visitors.[123] In August 2009, Xiaonei changed its name to RenRen, which means "everyone" in Chinese, to reflect Chen's expanded ambition. He was no longer satisfied with just a student network, but wanted people from all walks of life to be members. This meant that Xiaonei, which means "inside the school," was no longer a suitable name.

Compared to Facebook, Chen noted two differences in his users' behaviors. First, he notes, "as digital cameras are less widespread in China than America, our users write more blogs and post fewer photos on the site." Second, and more importantly, while Facebook solely depends on advertising for revenue, Chen's social network site also earns revenue from online games.

Gen-3 mashup: social networks + games

"In China, online games are huge. Social games and web games can be an important way to generate revenue on our site," said Chen. "A small percentage of paying users is enough."

Selling virtual items in online games can be a huge business, as many of the Chinese online game companies have discovered. Six of the ten

[121] Source: *http://www.facebook.com/press/info.php?statistics*

[122] Source: "Softbank invested US$3.84 million into Oak Pacific," *Sina News*, Apr 30, 2008.

[123] Source: *http://xiaonei.com/info/About.do*

largest internet companies (by revenue) operate online games as a major part of their business. Chen acquired a web game developer, Peagame.com, in mid 2008 and planned to buy more.[124] "We are also China's largest web game developer," he said.

The surge in popularity of social networking site Kaixing001.com further convinced Chen that social networking sites that incorporated games were the way to go. Kaixing001.com was founded by a group of former Sina executives, backed by venture capital.[125] It built up its popularity quickly by including "social" games such as Friends for Sale and Parking War.

Chen started his own competing version, Kaixin.com. He was not alone. Another major social network site in China, 51.com, also merged social networking with gaming. "Besides making money for us, the online games can make users stay longer on our site and hence help our online advertising revenue," said Pang Shengdong, cofounder of 51.com. 51.com was started by Zhang Jiangfu in 2003 in Fujian as 10770.com. Pang changed the name after he acquired the site in August 2005 and moved its headquarters to Shanghai.[126]

This MySpace-like website was China's largest social network site by user numbers, though its users tended to be less active than Xiaonei's. As of June 2008, 51.com had over 120 million registered users, of whom 31.5 million logged in at least once a month.[127] "While other social network sites focus on a particular niche, for example, Xiaonei.com for high school and college kids and Hainei.com for

[124] Source: Chen Shasha, "Oak Pacific aims to extend online roots with Peagame purchase," *Interfax China*, Jul 14, 2008.
[125] Investors include Qiming Venture Partners, Northern Light Venture Capital, and Ceyuan Ventures. Over US$20 million was raised by April 2009, according to JLM Pacific Epoch.
[126] We should make a quick comment on the proliferation of cryptic numbers in Chinese domain names. Why anyone would choose a domain name like 10770.com is bewildering to most Westerners. But numbers play an important role in Chinese culture, and are part of the history and linguistic studies that every child is brought up on. Numbers are lucky or unlucky, and figure into the heavenly stems and branches of the calendar. Stanislas Dehaene , in his book *The Number Sense*, suggests the Chinese are much better at remembering numbers because number words in the Chinese language are remarkably brief. Most of them can be uttered in less than one-quarter of a second (for instance, 4 is "si" and 7 "qi"). Their English equivalents—"four," "seven"—are longer: pronouncing them takes about one-third of a second. The number facility gap between English and Chinese apparently is entirely due to this difference in length, because the human mind tends to remember best if a list is presented in less than two seconds. There is also the suggestion that at least some of the Chinese facility in math may be attributable to a better handle on numbers. The Chinese facility with numbers shows through in their penchant for numerical domain names.
[127] Source: *http://company.51.com/index_en.php*

people with an IT background, we are for general internet users," said Pang.

51.com used the charm of beautiful girls to build its popularity. "When 51.com started, it convinced a lot of beautiful girls to put their blogs on the site. This attracted many other users," said an analyst. We suspect most of those other users were young and male (!).

Like Xiaonei, 51.com also attracted many investors. It raised US$21 million from venture capital firms Intel Capital, Redpoint, Sequoia, and SIG in two rounds of funding in 2006 and 2007. In mid 2008, it raised another US$51 million by selling a 25 percent stake to Giant Interactive, a Shanghai-based online game company listed on the New York Stock Exchange.

51.com gets its revenue from online advertising and selling virtual items (such as avatars) to its users. Its advertisers include Coca-Cola, Pepsi-Cola, Samsung, Motorola, and Kentucky Fried Chicken. With the help of Giant Interactive, it is also developing online games. "Many online game companies advertise on the social networking sites because of their huge traffic and the similarity of their user bases," said Huang of IDC. "So it is quite natural for social networking sites such as 51.com to develop online games. After all, online games are still the most profitable among all the different internet businesses."

Besides social networking sites, another Web 2.0 trend, video sharing, grew in popularity around 2005.

Sharing videos

An early mover in video sharing was Shanghai-based Tudou. (Its name means "potato" in Chinese[128], presumably a reference to the couch potatoes using their service.) Their slogan was, appropriately, "Everyone is the Director of Life." Tudou was founded by Gary Wang and Dutchman Marc Van der Chijs in April 2005. The two knew each other through Van der Chijs' wife, who worked with Wang in the China operation of Germany's Bertelsmann Media Group.

Van der Chijs was an active blogger who had been writing about his life in China. "I was thinking of making a podcast for my blog, but Gary said that was too easy," said Van der Chijs. Wang thought podcast software for bloggers was just too much of a niche market. Instead, he

128 Tudou's stated goal was to move couch potatoes from the television screen to the computer screen.

went ahead and built a full feature video sharing site, not much different from YouTube's.

"Since blogging became popular, internet innovation is no longer limited to Silicon Valley. People can read about what are the latest trends in the industry from the famous bloggers and apply those concepts in their ventures," said Van der Chijs, explaining the similarity.

Wang said his inspiration was not YouTube, which at the time was not well known. "There were many video sharing sites at the time. YouTube was just one of them," he said. Rather, he borrowed some of the ideas of photo sharing site Flickr to design Tudou's navigation system and organize video clips.

Whatever Tudou's origins, like YouTube it was focused on user-generated content—homemade videos. Wang quit his day job in January 2005 to concentrate on Tudou, and the first version was launched in April 2005. Van der Chijs became a silent partner, continuing to work on his own business. That same year, a video uploaded by two students at the Guangzhou Arts Institute captured the attention of the country and later the world. The Back Dorm Boys—Wei Wei and Huang Yi-xin—mugged for the web cam in their dorm room and lip-synched the Backstreet Boys' song "I Want It That Way."

Their grainy web cam broadcasts struck a chord with people around the world, becoming among the most viral on the web. With their matching Houston Rockets jerseys, synchronized swaying, bobbing heads, protruding lips, and exaggerated facial expressions, one couldn't help but laugh. *Good Morning America* aired their clips on American television. Motorola also took notice, and soon Wei and Huang were lip-synching their way through TV ads for the handset maker.

Afterwards, a few more homemade videos gave different people their "15 minutes of fame" in China. This was good news for Wang and Van der Chijs. Rather than letting fame turn their heads, the two pursued backing from venture capital investors[129] who were looking for the next big thing in China.

Competitors soon followed, especially after Google's US$1.65 billion acquisition of YouTube in late 2006. Video sharing sites were not only popular, but also valuable. At the peak of enthusiasm, over

129 Tudou's first batch of investment was a seed round of US$500,000 in 2005, then, in May 2006, it raised US$8.5 million from Granite Global Ventures, JAFCO, and IDG VC (according to "Toodou Closes US$8.5M Round," JLM Pacific Epoch, May 15, 2006 and "Tudou Announced $57 Million Financing," *China Web2.0 Review*, Apr 29, 2008).

100 wannabe YouTube sites were operating in China. Most looked exactly like their American model.

Pure homemade video was no longer the main attraction. All kinds of pirated materials and erotic content were uploaded to grab attention and market share. Viewers could watch movies that were still showing in the cinemas. Watching TV shows and movies on video sharing sites became a favorite pastime of the young. By the end of 2008, 238 million people—80 percent of China's online population—were visiting video sharing sites, according to IDC.

Because supporting national networks to deliver video content was very expensive, the industry started to consolidate in 2007. Only players with the strongest backing could survive. These included ku6.com, 6.cn, 56.com, and Youku. They set up shop with venture capital money and started to assault Tudou's position as the number one video sharing operator. Among them, Beijing-based Youku, founded by former Sohu president Victor Koo, was the most serious contestant.

Excellent first, cool later

Youku literally means "excellent and cool," with homage to *Bill & Ted's Excellent Adventure*, an American comedy and science fiction movie. But as Koo explained it, he wanted his site to be excellent first and cool later, meaning serving the mainstream audience with good quality content and network first, before going after niche user groups, those he refers to as the "cool" guys. In fact, he said, "We are not cool. We are mainstream." And to serve the mainstream audience, homemade video is not the answer.

"Homemade video in America has a history of 10 to 20 years. But it only became popular in China in the last two or three years. Good user-generated video content is much less plentiful in China than in America," said Koo. Youku focuses on professional content, partnering with local television stations and production houses to obtain programs and movies. "The mainstream people in China still love their TV dramas and movies the most. Some also like programs from Hong Kong, Taiwan, and Korea. But American programs have very few followers in China," said Koo.

Koo's previous experience with Sohu, which stocked its online portal with content from local newspapers and magazines, convinced him that he could have just as much success with professionally produced video. "China's film and television industry is very fragmented. It is not difficult to convince local television stations and production houses to partner with us," said Koo.

While the American television industry is dominated by a few powerful groups such as Walt Disney, CBS, NBC Universal, and Time Warner, China has 298 TV companies providing over 2,000 channels. "Every province and city has its own TV station." said Koo. And whereas the American film industry is concentrated in the hands of a few Hollywood studios, China has over 1,000 film and television production houses. Koo saw the fragmentation of the media industry as an opportunity. "The more the fragmentation, the more value we deliver as an integrator of video content."

By the end of 2008, Youku had signed up over 70 percent of local television companies and most of the film and TV production houses. It later expanded to media companies overseas.[130] Youku offers its partners a small down payment for the right to show their programs, and shares the advertising revenue with them.

Youku also had a different approach to its network from YouTube—it built its own network to deliver video content. "Unlike America, there are not many professional content delivery network providers in China," said Koo. "We built our own network to lower costs." By December 2005, Youku's national network was mostly in place and in the following 18 months it continued to expand rapidly in capacity and coverage. This ensured that Youku users could watch smooth videos, no matter where they were in the country.

Tudou's network infrastructure was originally provided by Beijing-based ChinaCache, a content delivery network provider that had set up thousands of servers and dedicated networks across the country. But soon Tudou discovered it could lower its costs by building its own network. Nowadays it relies on its own network for 85 percent of the traffic, and uses ChinaCache for the remaining 15 percent, according to Tudou co-founder Marc Van der Chijs.

With a decent network and lots of professional content, Youku's popularity soared. By the end of 2008, Youku was attracting 23 million visitors a day, who on average spent an hour a day on the site. As many as 150 million people, almost half of China's online population, visited the site every month.

130 Youku content partners include: TV stations such as Beijing TV, Jiangsu TV, and many other provincial or municipal television stations; branded content producers such as Hong Kong-based TVB; online copyright distributors such as Net Movie, 51.TV; and all major music companies including Warner Music, EMI, Universal, and so on.

"Over 70 percent of the videos people view on our site are professional content, such as TV dramas and movies," said Koo.

While Tudou continued to encourage user-generated content, it shifted its main focus to TV programs and movies. In late 2008, it launched a high-resolution service called black bean to play professional content. Showing TV shows and movies has an extra benefit. "As our content is similar to that of the mainstream media, it is easier to get advertising," said Koo.

Both Youku and Tudou formally introduced advertising programs in 2008. While Youku had ads from Google and Baidu, its revenue was mainly from display ads and video ads[131] for major brands, such as Samsung, Lenovo, Nike, Adidas, Li-Ning, Coca-Cola, and Ford. This is very different from YouTube, which relies mainly on ads from Google's AdSense network, Koo said. Youku's ad revenue target for 2009 was RMB100 million (or US$14.6 million).

Tudou had no Google or Baidu ads at all. It showed video player embedded pre-roll ads while the requested video loaded, as well as full screen wallpaper ads around the video during playback. Advertisers include Adidas, Ford, HP, KFC, Lenovo, Nokia, Nike, Olay, Pepsi, P&G, Samsung, Sony, and Unilever.

Nevertheless, neither Tudou nor Youku has given up user-generated content (UGC) completely. "While what people watch [is] mainly TV content, what they remember [is] UGC. For example, someone would tell his friends, 'yesterday I watched a funny video clip on Tudou.' UGC, in particular unique content, is [a] very powerful marketing tool," said Gary Wang of Tudou. The company is making special videos, mostly entertainment related, for users to view on its sites. "The latest one is called *Sophie's Diary*, it is a 5-minutes-per-episode mini video series, and our users can vote to decide how the story develops," said Van der Chijs.

Youku said it wants UGC, too. "We also like UGC. But rather than homemade video, we want our users to go out of their home and shoot real life incidents unfolding in the Chinese society. I think these are more interesting than any homemade video," said Koo. Television stations also use some of Youku's footage when reporting news. "There is one incident, a city was blocked in the heavy snow storm in January 2008. The crew of CCTV cannot reach the city in time, as the roads were blocked. So, they used our videos instead," said Koo.

[131] Video ads are pre-roll, post-roll, and seed ads. In-video ads include in-video banner, overlay ads, and pause ads.

Youku has made considerable changes to the business model pioneered by YouTube.

	Youku	YouTube	Remarks
Content	Focus on professional content	Focus on user-generated content (UGC), although professional content is increasing	Lack of good quality UGC in China. Fragmentation of media industry in China makes partnership with TV stations and production houses easy
Revenue	Mainly from brand advertising	Mainly from Google AdSense network	Professional content makes advertisers more confident about placing brand ads
Network infrastructure	Self-built	Relies on third-party content delivery network	Few third-party content delivery networks in China
User behavior	Longer stays	Shorter stays	TV dramas and movies attract Chinese users

***Table 11.2:* Comparison between Youku and YouTube—business models**

Financial crisis

Although their ad revenue has started to grow, most analysts believe Tudou and Youku are still making losses because of their high bandwidth requirements. "It takes US$1–2 million a month to run their operations," said an industry expert. Luckily, both have raised substantial capital from investors. Tudou had raised a total of US$85 million over four rounds of funding by early 2008.[132] Youku had US$70 million equity investment and another US$10 million in loans.[133]

By late 2008, the financial crisis that began in America's subprime lending market was affecting the investment atmosphere all over the world, including China. As easy money disappeared, video sharing

132 From Tudou's website: "Tudou has raised several rounds of funding, the latest being $57 million in spring 2008 for a total of $85 million over four rounds of funding. Tudou investors include IDG China, Granite Global Ventures, JAFCO, General Catalyst Partners, and Capital Today."

133 Youku's investors include Brookside (Bain) Capital, Chengwei Ventures, Farallon Capital, Maverick Capital, and Sutter Hill Ventures.

sites stopped blindly grabbing at market share. Tudou started to curtail its appetite for bandwidth. "I could easily increase our traffic immediately. Just give a phone call to the telecom operators and tell them to increase our bandwidth. But what is the point? Not all traffic is worth pursuing," said Wang.

"Youku was more aggressive in spending money. Tudou chose to test the business model before letting the bandwidth flow freely," said Helen Wong of GGVC, a venture capital investor in Tudou.

"In 2007, we competed with our rivals on traffic. But by early 2008, I realized that competition on traffic was a black hole. Unless you have the support of Google," said Wang, alluding to YouTube's corporate parentage, "the business model is not sustainable. We started to rethink our strategies. Who are our users? What is our content? What kind of users are too expensive to serve? Right now the key is not grabbing traffic, but generating revenue." Attitudes toward pirated content have changed as well. "Pirated material serves no purpose. We can't sell advertising on it and it uses up our bandwidth. We don't like being called the world's largest pirate video site either," said Wang.

Tudou is working with organizations such as the Motion Picture Association to purge its site of pirated content. Some improvement has been noted. For example, *Kung Fu Panda*, a 2008 American animated comedy blockbuster from DreamWorks Animation, disappeared off Tudou, where it could be viewed for free. However, not all video sharing sites are committed to cleaning up their act. With persistence, fans could still find the Panda movie on other video sharing sites.

May you come to the attention of the authorities

There is a Chinese curse—"may you come to the attention of the authorities," and indeed this is exactly what happened to Guangdong-based 56.com, which was also once a key player in the video sharing sector.

A report by the China Internet Society in March 2008 said that 56.com had a 30.9 percent market share in the video sharing sector, compared with Youku's 37.3 and Tudou's 32.9. But it was wiped out when the government decided to regulate the sector in mid 2008.

New regulations imposed by the State Administration of Radio, Film, and Television (SARFT), effective from late January 2008, require all video sharing sites doing business to have a license. Of the three, only Youku was not shut down by the government before getting its license. Tudou was shut down for a day and its uploading service was suspended for a week. 56.com was shut down for the entire month of June 2008. Afterwards, 56.com's market share dropped to single digits and many of its key executives quit.

"We thought obtaining a license from the local SARFT office in Guangdong would be enough," said a 56.com executive, "so we didn't go to the central SARFT office in Beijing. They found that offensive and shut us down. The other players had been courting the central SARFT office for a long time for their licenses," he added.

Lessons learned

1 Hybrid business models work best in China.

In making any business work, the best solution is usually a hybrid model—something that combines international best practice with local adaptations, according to Joe Chen of Oak Pacific. Asked why Tudou's interface looked so much like that of YouTube, its cofounder, Marc Van der Chijs, said that it was simply because it was the best design for the application.

No points for reinventing the wheel. Many Chinese internet businesses have built their basic operations according to successful foreign blueprints. This turns out to be the easy part of the task. According to Chen, apart from search engines, most other internet businesses present no technological barriers.

The real challenge is adaptation—how to make a service work in China's unique business and social environment. When it comes to adaptation, the local companies naturally have an edge over the foreign players. They understand the market better and can implement their decisions faster. "The American companies always make their decisions at their headquarters, which are on the other side of the Pacific Ocean," said Youku founder Victor Koo. "Therefore, they are always slow to respond."

Moreover, many of the American companies' subsidiaries in China are not as well funded as their local rivals. Successful Chinese internet companies had no problem attracting venture capital or getting listed on the stock market. By the time Rupert Murdoch's MySpace set up its China division in 2007, hardly anyone in the market expected it to be a serious threat to local rivals such as Xiaonei and 51.com. MySpace's market share remained small in China.

2 Westerners' triumph.

To be fair, the Chinese market has not been a total failure for the American internet companies that entered it. Despite being overshadowed by their Chinese counterparts, Google and eBay both do good business in the country. Many small businesses in China use them as a platform for overseas sales, a capability that the likes of Baidu and Taobao lack. Game developer Blizzard also found millions of customers for its online game World of Warcraft by partnering with local operators.

Although Yahoo failed to attract many visitors to its Chinese portal sites, it turned around its track record in China by investing US$1 billion in 40 percent of the Alibaba group, the country's e-commerce king, in 2005. Just counting Alibaba's listed B2B subsidiary alone, that investment amounted to almost US$5 billion in August 2009. And most analysts believe Alibaba's C2C site Taobao would be an even more valuable jewel, once it turns profitable.

The largest shareholder in China's biggest internet company, Tencent, is Naspers, a media group based in South Africa. In 2001 Naspers acquired the 20 percent stake owned by PCCW, a Hong Kong telecommunication company, when it was too short-sighted to hold on to a piece of the country's dominant online chat provider after the dotcom bubble burst.[134] Naspers increased its stake in Tencent by buying shares from other investors and Tencent's management. It held 50 percent of Tencent, just before the company listed in Hong Kong in 2004. In August 2009, Tencent's market capitalization reached US$27 billion, making Naspers, which still owned 35 percent of Tencent, one of the biggest winners (albeit a low profile one) in the China internet sector.

In the next chapter, we look at the stories of several Westerners who founded their own companies in China—people who had only a smattering of Mandarin at the start, who wound up running companies where everyone else is Chinese.

[134] Adding insult to injury, when Hong Kong's Hang Seng Index readjusted its compositions in May 2008, it replaced PCCW with Tencent. Source: Chris Oliver, "Tencent, Chalco added to Hang Seng Index, CKI Holdings, PCCW gets the boot in surprise move," *MarketWatch*, May 10, 2008.

12. The expats

China is now the world's largest internet market. But its more than 338 million users are still only about 25 percent of the population. Inevitably these numbers will swell in the next decade. The Chinese internet is fertile ground for entrepreneurs, both local and foreign. There are roles for foreigners to play. Many foreigners worked in the country's first internet ventures, and many others have arrived since. In this chapter, we share some of their stories.

Marc van der Chijs

Dutchman Marc van der Chijs arrived in China in 1999, sent out by Mercedes Benz. At the time he was 27 years old and employed at the headquarters of the German luxury car maker. When Mercedes posted an opening for a financial controller in its North Asia regional office in Beijing, he applied and got the job.

"It was an interesting job," said van der Chijs. "I traveled around the region a lot and did a lot of presentations." His was a comfortable expatriate life, with good money and a nice house. But something was missing.

"I felt I could do more than just write reports," he said. "Besides, many of the people at DaimlerChrysler, [then] the parent company of Mercedes, were unhappy. They did not like China that much. They were there only for the money, the status. I don't know ... I was different. I really loved it. I was happy in China."

Van der Chijs was dazzled by China's vibrancy. Everything was growing; construction sites were everywhere. "It was the place to be for entrepreneurs. It seemed like everything was possible. There was lots of potential." When his contract expired in 2002, he quit Mercedes but stayed in China. "I was going to study Chinese and probably start my own business," said van der Chijs. But, in fact, he did not have a plan. He enrolled in a Mandarin course at Beijing Foreign Studies University. But student life was rather boring for someone accustomed to the demands of the business world. "I was used to working long hours," he said. "School finished at three o'clock. And there was still a half-day left to fill."

So van der Chijs started his first company—a small consulting and trading outfit. Business grew quickly, and within a few months he was feeling the need for frequent business trips, which clashed with his studies. "The first time, the university let me take several days off. But the next time they didn't allow it, although I was probably the best student in the class."

So he quit school and went back to work full time—a decision he still regrets. "That is why my Mandarin has never been fluent. Now I have a son—I'd like to be able to understand what he says when he talks in Chinese."

Van der Chijs traded different products from China mainly with Europe. He also consulted for companies looking to enter Chinese markets—"advising them on what kind of business structure they should set up, helping them to find the right people. Whatever is needed when companies arrive in China. The purpose was to make some money while I figured out what I was going to do— and what I could do."

For the next three years, Van der Chijs did a lot of different things—including making the first reality TV show in China. "It was a show sponsored by Ford, Sheraton, and Nike. We flew to Hainan (a resort island in South China) for the filming. There were 12 contestants competing with each other for 12 days. The winner got a car. It was like *Big Brother*."

He also started his blog—Marc van der Chijs' Shanghaied Weblog (marc.cn), where he wrote about his life in China. "I like writing and I met a lot of people through my blog. I love getting feedback from others."

Then he met his business partner, Gary Wang. Together they would found one of the largest video sharing sites in China, Tudou.com. "I met Gary through my wife. They were colleagues at Bertelsmann. I was sitting next to him at the first-ever Formula One race in Shanghai," said van der Chijs.

The pair subsequently met for beers and went to a few parties together. During a golf game, van der Chijs suggested that they collaborate on a podcast site. "He really liked the idea and started working on it the next day," van der Chijs said. In the end, Wang launched not a podcast site but a full feature video sharing site, just like YouTube's.

"The Chinese do not like audio much. They like video much more—something they can watch," said van der Chijs.

The pair were quickly able to get venture capital backing. (Tudou in total raised US$85 million from four rounds of venture capital investment up to mid 2008.[135]) Wang quit his day job in early 2005 to devote himself to Tudou, while Van der Chijs remained a silent partner. "I was only a board member. Gary was the one who really built up Tudou," he said.

In 2005–06, Van der Chijs made another career breakthrough. Spil Games, a small online games company in the Netherlands, wanted to set up a website in China. "I was in Holland at the time and I went to meet them. I realized they really understood games, and they had good ideas," he said.

Besides, there was no one big player in the simple flash-based games business in China. The growth potential was huge. "I figured, they know about games and I know something about China, so we might just be able to make it work," said van der Chijs.

He and the Dutch company set up Spil Games Asia in Shanghai in January 2006 and established the website game.com.cn, or Game in China, as its Chinese name suggested. Van der Chijs worked part time on Spil Games Asia at first, continuing to run his trading business and help oversee Tudou. But the gaming company's prospects were so bright that he soon took it on full time.

Spil Games Asia later acquired a small game development firm in Shandong, a province in North China, which came with the domain name xiaoyouxi.com, which means "little games" in Chinese. "Now, we have 75 staff in total, two websites and about 32 million visitors monthly," said van der Chijs in late 2008. "Our traffic is about 40 percent of Tudou's."

Almost all of van der Chijs's staff are local Chinese—people he hired not for their English skills, but for their business acumen. "Many foreigners judge their staff by their ability to speak English. And they promote the wrong people as a result."

By the end of 2008, Spil Games Asia was already breaking even. Its revenue came from advertising, which van der Chijs used to market the sites and to attract more users. The next year it began to allow independent developers to contribute their games to the site and share the revenue with the owners.

135 Source: "Tudou Announced $57 Million Financing," *China Web2.0 Review*, Apr 29, 2008.

"There are many game developers in China who make good games, but can only share them with a few of their friends. We can make money for them—as the word spreads more developers will contribute their games to us." Van der Chijs expects this to be a new source of quality games at low cost.

Being a foreign entrepreneur is not always an easy lot. "As a foreigner, people always see you differently. Even if you live in China for a long time and marry a local Chinese woman, like I did," he said. Among the many obstacles, foreigners are not allowed to open companies with the same ease as local entrepreneurs. "You cannot open a local company in China. You have to set up your business in another legal structure—WOFE."[136]

And dealing with the government is always more difficult for foreigners. Van der Chijs had what he calls a "close encounter" with the government in mid 2008.

In May that year, China suffered its largest earthquake in 30 years. The disaster in Sichuan, a province in southwestern China, killed 69,227 people and injured 374,176, while another 18,222 were listed as missing. It left about 4.8 million people homeless. The government declared a three-day mourning period for the victims from May 19–21.[137] Van der Chijs received an email from the government telling him to close down Spil Games Asia for those three days. All online game companies received the same order. "Instead of our normal games content, we put a special page on our website to express our concern," he said. (Tudou, the video sharing site van der Chijs set up with Gary Wang, was also contacted. Although not required to shut down, Tudou made some adjustments, toning down its color scheme, for example, and posting messages of mourning and special earthquake-related videos.)

Van der Chijs does not normally deal with the government directly, leaving that to lawyers or consultants. "Although it is more expensive, the result is good," he said. He has met with government officials in the past, but only to say hello and pay his respects.

[136] A WOFE, or Wholly Foreign Owned Enterprise, is a limited liability company wholly owned by a foreign investor. In China, WOFEs were originally conceived for encouraging manufacturing activities that were either export orientated or that introduced advanced technology. However, with China's entry into the WTO, these conditions were gradually abolished and the WOFE is increasingly being used for service providers, such as a variety of consulting and management services, software development, and trading as well.

[137] Source: "Chinese Game Operations Suspended For 3 Days Of Mourning In China," ChinaCRS.com, May 19, 2008.

Despite such inconveniences, however, there are some advantages to being a foreign entrepreneur in China. "I always try to get ideas from my friends in other countries and apply them in China," said van der Chijs. "I believe it is easier to attract venture capital investment in general." He went on to say that for the many foreign venture capital firms that are new to China, people who speak their language and share their background are perceived as safer to work with. That logic applies to his partnership with Spil Games. "I am Dutch and they are Dutch. A local Chinese would not be able to do the same thing, even though he might be better," said van der Chijs.

He said foreigners must learn to respect the locals and their culture. "Many foreigners make the mistake of thinking they are better than the average local Chinese. That is stupid. I've changed a lot since I came. I was quite arrogant at first, working for Mercedes, etc. Now I am much humbler."

Outspoken people may be the most successful in Germany. But the Chinese are much more subtle. "You need to respect your employees and make them respect you. That does not mean you cannot be angry with them. But shouting at them in public is not the way to go," he said.

T. R. Harrington

American T. R. Harrington's first trip to China was in June 1994. A university roommate invited him to spend a month exploring the country. "I thought I'd never get such an invitation again," said Harrington, who was working at a law firm, but had decided he didn't really want to be a lawyer. "I was not very excited about my work in America, so I decided to travel. That month was really breathtaking. China was nothing like what I had imagined."

Everywhere Harrington and his friend went, construction sites were buzzing 24 hours a day, seven days a week. "I thought, in another 15 years. China would be really interesting," said Harrington. "It took less than 15 years—a lot less than 15 years."

He returned to China in December 2000. "Pudong[138] was completely different. In 1994, there was only a television tower. By 2000, there were office buildings, tower after tower, and it was the new financial center of Shanghai. The new Pudong airport had been built."

138 A new development zone in Shanghai.

"The environment was much more entrepreneurial and new-business driven. It was very different from 1994, when there had been much more structure and government influence over business. Few industries were open to foreign businesses then. But in 2000, I met several expatriates who were running their own businesses in China. I definitely saw the potential."

By the time of his second trip to China, Harrington had lived through the whole dot.com bubble in America. Harrington moved to San Francisco and worked in online marketing for four different startups from 1996–2000. In October 2001, he came back again to study Chinese, still undecided on whether to get a business degree or do something in China.

"In early 2002, I was accepted by one of my top choices for business school," said Harrington. He decided to go back to America and pursue his MBA at the University of Virginia. "I was getting older—I thought if I didn't do it now I would likely never take the opportunity to do it later."

In 2003, he returned to China as an exchange student in the MBA program at China Europe International Business School (CEIBS) in Shanghai. "Chinese internet companies, such as Sina, Sohu, and Netease, were pursuing different models in 2004. Apart from online advertising, they also had large mobile data businesses," he said. "I had worked on integrating online with wireless in 1999. I thought that by coming to China I could continue along that path."

He also met his future wife—which made him decide to stay, even though it might have been financially wiser to go home for a while. "Originally, I'd planned to go back to America, work a couple years, pay down some of my debt and hopefully save $200,000 to $300,000 before coming back. But my personal life fast-forwarded my plans for China." Without much cash or any specific plans, "I started to network with people here, while figuring out where I could fit in."

With a few former classmates from the exchange program at CEIBS, he started doing some independent consulting. "It was good for meeting people and looking for opportunities. At the same time, I was networking with people from eBay, Alibaba, and so on to find out how e-commerce worked in China."

By 2005, the Chinese internet market had shifted fundamentally. It had reached a critical mass of over 100 million online users. Alibaba had created an e-payment platform, Alipay, and in its wake eBay introduced PayPal to the country. Logistics services, whether offered by China's EMS or international providers such as Fedex, UPS, and TNT, had improved to such an extent that if you bought something online, you could have it delivered in two or three days. Taxes and provincial borders, which had prevented the smooth flow of goods from one place to another, had been removed. And banks started promoting credit cards in the major cities.

"You have the pillars of e-commerce ready. My theory was that once e-commerce starts to grab a foothold in China, the market would need a more efficient and measurable means of online advertising. I wrote a business plan in June-to-August 2005," said Harrington.

The plan became his company, Darwin Marketing, specializing in online marketing. "I started pitching my ideas to my network of friends and let them know I was looking for a local partner," said Harrington. He soon met Charles Shen of eBay China, who had been born and raised in Shanghai. Before eBay, Shen had worked for UK-based Research International and Germany's Bertelsmann.

"He worked in the data warehousing department of eBay. He understands the value of data and how to use data. We can add value to advertisers," said Harrington. In the next few months, the two had many lunches and dinners together, discussing different business models.

At the same time, Harrington saved US$50,000 from a few consulting projects he did. With that and Shen's savings, they started their business. "We hired our first employees in March 2006. We hired several developers. We finished our first platform in June 2006," said Harrington. It was an online-affiliate network, like that of US-based ValueClick. Publishers put the advertisers' ads on their websites and got paid as the ad was shown repeatedly, clicked on, or led to a sale online. "We had ten advertisers and started recruiting publishers among the Chinese websites," said Harrington.

In the next four to six months they started another online marketing business, a search engine marketing software plus services platform. The software helps clients to manage keywords in search engines such as Baidu and Google. In general, they can improve their clients' effectiveness by 20 percent or more, that is, get advertisers 20 percent more sales leads for the same budget. They achieve these improvements by testing thousands of different keywords and monitoring the performance of each continuously.

"We started with three search clients in November 2006," said Harrington. Search marketing became Darwin's major business, contributing 80 percent of its revenue in 2008.

"In 2007, we added another business, search engine optimization," said Harrington. This is designed to improve clients' rankings on search engines by redesigning their websites. "We now have three business units, two offices in Shanghai and Beijing, and roughly 50 advertisers. We are managing roughly RMB2 million (US$290,000) in media budget per month for our advertisers."

The company got an undisclosed amount of venture capital investment in July 2008. "The money should be enough for our development in the next two years," said Harrington.

Almost all of Harrington's staff are local Chinese. "I can speak some Mandarin and if there is something I cannot communicate, I can always grab someone like Charles [Shen] to help. I hire them to do business primarily in Chinese, not in English." Harrington said having a Chinese partner like Shen, who speaks fluent English, has helped him a lot. The two complement each other. "He used his guanxi and I used mine," said Harrington. Guanxi is a Chinese concept of personal or professional networks, a form of connection. And while Shen took care of the day-to-day operations side of the business, Harrington worked more on the strategy and sales side.

"Being a foreigner, I have access to something my local team do not get easy access to," said Harrington. "The expatriate network in China is heavily tilted toward the advertising industry. Many international advertising companies are entering the China market. I share similar backgrounds as them. I worked in [the] online advertising industry in America and I can talk to them in language they understand."

Harrington has been expanding his network beyond the expatriate community. "I belong to two associations where I am surrounded by local Chinese—the Founders Club, which is a group of entrepreneurs, and my MBA alumni at the University ofVirginia."

Richard Robinson

After Richard Robinson graduated from the University of Southern California in 1989, he did not get a "real" job like many of his classmates. Instead, he traveled around the world, while supporting himself with all kinds of peculiar jobs—he was a bartender in the Virgin

Islands, a door-to-door cable TV salesman in Boston, a concierge/ski bum in a Swiss hotel, an English teacher in post-revolution Prague, a house painter in Norway, a grape picker in France, and a BMW factory worker in Munich.

"I was taking dessert first before the main course. Having retirement first before working," said Robinson.

His first trip to China was during one of his Europe–Asia tours. "I hitched to Prague and then took a train two days to Moscow and stayed for a few days, then I hopped on the trans-Siberian Express through Siberia via Mongolia to China. Overall I spent 11 days on the train from Prague to Hong Kong over a one-month period. I had an epiphany and instantly fell in love with China as soon as I rolled over the border. From China I traveled to Thailand, Cambodia, Vietnam, Laos, Indonesia, Hawaii, LA, then back to Boston."

In 1994, he was finally ready to grow up. He went for the MBA program at the Rotterdam School of Management at Erasmus University in the Netherlands—one of the top business schools in Europe. He also had his first encounter with the internet. "I got a job working in the school library, spending too much time online right when Netscape's first browser came out and was hooked on the web. From then on I knew I wanted to be involved in the internet industry and somehow do it in China," said Robinson.

During the MBA program, he got an internship doing an internet-related consulting project for the Hong Kong Trade Development Council. Then, he had his last big adventure with a trip to the Middle East and a solo bicycle trip through Africa, before embarking into the real world.

Robinson's first position was in Hong Kong. Through the connection he had made during his internship, he got a job with a New York-based internet consulting firm called Poppe Tyson, helping to open their Asian office in Hong Kong. The company was soon acquired by Modem Media and Robinson's team was expanded to 45 people. They did consulting, development, and interactive marketing for major corporations such as IBM, Citibank, AT&T, Intel, etc. Robinson traveled a lot to China, Taiwan, Japan, Australia, and New York. After two and half years, the company listed on Nasdaq and internet fever was at its peak.

Robinson left and joined another internet startup. "During that time I met two former McKinsey consultants who were starting a Chinese version of GeoCities called renren.com or 'everybody' in Chinese. I became the first vice president they hired and part of the founding team," said Robinson. "We had very little funding and only eight people, but from there we went on a crazy dot.com ride from eight people to 350 in eight months by closing a US$6 million A round, a US$31 million B round, and then listing on the Hong Kong Stock Exchange. Until Nasdaq crashed, we were briefly worth over a billion US dollars."

After the bubble burst, most of renren's staff were laid off. "The good news is that we were fully acquired in May of 2001, so we all got to exit," said Robinson.

With a bit of cash and time, Robinson started his first venture—a comedy production house. "We invested some cash and started to bring over North American acts to perform in Hong Kong," said Robinson. He later expanded it to Japan, Bangkok, Beijing, Shanghai, and Singapore. "One of my favorites was when I brought out Colin Quinn for a tour of Beijing, Shanghai, and Hong Kong," said Robinson.

In early 2001, he started another venture—a wireless game company in Beijing called Mobile interactive Games (MiG), in partnership with a PricewaterhouseCoopers Consulting investment incubator called MINT. MiG grew along with the wireless market in China. It was fully acquired about a year later by the Sun Microsystems-backed Softgame, which was Sun's first investment in the wireless space outside of America. In 2007, MiG was ultimately acquired for US$40 million by Nasdaq-listed Glu Mobile.

At MiG, Robinson closed an exclusive deal with Yao Ming to create a suite of cellphone services for the Chinese market based around the NBA All-Stars, and also created a cellphone tie-in with the release of *Spiderman*—the first such tie-in for a major Hollywood movie in China.

"After one year I could leave, and my wife wanted me to do something more stable so I took a position as vice president of the international department of China's first/leading mobile entertainment company—Linktone," said Robinson. His role was to source and manage partnerships with international companies such as Cartoon Network, the big four music labels, Japanese cartoon companies, Indian tech companies, Disney, McDonald's, News Corp, and so on.

"We were the first wireless entertainment company globally to list on Nasdaq, and it was an interesting ride. We grew from 180 to about

1,000 people and I was the only foreigner, so that had its own challenges," said Robinson.

He felt constrained at Linktone and left after working there for two and half years. During that time, he founded his third venture, DragonPorts (now Shouji Mobile Entertainment). "While I was at Linktone, I met a lot of foreign companies with a similar problem. They needed to [adjust] their wireless applications to different models of cellphone, which is a tedious process. So I founded DragonPorts with a partner and we recruited a group of Chinese engineers to work on those projects." DragonPorts or Shouji had about 70 staff in early 2009, with revenues of nearly US$2 million. Its clients include EA Mobile, Disney Mobile, THQ Mobile, and Vivendi Games Mobile.

Afterward, Robinson founded a few more companies, including Kooky Panda and Dada Asia. Kooky Panda is a casual mobile games developer in Beijing. Robinson built up Dada's operation in ten countries in the region, covering India, and Australia to Greater China. In addition, he was involved with a few companies as an investor/adviser on the side. Robinson is also the cofounder of the first Beijing Chapter for Entrepreneurs' Organization, the world's largest community for entrepreneurs.

The serial entrepreneur now lives with his wife and two sons in Beijing. "We built a courtyard home here in Beijing, have four big dogs, an SUV, and a BBQ," said Robinson, "so I'm pretty much living the suburban nightmare that I've been able to avoid in America all these years and I'm digging it!"

Fritz Demopoulos

A native of Los Angeles, Fritz Demopoulos describes himself as a constant shifter between working for others and working for himself. After graduating from the University of California, Los Angeles, Demopoulos joined News Corporation and was sent to China for business development. He was involved with a range of News Corp companies including Twentieth Century Fox, STAR TV, NDS, and ChinaByte.

During the dot.com boom in the late 1990s, Demopoulos could no longer take the passenger seat and he founded his own company with a few friends. They started a sports portal Shawei.com, which means "brave shark" in Chinese. "One inspiration was from Sina, which also built up its reputation from covering sport. Murdoch's commitment to sports media was another," said Demopoulos. Sina was China's top online portal. Shawei soon attracted investment from Intel, IDG, and Softbank. By 2000, it was sold to Tom.com, an internet startup backed by Hong Kong tycoon, Li Kashing.

Demopoulos went back to working for others again. He joined Netease, the country's leading online games company and the third largest portal, as a senior vice president for business development. During that time, he met a lot of companies interested in partnering with Netease. He evaluated a lot of business proposals, and also came across a lot of ventures seeking investment.

By 2005, he was ready to start a new venture again. He contacted his old mates at Shawei, Douglas Khoo and Chen Chaozhuang. Khoo is a cofounder of Shawei, a Malaysian of Chinese descent. He has been involved in both the interactive and traditional advertising and marketing communications business for almost 20 years. Chen is the chief technology officer of Shawei. He is a native of Shanghai, he was working for the World Bank in Washington DC, building its intranet at that time.[139]

The three founded another internet business, called Qunar.com. It was a travel search engine, like that of American-based Kayah.com. Qunar aggregates information from other travel sites belonging to travel agencies, airlines, and hotels, so that consumers can easily compare the prices of flights and hotels between different providers.

Qunar soon became popular among travelers looking for cheaper air tickets and hotel rooms. By 2008, it was the country's most trafficked travel site. The number of unique visitors surpassed 12 million in October 2007, and reached 26 million in November 2008.[140]

Qunar does not sell directly to consumers; instead, it redirects the consumers to their preferred website to make their reservation. Thus, it makes money from pay-per-click advertising, when the consumer clicks through to one of the compared websites.

It attracted US$2 million investment from GSR Ventures and Mayfield in June 2006, and another US$10 million from the two and Lehman Brothers in late 2007. By late 2008, Demopoulos said the operation had basically broken even, but it might fluctuate due to seasonal factors. He looked forward to listing the company in a few years.

[139] Source: *http://www.qunar.com/site/en/Founders_1.3.shtml*
[140] Source: *http://www.qunar.com/site/en/enMilestones.shtml*

What have we learned?

Chinese internet entrepreneurs haven't always—or even generally—been successful. That should not come as a surprise. The internet is a new and rapidly evolving set of technology platforms, with challenges and opportunities that change by the day. There is arguably no other business quite as challenging or competitive.

Yet a glance at the internet playing field in China today should convince you that few can be successful in China without being steeped in the local culture. Foreign firms have, to their chagrin, found that business plans that have worked in the West can fail spectacularly in China. Yahoo, Google, and Microsoft have all experienced this, without clearly understanding why their previous success stories couldn't be extended into China. Indeed, their Chinese rivals' successes are predicated on abandoning American experiences and practices.

In this chapter, we will try to sum up the key differences in China and how successful Chinese internet competitors synthesized components from their Western counterparts, all the while innovating to accommodate the unique characteristics of the Chinese market.

We will also lay out some insights for the aspiring entrepreneur on how to "get right" your plans for entry into China's hypercompetitive web business markets.

The Chinese differences

First of all, Chinese internet users are different and their needs are different.

1 The internet is for young people looking for fun and friends.

While over 70 percent of the American internet population is over 30 years old, the opposite is true in China, where 70 percent of the internet population is under 30 years old. They look for entertainment and companionship online, especially as most of them come from single-child families.

This explains why online games, which provide the perfect playground for young people seeking friends and fun, is the most vibrant sector of the Chinese internet. In fact, out of China's ten largest internet companies by revenue, six offer online games as their major business. The largest, Tencent, was able to turn its online chat services into a goldmine, because it treated online chat as a community for young people, not a tool for adults. Tencent, too, derived a significant part of its revenue from online games. The rest of its revenue is mostly entertainment related, such as avatars, ringtones, and so forth.

Even search engine Baidu is heavily focused on the fun and friends concept. In the early days, it built its popularity through MP3 downloads, and many of its popular applications are built around community. For example, its Postbar (Tieba), a virtual forum where users discuss all kinds of topics, now accounts for 14 percent of the site's total traffic. Another service, Baidu Knows (Zhidao), a community-driven knowledge base where users answer each other's questions, has also been a hit.

2 The competitive landscapes of many industries are different in China.

Another point Westerners should be aware of is that many industries in China have a very different competitive landscape from that in the developed Western world. One example is the media sector.

While the media industry in the West is concentrated in the hands of a few powerful people and companies, China's media sector is highly fragmented, with very few strong players. The weak media sector created an opportunity for web portal Sina to offer an online alternative.

It built its business by gathering content from newspapers and magazines across the country. By focusing on topics of interest to the wider public, it stands out easily from the traditional media companies that are either too small or too identified with the government. In fact, most of these media companies have become Sina's partners, believing this can boost their reputation and influence.

Similarly, China's dominant video sharing site, Youku, built its popularity by partnering with television stations. Most videos watched in Youku are TV programs made in China, rather than homemade video clips uploaded by users.

3 Much of the infrastructure we take for granted in America has not yet been developed in China.

Another major difference can be found in China's infrastructure.

In America, payment by credit card was well developed before the internet emerged. But, payment solutions were still immature in China when the internet became popular there. So there have been many innovations in the Chinese internet sector aimed at resolving the payment issue.

For example, the innovation of Chen Tianqiao, founder of Shanda, the first major online game company in China, was not the games, but how to get paid. Its games were licensed from Korea, where MMORPG, or Massive Multiplayer Online Role-Playing Games, had been going strong for several years.

Chen's payment solution was rather simple, but very much adapted to the business and social realities in China—prepaid cards bearing an access code and password, and sold through hundreds of thousands of retail outlets. Chen also created a computer program to sell prepaid cards virtually in internet cafés, the main venue for online games in China.

As cellphone operators in China opened their platforms for third parties to provide data services, cellphones also became an alternative payment channel. Tencent, which operated China's largest online chat service QQ, used the cellphone platform as a way for its users to pay premium service fees and buy its virtual currency (Q coins) to enjoy other benefits.

Collecting a tiny amount (RMB5–10) from millions of users could be time-consuming and tedious work. But now, China Mobile and China Unicom can do this for Tencent through their payment channels and give Tencent the sum at the end of each month.

4 People still do most of the work in China's internet businesses.

As labor costs are low in China, many of the problems faced by internet companies are solved using people.

For example, selling keywords is problematic in China. In North America and Europe, tens of thousands of small advertisers bid for keywords online via Google's AdWords and pay by credit card. However, the vast bulk of potential Chinese users has yet to attain that level of sophistication.

Knowing very few would voluntarily go online and bid for keywords in China, Baidu used a third-party sales agent to cold-call anyone who might listen, and even to go door-to-door if necessary. The agents taught potential customers the keyword bidding process step-by-step, and when that was too difficult they simply did the work for them. They also collected payment on Baidu's behalf. Later, Baidu took part of the operation in-house and created its own sales force to cold-call potential customers.

Another example of people power is online travel agent Ctrip. After realizing that very few consumers were booking hotels and flights online, Ctrip sent promoters to greet travelers at train stations and airports. The promoters handed them a membership card, along with a booklet of hotel prices and a telephone number for reservations.

To handle the travelers' calls, Ctrip set up a massive call center with thousands of staff. Most of the world's online travel agents give customers a number they can call—but that is usually just for exceptional situations. In Ctrip's case, the opposite is true. The website is the exception and the call center, which handles more than 70 percent of the reservations, is the rule.

5 The internet café is an important part of Chinese cyberspace.

In America, the use of internet cafés is often limited to tourists checking emails. In China, however, 42.4 percent of the country's 298 million internet users go online in internet cafés, according to a survey carried out by CNNIC in 2008. With limited sports facilities and other entertainment options, an internet café is usually where the kids and teenagers in the neighborhood hang out.

Internet cafés have played a vital role in the development of the internet in China. For many, especially the poorest people, internet cafés are the first place they encounter computers and the online world.

Aware of their importance, Baidu formed alliances with a number of directory websites, which are popular in internet cafés. The café owners usually refer the novices to directory websites that show them how to find the sites that appeal to their particular interests. By partnering with these directory sites, Baidu has built up a strong following among internet newbies. Just before the IPO, Baidu purchased the most popular directory site Hao123.com. Baidu also persuaded many internet café owners to make Baidu.com the default site on their web browsers. This partly contributed to Baidu's lead over Google in China.

As internet cafés are the entertainment hubs for kids and teenagers, trends can easily spread there—making them a perfect marketing channel. When online game operator Giant Interactive wanted to promote its game ZT Online, it chose internet cafés. A 2,000-strong army of promoters was sent to internet cafés in every city and every town to encourage players to join the new game.

The promotion worked very well. A year and a half after its official launch, ZT Online became the second game in China's internet history to have more than one million players during its peak hour.

6 Government policies and market conditions can change quickly in China.

The boom and bust cycle of the mobile data sector is primarily the result of the changing policies of the cellphone operators, China Mobile and China Unicom.

In early 2001, they wanted to encourage third-party participation and the terms were very generous. A whole generation of new companies flourished. But, by the beginning of 2004, the cellphone operators wanted to tighten their hold and took part of the mobile data business back in-house. (To be fair, some of the cellphone operators' control measures were necessary, as abuse of users rights was common.) This led to the collapse of the sector. The fate of third-party mobile data service providers changed overnight, and many have been running at a loss since mid 2006.

Although China is becoming more and more open in its economic system, many businesses in China still depend a lot on government policies. Investors should beware of businesses that are booming only because of favorable government policies or market conditions, because such policies or conditions might change in a few years, leaving them with losses.

The video sharing business provides another example of how quickly conditions may change. After YouTube became popular in 2005, many similar services emerged in China. At first they were scarcely regulated, but in 2008 the government began to assert its control. Leading operators Youku and Tudou were able to conform to the government's regulations and received their licenses without experiencing much interruption of service. But 56.com, the third largest video sharing site at the time, ran into problems that caused the government to shut it down for a month. Afterwards, 56.com's market share plunged and it ceased to be a major player. Many of its top executives deserted the company.

7 The problem of rampant piracy.

Piracy is such a big problem in China that the usual rules about how to profit from intellectual property do not apply.

With rampant piracy, selling a song over the internet is almost impossible in China. But using the internet to promote a song worked like magic, as the internet song phenomenon showed. Before he wrote the song "Mice Love Rice," singer/composer Yang Chengang was unknown and broke. But his decision to give up his copyright and let people freely download the song ultimately made him rich.

Ironically, Baidu's MP3 search engine, condemned by record companies the world over as a facilitator of piracy, was the powerful tool that made Yang a star. Within a few months, every youth in the country had heard the song. This kind of publicity would have cost Yang millions of dollars if he had promoted his song in the traditional way, through advertising and media events.

Ultimately, the best way of profiting from the song was through cellphones—ringtone downloads and ring-back tones—where piracy was much less of a problem. In fact, the online game sector has worked in a similar way. Game software is free to download, but users must pay for the privilege of playing with thousands of other users.

As the government tightens regulations and enforces laws, China's piracy problem might eventually improve. But for the time being, instead of fighting piracy over the internet, the best tactic is simply to use the internet as a channel for free promotion and profit via other means, for example through ringtones or live concerts.

Dos and don'ts

By now, we have hopefully dispelled any illusions you may have had that China's "one billion customers" will easily yield to your innovations. The going will be rougher than at home, with cultural pitfalls, mixed communications, and aggressive competitors taking aim at exactly the same customers as you.

If you are not from China, you are going to have to innovate more creatively, work harder, and offer better services to overcome your inherent limitations. And it will all be worth it, because in the end, there are "one billion customers" (1.3 billion, more precisely) and these customers are worth having. Besides, you will have a chance to learn, live, and embrace one of the world's great cultures in the process—in a country that will be a major force on the world stage over the coming century.

The stories in this book provide a wealth of insight for the aspiring entrepreneur planning an entry into China's hypercompetitive web business markets on how to "get it right." So how do you get started? Read on.

1 Keen powers of observation are the key to developing any good business model.

First of all, you should study carefully the market you are addressing.

At Alibaba, it was Jack Ma and his closest advisers who kept an eye out for any useful adaptations to their business model. Ma's own experience gave him insight into the informational and logistic problems of China's trade, and Alibaba was his choice of how to solve it—his version of a B2B platform, an electronic message board for buyers and suppliers to exchange information freely.

Western internet companies have been slow to move into Ma's competitive space, to assist the thousands of small factories looking for new trading partners. Probably because they have never seen how traders and manufacturers work in China—what problems they are facing and what their key concerns are.

On the other hand, Jack Ma's insight likely arose directly as a result of his proximity to Hangzho, which was full of small factories making everything from buttons to television sets, most of them for export. Global Sources developed similar platforms from its trade magazine business that it had grown over 40 years of operating out of the trading center of Hong Kong.

Somewhat related is the second rule:

2 When adapting a business for China, remember to keep your eyes open. What is great in your home country may not be desirable in China. Conversely, what is not an option in your home country may be a great opportunity in China.

Sina started its business by imitating Yahoo. But very soon, its founder Wang Zhidong realized one thing stood out—news. The Chinese internet users had a much greater appetite for news than for other services, so instead of imitating Yahoo's scattergun approach, he focused on news alone. Hundreds of editors painstakingly gathered news from all the leading newspapers and magazines in China for his site. By taking this approach, Sina.com became not only the largest online portal in China, but also the country's dominant online media firm.

The same opportunities might not exist for Yahoo. The media industry in the West is concentrated in the hands of a few powerhouses. If Yahoo had wanted to use their content on its site, it would have had to pay a high price.

Google has tried something similar with its news search by aggregating many news sources on the web, which caused some problems with major media companies. In April 2009, media mogul Rupert Murdoch accused Google of committing copyright theft by borrowing material from news stories to assemble search rankings. Shortly after, Associated Press, a 163-year-old cooperative owned by news organizations, weighed in with a similar charge—though it did not mention Google—announcing a content protection initiative and threatening legal and legislative action against news aggregators.[141]

As the power of traditional media firms declines in the West, they might be more willing to cooperate with online portals. Recently, Yahoo has been successful in partnering with some smaller publications in America to show their content on its site.[142]

3 Don't underestimate the size and complexity of the Chinese market. Don't try to force too many of your own ways on your China divisions. Listen to your Chinese team members.

When a multinational arrives in a new market, it must decide how much it wants to adapt its original model to local tastes.

Many Asian cities (such as Hong Kong and Singapore) have a small internet population, which makes developing new features for local markets expensive. So most American internet companies just moved in with their existing models. Their only major concession to local needs was to change the language of the web page. They usually have a small office for sales and marketing and rely on headquarters for everything else. This might work, because most local markets are too small to support their own internet alternatives.

[141] Source: Dirk Smillie, "AP's Curley Has Fightin' Words For Google," *Forbes.com*, April 30, 2009.

[142] Source: Evan Hessel, "Yahoo!'s Dangerous Newspaper Deal?" *Forbes.com*, Jun 22, 2009.

China is very different though. At over 338 million users, its internet population is already the largest in the world.[143] It can support its own local internet firms, with unique business models that suit local tastes. In fact, before the multinationals came in, the market was already packed with local rivals competing vigorously among themselves. The structure of the multinationals' divisions in other Asian cities—small offices totally controlled by headquarters—does not apply to China.

However, many American internet companies underestimated the Chinese market and tried to do things their own way.

At eBay China, the local team had to face an aggressive rival, Taobao, with their hands tied. eBay China's technology platform was moved to America, and every decision had to go through headquarters. A lot of information was lost in the communication process, particularly as eBay China's junior staff did not speak English well and thus were not able to make compelling arguments in a foreign language.

By trying too hard to consolidate its operations at headquarters, eBay quickly lost its dominance in China. On the day of the platform move, traffic to eBay China dropped by half. What had been information flow within China became traffic across borders and across the Pacific Ocean. However, the internet infrastructure between China and America was not very good at the time. The loading speed of eBay China's web page, one of the most important user issues, slowed dramatically.

Six months after the move, Taobao had turned the tables on eBay China, capturing 60 percent of the market while its rival languished at 30 percent. eBay's China team could have warned its headquarters and stopped them from moving the platform prematurely. (eBay's China team had raised concerns about transmission speed issues across the Pacific Ocean.) Such concerns, however, were downplayed during the eBay technology team's presentation to eBay's then CEO, Meg Whitman.

eBay might have had better results in China if it had listened to its local staff more.

4 Foreign companies entering China should be warned: a better technology alone is not enough to ensure success.

Baidu's overwhelming lead over Google (60 to 30 percent) goes to show that those with inferior technology can win in China by having more customized solutions for the local market.

143 Source: CNNIC, end of June 2009.

Baidu's applications, such as MP3 search, virtual forum—Postbar (Tiebar)—and community driven knowledge base—Baidu Know (Zhidao)—are hardly advanced in technology. But they made Baidu popular in China, particularly among young people looking for entertainment and friendship.

Many other examples in China's internet sectors showed that the best solution might require no technology at all. For instance, Ctrip uses promoters to market its travel services in train stations and airports.

Shanda's solution to the payment issue in online games (prepaid cards plus an e-sale system at internet cafés) was hardly advanced in terms of technology, either.

5 Don't assume your brand to be a household name.

You might think you have a household name. But you still need to advertise your brand in China to reach the mass market.

Although many Chinese are studying English, their primary language used in day-to-day life is still predominantly Chinese alone. Western media is not popular in China. Most people either don't know or sometimes don't care what is popular in the Western market.

For example, Google is a synonym of search online in the Western world. But you would be amazed by how many Chinese could not even spell it right. Failure to advertise its name aggressively was blamed as the reason for Google's rather low market awareness in China.

"When Google started in America in 1996, it beat AltaVista, the dominant search engine then, by viral marketing alone. So, it believed having a great product alone was enough to win a market share. But, the situation in China was different," said T. R. Harrington, director of Darwin Marketing.

Internet penetration in China (about 25 percent in June 2009) was too low for viral or word-of-mouth marketing to be highly effective. Besides, according to Harrington, the difference between Baidu and Google was not large enough for people to switch immediately. In contrast, Baidu spent a lot on all kinds of advertising—TV, billboards, printed, online, and so on, after it raised enough money from an IPO. These greatly increased its brand recognition and ensured its rapid growth in market share after the IPO.

6 How to deal with aggressive local rivals with fewer competitive scruples.

Because China is an emerging market, there are many areas where laws are unclear and business practices unsound. To achieve what they want, local players are sometimes not afraid to cross lines or break the law.

Facing such a rival, don't just cry "this is unfair." Instead, identify all the tactics your opponents are using to win market share. *Some will be smart—and ethical—and worth imitating.*

For example, Google followed Baidu in using third-party sales agents to target small businesses in China. And after Baidu acquired the most popular directory site Hao123.com, Google bought the second most popular, 265.com, to attract internet novices.

As for tricks that might be considered improper or illegal in your home country, steer clear.

Google neither introduced illegal music search nor mixed search results with paid ads. And it continues to enjoy healthy profits and growth in China.

Finally, play to your strengths.

You undoubtedly have advantages your local rivals can't match. For example, Google has a global user network whereas Baidu's is China-only. Companies in China need Google to market their products and services overseas, and Google's better technology also gives it an edge on its ad platform and network sites.

Remember that as China becomes more integrated with the rest of world, its legal system will get tougher, and customers and competitors will be faster to denounce unethical practices. Companies whose success depends on their ability to walk a fine line between legality and illegality will not last.

7 A local partner can be very useful in entering China's market, but be careful.

Although the Korean game company Wemade's Mir 2 was a good quality game, for Mir 2 to succeed in China its local operator Shanda had to put in a lot of effort. Issues the firm had to solve included payment, working with internet cafés, partnering with fixed line operators, dealing with private servers, and cheating programs. These are difficult, if not impossible, for a foreign company to do in China.

Partnering with local operators seemed the way to go for many foreign game companies. As long as their games were good, they had no problem finding local partners under favorable terms, as Blizzard found out from its experience with World of Warcraft. It first partnered with Shanghai-based The9 and then Guangzhou-based Netease.

But there are hazards, too. Is the local partner honest about the quantity of product sold, the sales commission to local distributors, and so on? Local partners could start to produce copycats of your products, if they become successful in the market. After fighting bitterly with Wemade over loyalty issues, Shanda made Woool, its own sequel to Mir 2, out of despair. But other game companies have tried to make clones of games they licensed, just for higher profit.

Another example is Baidu. Using third-party agents helps Baidu to sell keywords successfully to hundreds of thousands of small and medium-sized businesses in China. However, it found out that some third-party sales agents had been telling potential clients that their sites would be deleted from the search engine's index and that access to their sites would be denied even to users who specifically searched for it, unless they agreed to join its advertising program. Though Baidu publicly denied this bogus claim, its reputation did suffer damage.

8 Serving the bottom of the pyramid could be a very profitable business.

The success of online game companies in China proved that serving low-end internet users in China could be a very profitable business.

Although this group, consisting mainly of students and young workers, cannot pay large amounts, their number is huge and they lack entertainment alternatives. Therefore, as long as the price is low, they are willing to try many new services. Besides online games, the mobile data services (e.g. ringtones) and online chat service QQ also benefit from serving this group.

The financial crisis has, in fact, had very little impact on those providing a low-cost entertainment alternative—as a student or an unemployed factory worker can still easily pay RMB50–100 a month. Tencent, operator of QQ, and the online games companies in China have been doing very well during the economic downturn that started in 2008.

Compared with Google, Baidu also served primarily the low-end market—the average spend of a Baidu client was just US$674 per quarter in late 2008. Nevertheless, its market share in China led Google by a huge margin. As of the end of 2008, Baidu controlled an estimated 60 percent of the search market, compared to 30 percent for Google, according to market research firm Analysys International.

9 Never neglect newbies.

The last lesson we want to share with entrepreneurs coming into China is: never neglect the needs of newbies.

Baidu has been smart to focus on first-time internet users right from the start. It has formed alliances with a number of directory websites, which are popular in the internet cafés where many Chinese teens get their first online experience. It has also persuaded many internet café owners to make Baidu.com the default site on their web browsers.

In addition, it created a new method for inputting Chinese in the search box, so that newbies can easily get their results. And there were plenty of other examples of Baidu making an effort to reach out to new users, addressing their needs and helping them to use search. Winning the allegiance of internet neophytes is good business for Baidu. It allowed Baidu, not Google, to be the synonym for search in China.

Internet usership is growing fast in China. Newbies account for a large part of the Chinese internet population. Of the 298 million Chinese online at the end of 2008, about 30 percent had come online within the previous 12 months, while 46 percent had less than 18 months of online experience.[144] The Chinese internet market is still in a high-growth phase, having just achieved around 25 percent penetration in June 2009. Every year brings a flood of new users. Being the first to reach them, please them, and win their loyalty will be the key to your success.

Similarly, this applies to other products and services in China. If it is still relatively new to the market, find out where a typical consumer first encountered the product or service—can you promote your brand in that channel? What is stopping consumers from using the product or service—can you do something to persuade them to use it?

144 Source: CNNIC.

Internet development: China's conundrum

In August 2009, the market value of the largest Chinese internet company, Tencent, at US$27 billion, had surpassed that of Yahoo (US$21 billion) and was rapidly approaching that of eBay (US$28 billion). Many Chinese internet entrepreneurs have expanded from their niche markets to become major players in the industry. But how did this rag-tag band of entrepreneurs grow so successful?

Surprisingly, it is because the Chinese government—long characterized, somewhat unfairly, as an overbearing, doctrinaire monolith—actually took a step back when the internet took off in 1995. Of course, it expressed concerns about politically sensitive news and discourse, which at times led to blatant censorship (for example, the Great Firewall, the Green Dam[145], the blocking of Google and Facebook, and so on). But when it comes to commercially important issues, the Chinese government knows when to get out of the way.

"While regulating the internet is important, government's role is also to provide a healthy environment for the industry to grow," said Kou Xiaowei, a deputy director of the General Administration of Press and Publication (GAPP). GAPP is a key government body in the regulation of online games in China.

And compared to other industrial sectors in China (telecoms, steel, and banks, to name a few), the internet is handled with kid gloves. In telecoms and heavy industry, government entities are both regulators and players (through state-owned enterprises). China's internet sector has more freedom, is more dynamic, and more successful. All the major internet players in China are private companies, many of which are listed on foreign stock exchanges—even their initial investments came largely from overseas sources, through venture capital funds. The major Chinese internet companies discussed in this book—Sina, Ctrip, Baidu, Shanda, Alibaba, Tencent, etc.—all received their orig-

[145] Green Dam is a content control software program developed in China. Under a directive from the Ministry of Industry and Information Technology (MIIT) that took effect on July 1, 2009, it is mandatory to have either the software or its setup files pre-installed on all new personal computers sold in China. However, because of strong protests from the public, the plan has been delayed to an undetermined date.

inal investment through venture capitalists, ultimately going public on either the NASDAQ or Hong Kong stock exchanges.

Timing was important, too. Deng Xiaoping completed his Southern Tour through China in 1992, kicking off China's economic boom. Shortly thereafter, American serial entrepreneur Jim Clark convinced computer scientist Marc Andreessen to commercialize the Mosaic web browser he had developed at the University of Illinois to provide an internet alternative to interactive TV. By 1995, both the Chinese economy and the World Wide Web were on a roll.

"At that time, China's paramount leader Deng Xiaoping had just finished his famous Southern Tour and reconfirmed the country's direction of continual reform and an open market," said J. P. Gan, managing director of Qiming Venture Partners, who has been investing in internet startups in the country since his days with Carlyle in 1999.

Deng's Southern Tour was more or less a private tour of China's most successful cities (Guangzhou, Shenzhen, Zhuhai in the south, and Shanghai in the north) following his retirement. His apocryphal phrase, "To get rich is glorious," took the public's fancy and kicked off a wave of entrepreneurship that opened up unprecedented opportunities for—among others—internet entrepreneurs.

Most impressive, though, is the awareness and understanding of America's internet innovations that many of these Chinese entrepreneurs demonstrated—innovations that were lost on many Americans, even. During the 1990s, the Chinese government felt that the internet was too small to consider it a threat—less than 1 percent of the country's population was online in 1999[146]—and took a hands-off approach that the tightly controlled media sector came to envy. Indeed, government bureaucrats saw the internet more as a technological innovation. The most involved government body at that time was the Ministry of Information Industry (MII), which oversaw the development of the country's telecoms infrastructure. MII saw the internet as another way of increasing China's telecoms usage, and thus its own revenues. It actually tried to encourage internet service usage.

With no state-owned enterprises as competitors, little direct government control, and relatively low barriers to entry, Chinese internet entrepreneurs flourished. They had access to Silicon Valley's capital

[146] Source: CNNIC.

and know-how, as many of the entrepreneurs were returnees from overseas. Our book discusses many of these "sea turtles", for example Baidu's Robin Li, Sohu's Charles Zhang, and Ctrip's James Liang. Indeed, many of them were valuable members of the American engineering community before they returned to China.

They competed vigorously against each other—spreading use of the internet in China, and at the same time pushing the limits of social and sometimes legal boundaries. The rivalry was brutal, and innovation thrived. The result: a burgeoning Chinese internet market with a bevy of competing services, and huge benefits to users who got high-quality services at bargain basement prices.

The strongest players, with the most creative ideas and best overall performance, eventually dominated their individual sectors—Baidu for search engines, Tencent for online chat, and Sina for online portals. In fact, today these companies are so strong that they have beaten their Western rivals—Google, eBay, Yahoo, and so on—in the relentless battle for the Chinese online consumer's loyalty.

As of mid 2009, China's internet is no longer a niche market. Over 25 percent of the country's population is online[147], and the numbers are increasing faster than anywhere else in the world. This is a mixed blessing, as the internet has now "come to the attention of the authorities." China's government has recognized the internet as a powerful media force, and something to be controlled; industry insiders are feeling the government's tightening grip. Regulation is no longer solely the domain of the business and technology friendly MII, which recently changed its name to the Ministry of Industry and Information Technology (MIIT). New, hard-line regulators are entering the fray, for example the State Administration of Radio, Film, and Television (SARFT).[148] SARFT traditionally regulated China's TV stations and it cares more about policy and political agenda than about promoting internet use.

The change was most apparent in the licensing of video sharing sites in 2008. SARFT initially required all video sharing sites to be government owned, as with TV stations. Strong protests from the industry,

[147] CNNIC found that there were 338 million internet users in China in June 2009, or 25.5 percent of the country's total population.

[148] Apart from MIIT and SARFT, other Chinese authorities overseeing the internet include the Police Department, the Ministry of Culture, and the General Administration of Press and Publication (GAPP). The propaganda department of the Chinese Communist Party is also involved.

though, forced it to cancel this strict requirement. Still, a frustrating litany of requirements needed to be met before licenses were issued. SARFT even made an example of one of the major players, to show that it meant business. Guangzhou-based 56.com, the third most popular video sharing site at the time, was suspended for a month in June 2008 before eventually getting its license. The effects were devastating—56.com lost its popularity and ceased to be a major player. SARFT's message was not lost on other companies. "People worried whether the government would continue its open market policy or decide to get more involved," said an industry insider.

Kou, however, did not think that the government's role in internet business had changed fundamentally in recent years. "The first internet regulation was issued in 2000 by the State Council. Since the industry was still in its infancy, there was no way to make detailed rules for different internet businesses. MIIT was most involved in the early days (1995–2000) because the internet was technology driven, and the major task in those days was building infrastructures, such as providing internet access to the public (i.e. ISPs)," said Kou. "As internet services develop and mature, the government can implement more detailed rules to regulate different internet businesses."

Kou believes there will be more regulations coming out in the next two to three years, as the government figures out how to regulate the industry in a more detailed manner. "The internet is like a double-edged sword. There is no doubt its development will benefit society and people. But, without proper control, it can also have a negative impact," said Kou.

The current regulatory environment reflects China's (and, indeed, most countries') consternation over exactly how much control is healthy in an industry. Over-controlling it would kill the creativity that has generated so much wealth, employment, and innovation. Under-controlling it allows media and technology to be used in acts that are harmful to society and to the government itself. The emerging challenge facing the Chinese government is how far it can balançe its urge to control the web, while keeping entrepreneurial spirits flourishing.

"Ultimately, the government does not want to kill the internet industry. We just try to rule out what is deemed improper," said Kou. (For more information about how the Chinese government regulates the country's internet sector, please refer to the "Dialogue with a Chinese official" on our website: *www.redwiredrevolution.com*.)

China's internet and the new regionalism

The 19th century belonged to England,
The 20th century belonged to the U.S., and
The 21st century belongs to China.
Invest accordingly.

Warren Buffett[149]

The internet was supposed to be an instrument for flattening out and homogenizing the world.

"When the world is flat, you can innovate without having to emigrate," argued Thomas Friedman.[150] The stories you have read throughout this book should have convinced you, though, that China's regional internet services are taking on their own economic and cultural forms. Cyberspace is emerging as a more varied and interesting place than we initially thought, with China playing its unique role in this transformation.

Since the early days of the Cold War, when the precursors of the internet were being assembled, international relations and commercial policy have toyed with concepts of regionalism (counterpoised by multilateralism and unilateralism). Regionalism builds on a common sense of identity and purpose, combined with the creation and implementation of institutions that express a particular identity and shape collective action within a geographical region. China's emergence as the major power—political, economic, and cultural—in the Asia-Pacific region defines a special role for its culture and policies. This will be projected onto the evolution of its contribution and role in the transition of economies and culture into cyberspace.

Our final chapter examines the emergence of China's web presence, and how it will affect the evolution of regional culture, economics, and social activity that revolves around the internet.

[149] Source: Chuck Saletta, "Why the 21st Century Belongs to China," *www.fool.com*, Feb 3, 2009.

[150] Source: T. L. Friedman, *The World Is Flat: A Brief History of the Twenty-first Century*, Farrar, Straus, and Giroux, 2005.

Governance or government?

Cold War era regionalism was traditionally about government—how to insert a layer exercising power into the hierarchy of state–local relations. In the future, regionalism will be about governance—about the coordination of people, economics, and activities impelled through vision, imagination, and insight. Regions will differentiate themselves by their vision and goals, and will market these intensely to each other. The emerging influence of governance—versus the raw power of government—recognizes the importance of quality of life and competitiveness in a region.

This will be a shared responsibility in all sectors of a region, where investment in vision and goals is implemented through marketing and collaborative decisions. Moreover, it requires the shared powers and talents of these sectors working strategically to ensure success.

China, arguably, has a longer tradition of innovation in both government and governance than nearly any other society. One thousand years ago, Song Dynasty China witnessed a flourishing of innovation unlike anything the world had ever known. Around its capital of Hangzhou, it saw an explosion of wealth and technology unknown again until the years following Deng Xiaoping's southern tour of China in the spring of 1992. Song China was the first government in world history to issue banknotes or paper money, and the first Chinese policy to establish a permanent standing navy. The Song developed revolutionary new military technologies augmented by the use of gunpowder. Innovations in agriculture doubled China's population and the number of inhabitants in Hangzhou—described by Marco Polo as "the City of Heaven, beyond dispute the finest and the noblest in the world"—grew to over 2 million, making it the largest city in the world.

Song Chinese governance of a millennium ago engendered a gregarious social scene, at once vibrant and intellectually expansive. Art flourished, and people intermingled at public festivals and private clubs; literature and knowledge spread through the innovation of woodblock printing and the Song innovation of movable type printing. Movable type printing made paper currency possible, which the Song Dynasty government began circulating among the traders in their monopolized salt industry.

Song China's governance was so influential that Kublai Khan, who founded the Mongol Yuan Dynasty, bought into the Song vision.

Kublai immersed himself in Song culture and was so embarrassed by his rustic Mongol kin that he built the Forbidden City (under the Mongols, a walled courtyard) to hide them from Chinese eyes. Kublai grew to such enormous girth on a diet of Chinese pastries that he was unable to ride a horse (unheard of for a Mongol), instead employing a "Grand Pavilion" supported by four elephants to transfer him about the Empire.

The West remained ignorant of Chinese innovations in governance because Song traditions gave way to power politics, and the evolution of Chinese innovation was fitful, with high spots in the Ming Dynasty followed by low spots in the Manchu Qing Dynasty and the brutal warlords of the twentieth century. The China we knew in the twentieth century never truly reflected China's innovations in governance. Deng Xiaoping's southern tour of China in 1992 set the tone for a new Song Dynasty that is only bearing fruit decades later. And we should not be a bit surprised that the journey has returned us to Marco Polo's "noble city," Hangzhou, where the transformative figure Jack Ma chose to stake his claim on the explosion of innovation surrounding the internet.

The fifth century BC philosopher Confucius argued that the best government was one that "impels" its citizens to do the right thing. In his *Analects*, he advises, "if the people be led by laws, and uniformity sought to be given them by punishments, they will try to avoid the punishment, but have no sense of shame. If they be led by virtue, and uniformity sought to be given them by the rules of propriety, they will have the sense of shame, and moreover will become good." Shame, in Confucius' mind, impels citizens to formulate their own goals in pursuit of their duties, rather than requiring the State to lay down every possible law that might be required (a doctrine that came to be known as Legalism in China). In this sense, one can rightly argue that governance is the goal of Confucian teachings, and that government—insertion of a legal system into the hierarchy—is antithetical to these teachings.

Process or structure?

In governance, process trumps structure. It's where you are heading, not the way that you do it, that counts. Cold War regionalism spent a great deal of time worrying about how governments should look at how close their institutions were to those in America. Unfortunately, rigid structure is inclined to protect the status quo—warts and all. If all you have ever seen is "X," then any other structure is going to look unfamiliar, and probably bad. Structure stifles innovation and technological advancement—both have become international coins of the realm in the twenty-first century.

China's "new regionalism" is more likely to incline toward Deng Xiaoping's sentiment that, "it does not matter whether the cat is black or white; as long as it catches the mouse, it is a good cat."[151] It is just as likely to select a structural alternative as a strategy for achieving an objective, but its main focus is on processes—visioning, strategic planning, conflict resolution, and consensus building—that will get it where it wants to go.

The biggest problem with structure is the sheer pace of technological advancement today. Research and development of technologies and their application to everyday problems comprise the processes most focused on in the twenty-first century. The competitive advantage of nations and firms is rooted in technology, which is always in flux. There is no preferred structure for advancing technology—technology itself changes the processes constantly, as new tools become available. Twenty years ago, pharmaceutical research took place in organic chemistry labs; today, it is as likely to take place inside computer algorithms.

China has, at times in its history, shown brilliance in contributing to the integration of technological advances into governance. The Song Dynasty produced scientists such as the polymathic Shen Kuo, who advanced technology, philosophy, mathematics, and engineering. No culture before had seen the brilliance of Shen Kuo—mathematician, astronomer, meteorologist, geologist, zoologist, botanist, pharmacologist, agronomist, ethnographer, encyclopedist, poet, general, diplomat, hydraulic engineer, inventor, academy chancellor, finance minister, and government state inspector. He described the magnetic needle compass a century before its discovery in Europe, discovered the concept of true north four hundred years prior to Edmund Halley's discoveries in Europe, accurately mapped the orbital paths of the moon and the planets, fixed the degree position of the Pole Star, and argued that the sun and moon were spherical in shape, not flat. He

[151] Deng Xiaoping on his southern tour, commenting on whether China should turn to capitalism or remain strictly in adherence with the economic ideologies of communism.

devised a geological theory of land formation not seen in the West until the late nineteenth century. He developed the dry dock to repair boats suspended out of water, wrote extensively about movable type printing, and experimented with camera obscura. Shen's brilliance was able to thrive because the Song governance stayed focused on objectives—on the "mouse catching"—rather than the means—the "cat." With luck, Shen's modern counterparts will initiate a new renaissance—indications are that they are well along in the process.

China's defining architectural monument, the Great Wall, was, shortly after Shen's day, the pinnacle of technological achievement. But it also reflects one of the greatest threats to the process of technological advance—China's surfeit of affordable labor. The human cost of constructing the Great Wall was immense. Over one million troops built it, with as many as 400,000 dying along the way. Legend holds that thousands were entombed within it. With an abundance of cheap labor, there is less incentive to explore processes and devise machines to take their place—a recurring conundrum for Chinese technological prowess that affects governance to this day.

Open or closed?

Emperor Qianlong expressed a long-held Chinese sentiment to Lord Macartney—that "all countries are peripheral in comparison to China." China's penchant for excluding the world is conveyed most dramatically in the Great Wall—the oldest architectural monument in China and one of the best-known structures in modern history. Its scale is monumental, snaking through rugged mountainous terrain and inaccessible locations for 4,000 miles (6,000 kilometers), from the Bohai Sea in Shanhaiguan to Jiayugan in Gansu province. Initially constructed for defensive purposes to help the Mings thwart their Manchu invaders[152], it unfortunately proved unsuccessful. Not through any technological flaws, but because a disgruntled general Wu Sangui opened the gates at Shanhaiguan, letting the Manchus invade. The Great Wall remains the most extravagant means by which China has distanced itself from the world (and the world from it).

152 The Great Wall of China was first built around the 5th century BC. It was rebuilt and maintained until the 16th century to protect the northern borders of the Chinese Empire during various successive dynasties. The current wall was built during the Ming Dynasty (1368–1644).

At other times, China has opened up to the world with great success. Ming emperor Zhu Di made favored eunuch Zheng He (known as Sinbad to the West through tales of his travels) the admiral of the gigantic Treasure Fleet of ships, designated for international tributary missions. No government-sponsored tributary mission of this grandeur and size had ever been assembled before, nor was it again until the twentieth century. To service seven different tributary missions abroad, the Nanjing shipyards constructed two thousand craft. The first voyage, from 1405 to 1407, comprised 317 vessels with a staff of 70 eunuchs, 180 medical personnel, 300 military officers commanding a total estimated force of 26,800 men, and last, but not least, five astrologers. Zhu's Treasure Fleet reflected a zenith in medieval Chinese diplomacy, advanced shipbuilding technology immensely, and left a lasting impression on all parts of the world it visited.

Will twenty-first-century China be open or closed? China's immediate history is reassuring. It has eschewed the Cold War regionalism concerned with defining boundaries and jurisdictions, with open invitations to the world to join in its progress. China's leaders realize that boundaries—social, political, geographic—are open, fuzzy, or elastic. What defines the extent of the region varies with the issue addressed or the characteristic considered. The fuzziness of boundaries makes it easier to put together the type of cross-sector governing coalitions that lead to economic progress.

Collaboration or coordination?

The philosopher Confucius articulated China's version of the Golden Rule—"Do not do to others what you do not want done to yourself." Since his era, Chinese culture has emphasized respectful relationships with others through the etiquette of daily behavior, and reverence for family and ancestors, as well as social and political institutions.

Confucian perspectives favor "coordination" around a strong familial loyalty, over the outspoken collaboration and debate of the West and, in particular, America. This contrasts sharply with the dictates of post-Cold War regionalism that focused on collaboration and voluntary agreement among equals. Collaboration abhors a hierarchy, because that suggests that someone, or some position, is in control. Collaboration thrives when all parties to it see each other as distinct, yet equal.

It is difficult for the West to grasp the consequences of a Confucian perspective. On the one hand, Westerners admire the polite and constructive society that it has engendered. On the other hand, they see Confucian dictates as so much excess baggage that stifles the expression of the individual spirit.

As we noted earlier, the philosopher Confucius argued that the best government was one that "impels" its citizens to do the right thing, with a significant emphasis on the goal. Perhaps this explains why China's leaders tend to be engineers, concerned with the most efficient way to structure a solution, whereas their Western counterparts tend to be lawyers, concerned that everyone has a voice in the solution. Western institutions may tend to be legalistic because of the coordination problems associated with letting everyone have a voice.

Confucian principles flavor the coordination, including technology, infrastructure development, services, and the like. Coordination typically implied hierarchy; for example, a regional authority with powers to implement decisions. There is considerable tension with the West's view of what they regard as an open internet and systems such as Creative Commons for sharing knowledge. China argues that their system works; Confucians might say to the West that, "When you have faults, do not fear to abandon them" (from the *Analects*).

Whatever the outcome, we are likely to see some of the most interesting debates over the internet concerning the role of Confucianism on its structure.

Trust or accountability?

Trust and shame were integral to Confucian teaching, asserting that if the people "be led by virtue, and uniformity sought to be given them by the rules of propriety, they will have the sense of shame, and moreover will become good." The implicit punishment of "shame" in consequence to actions that might undermine trust was to be preferred. Accountability demands huge resources, unaffordable as society grows more complex under the relentless advances of technology. Cold War regionalism's emphasis on coordination was often accompanied by demand for accountability—any accumulation of power would be kept in check through procedures of accountability. More often than not, accountability results in inflexibility.

Even the most conservative of Westerners have admitted the shortcomings of endless legalistic accountability. Ronald Reagan's signature phrase, "Trust, but verify" (actually a translation of a Russian proverb) suggests that trust is a necessary part of any political, social, or economic contract.

And trust is a binding element in relations among regional interests. Trust is becoming a central contention in the governance of the internet, and much of this is due to China. There is a "spook story" of sorts emerging on the Chinese internet—nuances and denouement as yet unknown, since the spies involved are reluctant to reveal themselves, their sponsors, or their motives. The internet's ubiquity is uniquely attractive to this clandestine caste, who are attracted to the internet's digital anonymity, where long-distance travel is unfettered by borders, passports, or transport slower than the speed of light. Such spies can crack safes anywhere in the world, purloin secrets without trace, and leave traps—safe and deadly—for the unsuspecting. For the victims, the internet is seductive in its false security—for now, at least.

The most recent escalation started in early 2009, when NATO's cyber warfare think tank in Estonia was deluged with requests for help from across the world.[153] Labeled GhostNet, this operation infiltrated 1,295 computers in 103 countries over 22 months, including the foreign ministries of Iran, Indonesia, and the Philippines; German, Indian, and Pakistani embassies; and organizations such as the Asian Development Bank and NATO.

Britain blamed the Chinese government and Beijing denied it; no one really seems to know the truth. Attackers used what are known as Targeted Trojans, emails sent to specific individuals that contain malicious software or "malware" hidden in an attached document or photo, or a link to an internet site to which the recipient is directed. Security experts were seeing one or two per week in 2005, a number that on average had grown by 2009 to 50 per day.[154]

Meanwhile, the fracas is fueling suspicion of the Chinese government, and industry is finding itself caught in the middle. In Britain, the

[153] Source: R. Deibert, "Tracking GhostNet: Investigating a Cyber Espionage Network," *Information Warfare Monitor*, University of Toronto, Mar 29, 2009. This report documents the GhostNet—a suspected cyber espionage network of over 1,295 infected computers in 103 countries, 30 percent of which are high-value targets, including ministries of foreign affairs, embassies, international organizations, news media, and NGOs.

[154] Source: Paul Woods, senior strategist for Message Labs Intelligence, London.

Chinese hardware maker Huawei is one of the main contractors in a $14 billion effort to upgrade the telephone system. Huawei is run by Ren Zhengfei, formerly an officer of the People's Liberation Army, causing Britain to fret that network equipment to be used by firms, households, and government departments could come with hidden "backdoors" that would let Chinese snoopers evade easy detection. In 2008, America's Congress blocked Huawei's plans to buy 3Com due to similar concerns.

Perhaps all this is merely sniping by competing spies. Sir James Brooke, the nineteenth-century White Raja of Sarawak, confided his own ambiguous sentiments when he opined, "I know not whether to admire the Chinese for their many virtues or to despise them for their glaring defects ... their industry exceeds that of any other people on the face of the earth, they are laborious, patient and cheerful; but on the other hand they are corrupt, supple and exacting, yielding to their superiors and tyrannical to those who fall into their power."[155] Inside and outside industry, the evolution of China's internet that we have documented here reflects the force of all of these influences. Can we truly be sure that—given cyber warfare's projected future—that mutual trust between regional internets might not be an early victim?

The new enlightenment

If the twenty-first century truly belongs to China, expect to look forward to the emergence of enlightening figures such as Shen Kuo who will define governance, technologies, societal interaction, and ideals of progress that will lead the world and parallel the renaissance of Song China a millennium ago.

Expect such figures to choose the internet for dissemination and exchange of ideas, with its global reach, interactive processes, and emerging abilities to initiate action anywhere on the globe with a variety of knock-on technologies.

Physicist Neils Bohr quipped that, "prediction is very difficult, especially about the future." History is only an imperfect guide to the future. We sit at one of history's great inflection points, where the Chinese internet has itself reached a critical mass with its 338 million users growing at 33 percent annually (according to CNNIC in June

[155] Source: G. L. Jacob, *The Raja of Sarawak*, Macmillan & Co, 1876.

2009), with rapid migration to non-traditional platforms such as telephones and personal digital assistants.

China's future will be true to history in one sense—its scale will boggle the mind with a population that is at once bigger, cleverer, more competitive, but also possibly more capricious, treacherous, and shadowy.

With this caveat, we in the West may ask ourselves, "to what end would the modern day genius of a Shen Kuo be put?" Would it be for good or evil; for selfish enrichment and aggrandizement; or for the betterment of the world? Or will it be some complex mix of all of the above that will envelope us all; for which the challenge of detangling is too complex for the certainty of either a happy or tragic end? Benjamin Franklin might have been similarly hard pressed to respond to the same question concerning the nascent America. When exiting the Constitutional Convention he was asked whether America "had a monarchy or a republic," to which he replied, "A republic, if you can keep it." China's outcome will be determined over many decades or centuries.

Whatever happens, China is entering a phase of intellectual and philosophical development where the internet is central, both as a vehicle and a technology, to impact moral, social, and political evolution. Individuals will be empowered at the same time they are challenged to innovate and take responsibility for the future in an entirely new vein.

China's new regionalism, as it evolves, can naturally be expected to direct its central emphasis toward individual rights, reason, common sense, and technology. The internet has already become a defining force and a powerful tool for speeding the departure of all nations away from centralized administrative and economic systems and censorship of ideas, toward an era of rational discourse and personal judgment, scientific method, and global collaboration.

Appendix: Chinese internet in figures

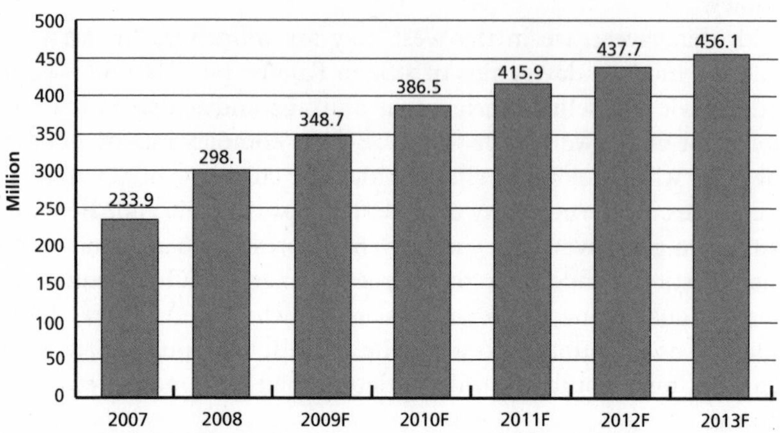

Figure A1: **China's internet population (2007–2013F)**

Data source: IDC

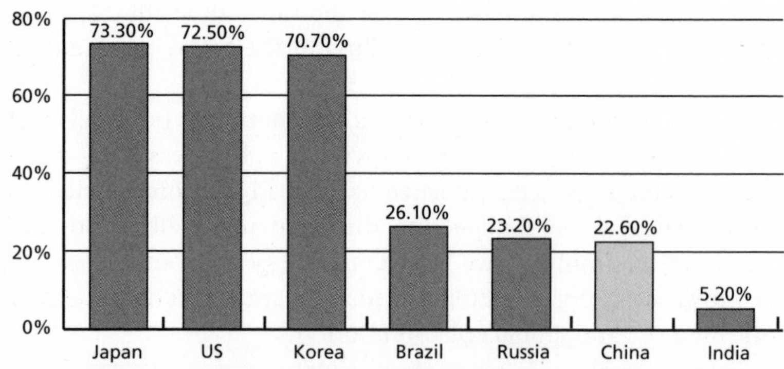

Figure A2: **Internet penetration in different countries (2008)**

Source: CNNIC–China Internet Network Information Center

Other major findings from a survey done by CNNIC in 2008:

- Broadband penetration reached 90.6 percent or 270 million, up from 163 million in 2007.
- Mobile internet user reached 117.6 million, increased from 50.4 million in 2007.

- Internet users in rural areas reached 84.6 million, up 60 percent from 52.6 million in 2007.
- Overall, 71.6 percent of internet users are from urban while 28.4 percent from rural areas.
- Male users account for 52.5 percent of the total and female 47.5 percent.
- On average, each user spends 16.6 hours online every week.

Demography of China's internet population

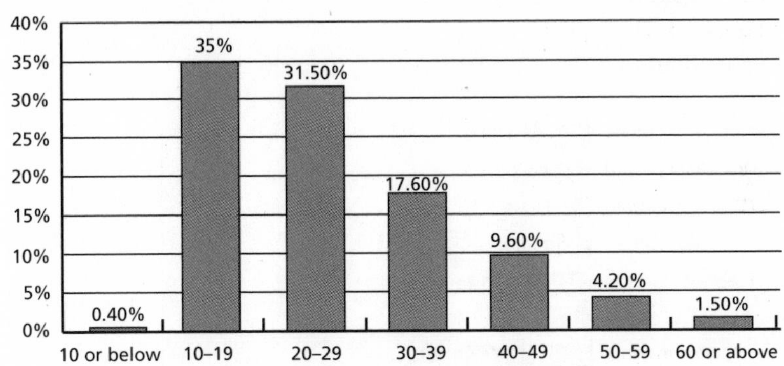

Figure A3: **Age distribution of China's online population (2008)**

Data source: CNNIC

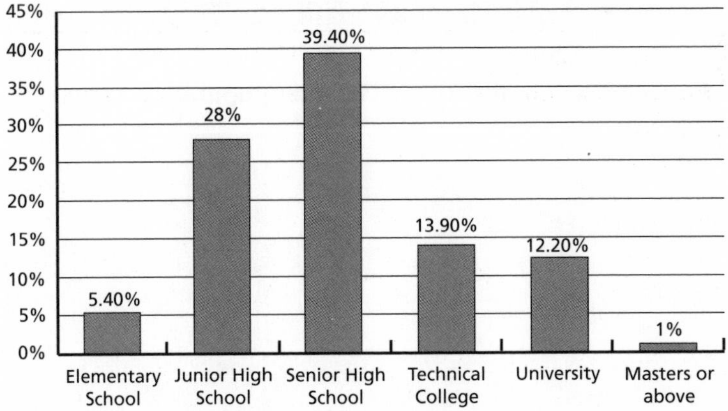

Figure A4: **Educational background of China's internet population (2008)**

Data source: CNNIC

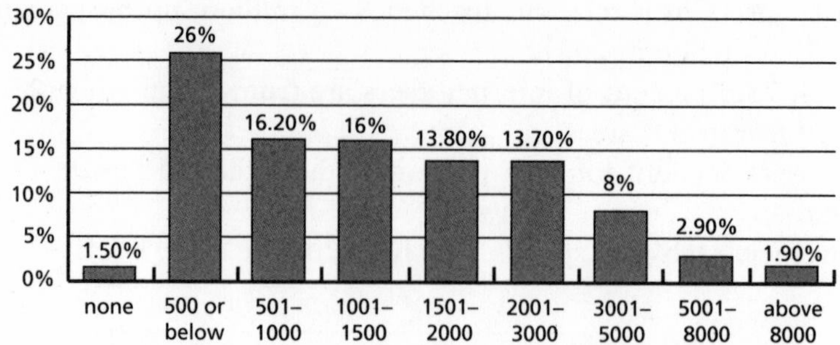

Figure A5: **Income (RMB per month) distribution of China's internet population**

Data source: CNNIC

Note: US$1 = RMB6.89

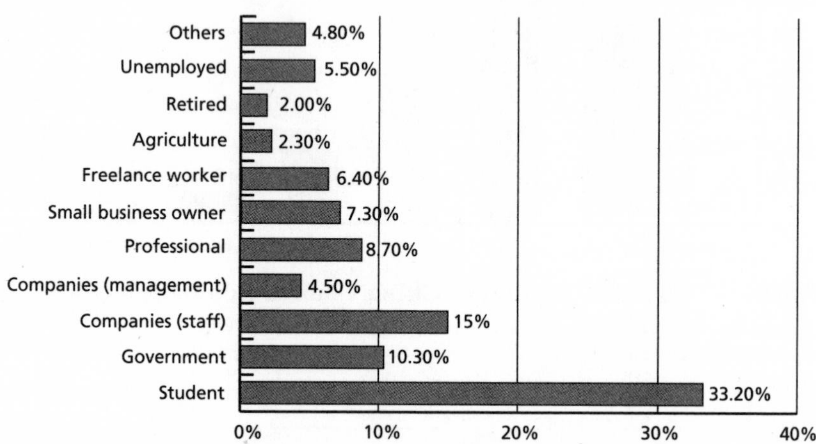

Figure A6: **Occupation of China's internet population (2008)**

Data source: CNNIC

User behavior

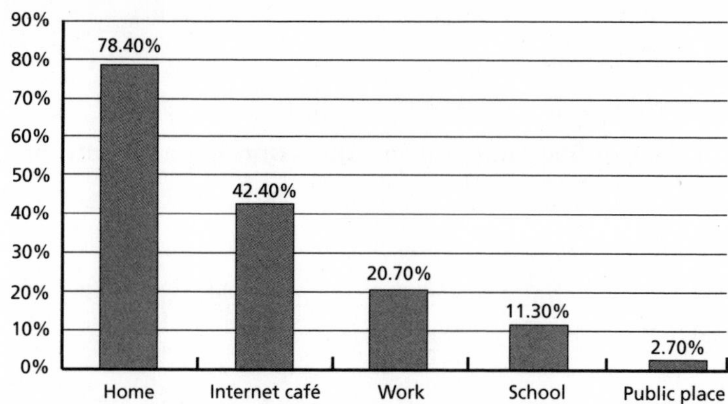

***Figure A7:* Places for going online (2008)**

Data source: CNNIC

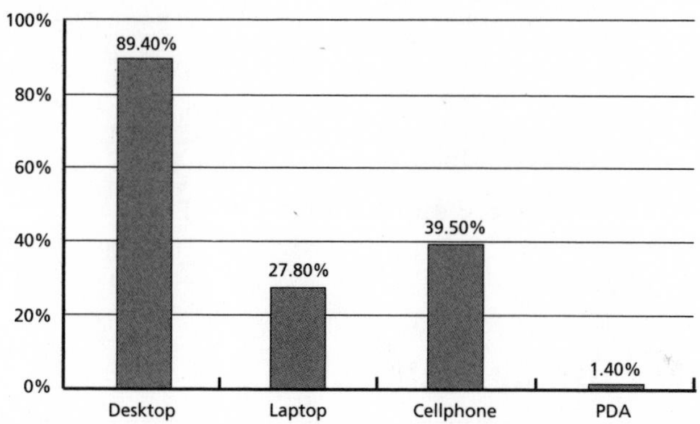

***Figure A8:* Devices for going online (2008)**

Data source: CNNIC

Internet application	Penetration	Number of users (million)
News	78.50%	234
Search engine	68%	203
Email	56.80%	169
Instant messaging	75.30%	224
Online banking	19.30%	58
Online security trading	11.40%	34
Online education	16.60%	49
Online recruitment	18.60%	55

***Table A1:* Usage of different internet applications (2008)**

Data source: CNNIC

Application	Penetration	Number of users (million)
Blog	54.30%	162
Update blog in last six month	35.20%	105
Forum/BBS	30.70%	91
Social networking site	19.30%	58

Table A2: **Usage of blogging and social networking applications (2008)**

Data source: CNNIC

Application	Penetration	Number of users (million)
Online games	62.80%	187
Music	83.70%	249
Video sharing site	67.70%	202

Table A3: **Usage of entertainment applications (2008)**

Data source: CNNIC

Application	Penetration	Number of users (million)
Buying online	24.80%	74
Selling online	3.70%	11
Online payment	17.60%	52
Online travel	5.60%	17

Table A4: **Usage of e-commerce applications (2008)**

Data source: CNNIC

Internet market size by sector

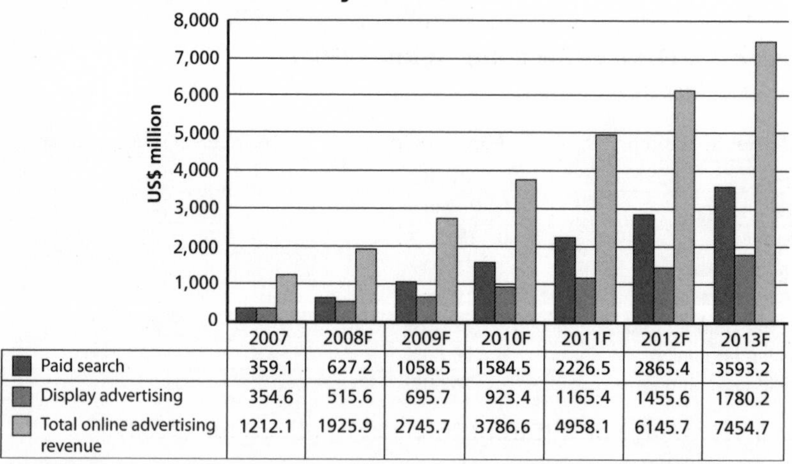

	2007	2008F	2009F	2010F	2011F	2012F	2013F
Paid search	359.1	627.2	1058.5	1584.5	2226.5	2865.4	3593.2
Display advertising	354.6	515.6	695.7	923.4	1165.4	1455.6	1780.2
Total online advertising revenue	1212.1	1925.9	2745.7	3786.6	4958.1	6145.7	7454.7

Figure A9: **China's online advertising market (2007–2013F)**

Data source: IDC

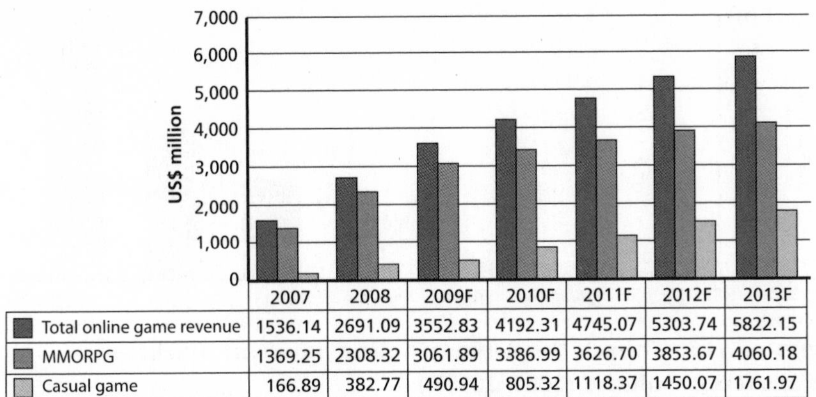

	2007	2008	2009F	2010F	2011F	2012F	2013F
Total online game revenue	1536.14	2691.09	3552.83	4192.31	4745.07	5303.74	5822.15
MMORPG	1369.25	2308.32	3061.89	3386.99	3626.70	3853.67	4060.18
Casual game	166.89	382.77	490.94	805.32	1118.37	1450.07	1761.97

Figure A10: **China's online game market (2007–2013F)**

Data source: IDC

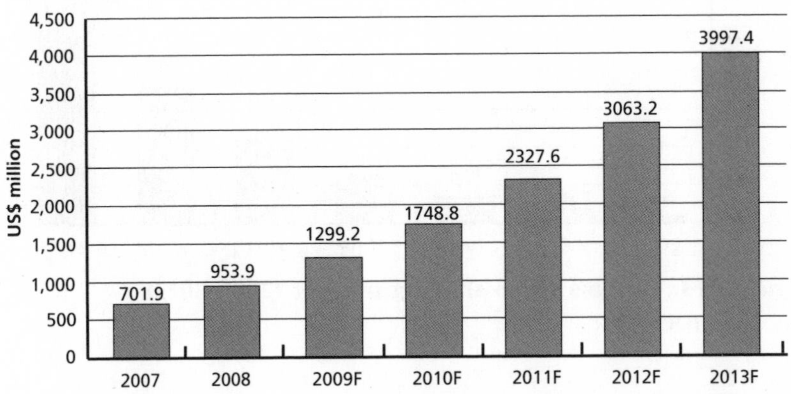

Figure A11: **China's instant messaging (online chat) market (2007–2013F)**

Data source: IDC

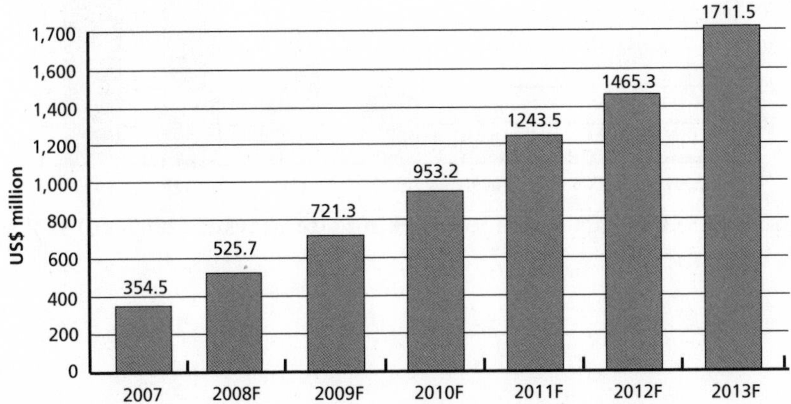

Figure A12: **China's online travel market (2007–2013F)**

Data source: IDC

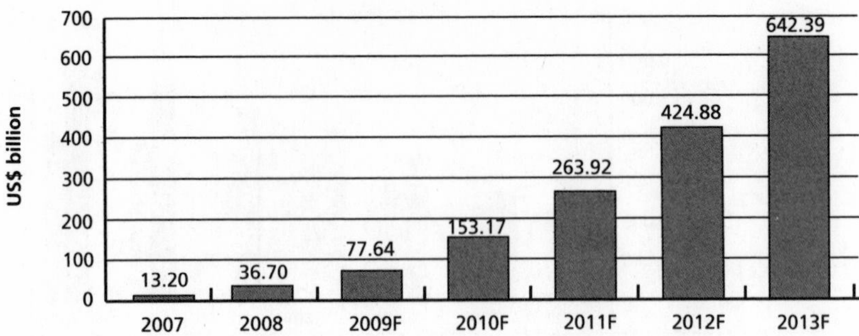

Figure A13: **China's third-party online payment market—transaction volume (2007–2013F)**

Data source: IDC

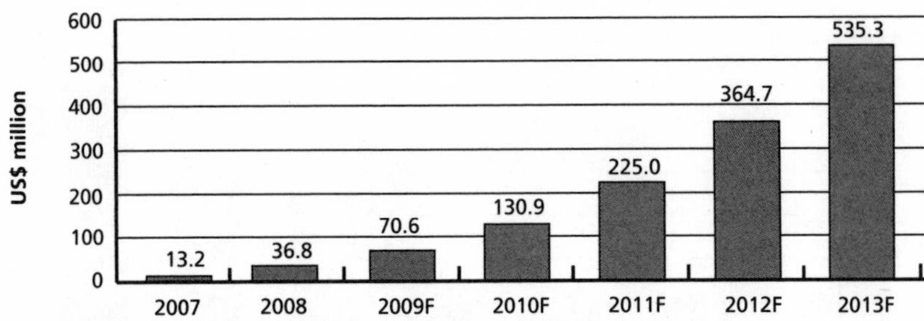

Figure A14: **China's video sharing market (2007–2013F)**

Data source: IDC

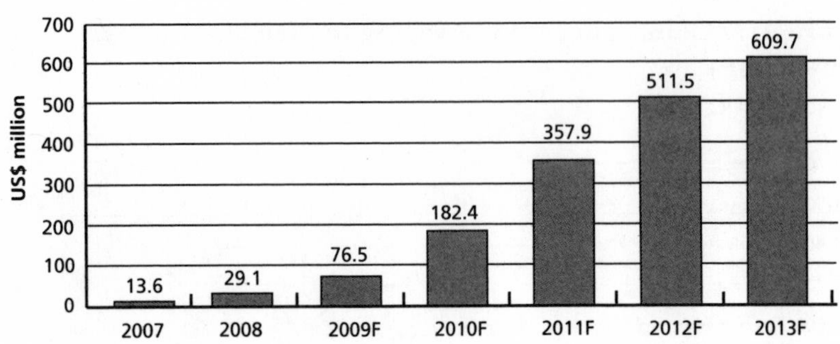

Figure A15: **China's social networking site market (2007–2013F)**

Data source: IDC

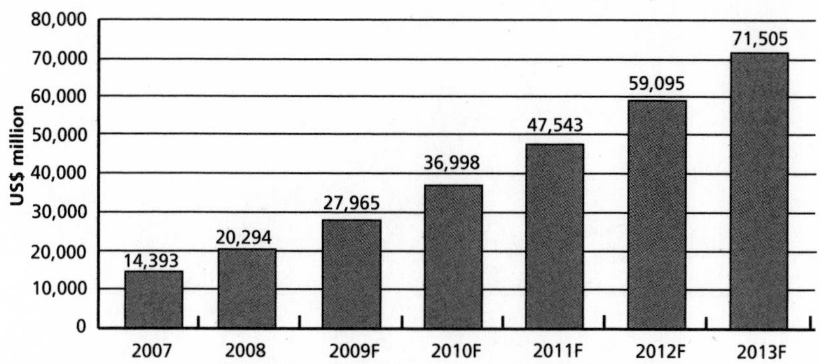

Figure A16: **Mobile data services market (2007–2013F)**

Data source: IDC

Market share of different internet sectors

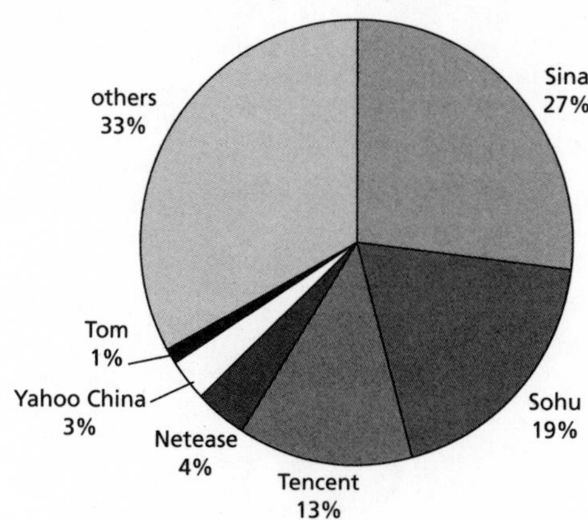

Figure A17: **Market share of online portals (2008)**

Data source: Analysys International

Note: by revenue of online Display Ad.

Yahoo China figure included display ads for Yahoo China, Alibaba, and Taobao.

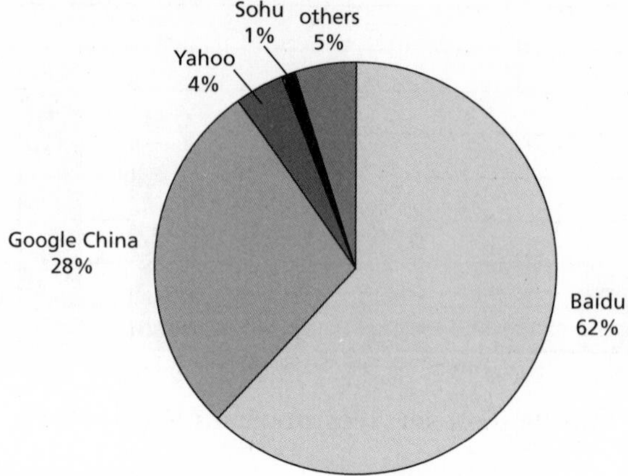

Figure A18: **Market share of search engines (2008)**

Data source: Analysys International

Note: by revenue of keyword search ad.

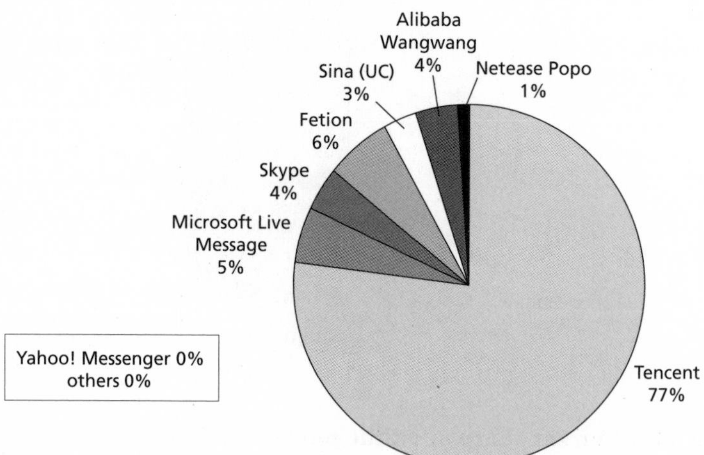

Figure A19: **Market share of instant messaging (online chat) services (2008)**

Data source: Analysys International

Note: by number of active users.

Reviews

Erik Brynjolfsson, MIT Sloan School, co-author of *Wired for Innovation: How Information Technology is Reshaping the Economy*, Director of the MIT Center for Digital Business, Chair of the MIT *Sloan Management Review*, and Editor of *Information Systems Network*.

"So and Westland have teamed up to create the essential roadmap to the largest internet market in the world. They reveal the unique challenges and opportunities of China's internet market that no business executive or policy-maker can ignore."

Jason D. Brueschke, Managing Director and Head of Asia Entertainment, Media and Telecom Research, Citi Investment Research, Citigroup.

"Broad in scope, rich in details and anecdotes, and thoughtful in analysis, *Red Wired* is a thoroughly readable and enjoyable journey through the Chinese internet landscape. The rise of successful Chinese internet companies is a story of both superior adaptation to the local environment and also the blunders committed by the larger, better financed American players. The lessons highlighted herein will prove invaluable to anyone seeking to penetrate China's large and fast growing domestic marketplace."

John Sviokla, Vice Chairman of Diamond Management & Technology Consultants, Inc.

"Don't read this book. Instead, simply wander blindly into the most vibrant parts of the largest market on the planet and miss the data, wisdom, and rich lessons of this book. Good luck without it!"

JP Gan, Managing Director, Qiming Venture Partners.

"The buzz word of the 90s was "internet"; the buzz word of the 21st century has been "China." *Red Wired* has got them both."

Helen Wong, Partner of GGV Capital, a venture capital investor in Alibaba, Tudou, and many other major China internet companies.

"Watching the largest internet population in the world allows one to look into China's future. The newest trends, the thoughts and ideas of the young generation are nurtured, aggregated and reinforced on the internet. This book is a timely read into how things began, and how they will develop in the future."

Bo Harald, Head of Executive Advisors for TietoEnator.

"China is immensely important to business and many of the next commercial applications of the internet – compelling reasons to read this timely and informative account of this vibrant development."